Snow Bodies

one woman's life on the streets

by Elizabeth Hudson

INTRODUCTION BY LAUREN CASEY

NEWEST PRESS

National Library of Canada Cataloguing in Publication
Hudson, Elizabeth, 1952-
Snow bodies : one women's life on the streets / Elizabeth Hudson.

ISBN 1-896300-74-X

1. Hudson, Elizabeth, 1952- 2. Homeless youth—Alberta—Calgary—
Biography. 3. Homeless women—Alberta—Calgary—Biography.
4. Homeless youth—British Columbia—Vancouver—Biography.
5. Homeless women—British Columbia—Vancouver—Biography.
I. Title.

HQ799.C3H83 2004   362.5'092   C2004-900765-3

Cover and interior design: Ruth Linka
Author photograph: Michael Figel
Cover photograph: J. Alleyne Photography

Some names and locations have been changed to protect identities. The author does not wish to cause embarrassment or to find fault. This is her story recalled from her point of view.

Canadian Heritage   Patrimoine canadien

NeWest Press acknowledges the support of the Canada Council for the Arts and the Alberta Foundation for the Arts, and the Edmonton Arts Council for our publishing program. We also acknowledge the financial support of the Government of Canada through the Book Publishing Industry Development Program (BPIDP) for our publishing activities.

NeWest Press
201–8540–109 Street
Edmonton, Alberta T6G 1E6
(780) 432-9427
www.newestpress.com

1 2 3 4 5 07 06 05 04

PRINTED AND BOUND IN CANADA
ON ANCIENT FOREST-FRIENDLY PAPER

To Mrs. R. my friend and mentor.

*With a heartfelt thank you to my husband John who has
steadfastly loved me in spite of myself.*

*Also a warm thank you to my sons, who are my proof that
mine has been a life worth living after all.*

Introduction

Snow Bodies is a powerful story of one woman's journey. It is a story of heartbreak, pain, and suffering. It is equally one of strength, courage, and determination. Through an agonizing process, Elizabeth Hudson escaped her life of addiction and sex work—and she lived to tell her story. Most women, however, do not. Every day, worldwide, thousands of women are mutilated, raped, beaten, strangled, and murdered while working in the sex trade. Think of the missing women from Vancouver's downtown eastside. Think of the missing women everywhere. Now try to imagine that one of these women is your sister, your wife, your aunt, your mother, or your friend. If you can imagine such lives, you are on the path to empathy and understanding.

I worked in the sex trade for fifteen years: on the street, in massage studios, and as an independent call girl. I made a lot of money and put myself through university. I travelled extensively, and I bought nice things. Over time, however, I was introduced to cocaine; within the next ten years I became hopelessly addicted to crack cocaine. I was thirty-eight years old when I "bottomed out" in California. I had nothing left inside or outside of me. I was a broken, destitute, lost soul. I have spent the last five years reconstructing my life after many episodes of violence, abuse, and stigmatization.

Western society has stigmatized sex workers, particularly those who are addicted to drugs. Subject to ridicule and public ignorance, sex workers have carried negative labels for centuries. Essentially, they have been made invisible. This invisibility has exacerbated the negative aspects of sex work and addiction both for the community and for the women themselves. Being invisible also means being inaudible. Things change for sex workers only after they begin to speak for themselves.

Contrary to the "bad girl" image journalists and criminologists commonly affix to sex workers, many women who engage in this work are doing so out of a need for money, not out of a need to buy more drugs. Economic problems or "knowing someone in the business" are common motivating factors for entry into the sex trade. Over time, however, many women are introduced to drugs due to the lifestyle associated with sex work. Women can become addicted to a particular substance; the money made in prostitution essentially goes to get their next "fix." Thus begins the endless round of hospitals, drug and alcohol rehabilitation centres, detoxification units, and jails.

Addicted women who have engaged in sex work must be understood as a group of women with multi-varied experiences. *Snow Bodies* illustrates that each woman has her own accounts and experiences. It also shows that anyone can become addicted to drugs, regardless of her social or material position in society. I do not label sex workers as "victims," for they are the greatest teachers in the world. And that's why Elizabeth Hudson's memoir resonates so strongly with me.

When the author left her life on the streets, there were no agencies like PEERS (Prostitutes, Empowerment, Education & Resource Society) to support her.

Sex workers need a place to withdraw—a place where they are not shunned or judged. They need to have a voice to educate the public about the realities of their situations. They need safer working conditions. They need to be treated as equals and not as sick, dirty, disgusting people. They are strong, independent survivors.

Those who have been addicted to drugs have gone through hell and carry the ashes on their shoulders to prove it. When cocaine had me in its grasp, I would have done anything for my next hit. But now I understand my story: I have learned not be afraid of my past, for it can no longer haunt me.

When I was initially approached to write this introduction, I agreed to read the manuscript first, then make my decision. I began reading it on a Saturday afternoon. I thought to myself, "I will read the first chapter or two, and then I will work on a couple of other deadlines I have to meet." Famous last words. I began reading at 3 PM and was unable to put the manuscript down until I had finished the story. I hope you will find the contents of this book as rewarding and challenging as I did.

Lauren Casey, MA

Executive Director, PEERS*

Victoria, BC

* PEERS is a non-profit society established by ex-prostitutes and community sup-
porters. We are dedicated to the empowerment, education and support of
prostitutes. We respect those involved in prostitution and we work to
improve their safety and working conditions. We assist individuals who
desire to leave the sex industry and we strive to increase public understanding of the trade and those who are in it.

I SAW A SICKLE MOON slice through the September clouds as my left eyelid cracked open, then clamped shut again.

"Where are we going?" My voice purred with the powerful effects of the drug injected an hour or so ago in the Esso men's room on Centre Street. There, around a stained and stinking urinal, Peter and I had fixed. For this brief piercing pleasure we'd peddled Valium around the bar for fifty cents a pop. The sell tonight would have been easier if they'd been "blues" worth a buck a piece, but those had sold out nights ago. Left with the not-as-popular "yellows," together we'd approached, hassled, and harassed each beer-filled table before selling a couple hundred tabs. Enough but never enough. "*Where are we going?*"

"Just driving, Beth. Just driving." Peter answered as he lounged beside me in the Volkswagen's back seat.

I snuggled under his arm and sank again into the feather down of the nod. But when Peter ordered, "Turn right," I pulled away, repelled as always by Fast Eddy's presence as chauffeur. An escapee from Prince Albert Penitentiary, Fast Eddy had restless green eyes, narrow lips, and a tongue that constantly darted out of his small mouth. I wondered how he got the prefix "Fast" because he seemed quite slow-witted. Street names could be like that, a reverse reflection of the self.

Peter kissed me lightly on the forehead. I was always unsettled by his tendency to keep me in the dark about the majority of the things he pulled off. His excuse was that if the pigs were on to him there wouldn't be much I could tell them. True, but the strategy left me no role in our relationship, except as a sometimes pill hawker. More often, I was the scavenger, waiting to feast off the plunder of his crimes. And with our habits escalating, my greatest fear—the possibility of losing him— loomed ever nearer.

I knew the cops were wise to Peter. Although he'd promised that he'd stopped kicking over Calgary drugstores, he continued to play a reckless game of chance with each break-in and rip-off. That evening, as I glided on the black wings of the high, I could almost hear the slow click-click-click of a roulette wheel.

My usual role was waiting in the bar while Peter disappeared; he'd return after a few hours, flush with money and drugs. "Heaven with a little bit of hell," I mumbled, and turned to him. I was drawn to Peter's determined young face and his intense bronze eyes.

He ignored me. "Slow down," he reprimanded Fast Eddy.

Apprehension was beginning to wash away the effects of the last fix. "What are you up to?"

"Relax . . . relax," he said, signaling to Fast Eddy, who dimmed the car's lights as we turned into a narrow alley. Through the open window I could hear trees swaying behind tall-fenced yards. From the recess of some back yard, wind chimes tinkled. A well-lit strip mall appeared at the other end of the gloomy lane as we coasted to a stop. Brown and yellow leaves blew along the pavement and tap-danced across the car's hood.

"I want you out here. I'll pick you up afterwards. Just be ready. Understand?"

"I'm tired of waiting, always waiting somewhere else," I said.

"Shit . . . just get rid of her," Fast Eddy barked.

"Fuck you," I retorted, my fingers curling into fists.

"Shut-up, both of you . . . we don't want to draw no heat . . . now out," Peter hissed and gave me a rough push.

"I ain't going nowhere," I said, pushing back with equal force.

He waved his arms. "Okay . . . you win. You want to stay, then stay. But in the car." He shook his finger; unconcerned, I nipped at it playfully.

"You bitch . . . I'm serious," he pinned my arms. His extended fingers probed around my sensitive ribs making me squeal in delight.

"Jesus Christ!" Fast Eddy smashed his knuckles against the glass. "I thought ya was a professional."

Somber again, Peter nodded grimly to Fast Eddy and the car rolled, tires crunching over loose stones as we moved farther along. Fast Eddy cut the engine well back in the darkness, stopping beside a white-painted fence. Hollyhocks had escaped from inside and were now going to seed. They clustered in an imposing bunch and provided some needed cover for the car.

Fast Eddy opened the door and crept out. He stood for a moment with his nose in the air, sniffing. Peter cautioned me one more time: "Stay down and don't let no one see ya."

Silence and shadows swallowed the car. My heart started to pound in a fierce steady rhythm. For sure they were gonna knock over a joint, but which one? Curious, I raised my head and peeped through the car's side window. Over to my right, two figures were pressed against a rail fence. At the sight of them, I felt braver and raised my head higher. As if expecting me to do just that, Peter turned and gestured angrily for me to get down. I ducked quickly behind the seat, but I'd seen enough. I knew what the hit would be.

We were at the small shopping centre on the corner of Elbow Drive and Glenmore Trail. When I dared look again, they'd vanished. Along, and yet still playing the waiting game, I thought bitterly: waiting in Peter's bedroom, waiting at the Summit Hotel, now waiting in the damned car. I sensed the danger, as surely as Fast Eddy could smell it, and stifled a sudden urge to throw up. Finally, when I could stand the fear and tension no longer, I opened the door and slid out.

I edged along the rough fence and skirted the hollyhocks. Arranged in an L shape, neon signs illuminated the small businesses that joined each other in glass-fronted blocks. There were no cars in the parking lot. I expected the dreaded wails of police cars any minute. I could feel my feather earrings gyrating as my nerves stretched and quivered. Unable to stand the suspense any longer, I stepped away from the corner of the fence. Caught momentarily in the glare of an overhead street light, I jumped back towards the shadows. Through the grainy darkness, I saw the shape of a woman carrying two orange plastic trash bags. As I heard the garbage cans rattle, I froze, convinced my heart would stop. Suddenly, two men with nylons pulled over their faces bolted from the Chicken on the Way takeout restaurant and quickly overtook me.

"Shit!" Peter said angrily and grabbed my arm, dragging me to the safety of the car.

Fast Eddy was already wedged in the back as Peter threw me in the driver's side. I scrambled over the stick shift as he flung himself into the seat and revved the engine. We roared through the lane to merge with the heavy traffic on Glenmore. Faintly, in the distance, I heard the first sirens.

"Christ . . . don't you ever do what you're told?"

Fast Eddy snorted, "Ya could have fucked up everything."

"I didn't though," I snapped. I felt giddy with fear. As I glanced over my shoulder, certain a police cruiser would overtake us any minute, my deep, wheezy breaths combined with hiccups.

"Get a grip, Beth . . . for Christ's sake," Peter ordered.

"You didn't hurt no one?"

"Thought the old lady would have a stroke when she saw the knife," Fast Eddy sneered, "or at least piss herself."

"What?"

"Forget it . . . she wasn't hurt. Just dished us the money as fast as she could." Peter manoeuvred onto Crowchild Trail. My anxiety diminished as Elbow Drive receded in the distance. Another exit, Seventeenth Avenue, and the suburbs of Scarboro were in sight.

"It took so long," I complained.

"Just to you," Peter said. The tension in my hands evaporated as we cruised into the quiet suburban streets. A few more turns and we swerved into another murky alley.

Fast Eddy dumped the money from a brown paper bag in his lap to split the take. "Seventy-five bucks each. Not bad." His grin exposed his tobacco-stained teeth. He patted Peter's shoulder in a clumsy attempt at backslapping. "Let me off here. I'll find my own way."

Peter whistled low through his tight lips, "You forgot something." As if laughter could hide his oversight, Fast Eddy chortled loudly and delivered some bills into the waiting palm.

Peter counted the cash and, then satisfied, flipped his seat forward. As Fast Eddy slithered past, I heard him mutter just loud enough for me to hear, "Nice doing business with ya . . . but next time ditch the broad."

Peter arched an eyebrow and gave a brief two-fingered salute.

"I don't like him."

"No kidding. It's only a business arrangement. Now I know why I've kept you out of it. You're too high strung." I watched his cheek twitch, the way it did when he was irritated.

I eyed him and shrugged. Maybe I was high strung, nervous, or whatever he wanted to call it. I squinted down the dark funnel of the lane, wishing now he had kept me out of it. That I'd kept out of it. I rested my head on his shoulder. The car idled quietly while my excitement, fear, and guilt settled between us. With the tops of our heads touching, we listened to the seductive calls of the receding high and stared absently through the windshield into the dark. Suddenly, a gust of wind rocked the car and, startled, I belched.

"What a fucking thrill," Peter said. "Beats the midway all to hell . . . wouldn't you say so, darling? Did ya ever feel so alive as when we was making our getaway? Cat got your tongue? C'mon admit it to me . . . c'mon."

His excitement refueled my own. That was it: the excitement was the electrifying wallop that overwhelmed every other sense. No drug could give me that high, that adrenaline overdose. I'd never felt such a rush. I moved my lips to his, suddenly aroused.

Delighted, Peter chuckled: "Well, now that you've seen your old man in action, how about a burger and a shake?"

Chapter Two

LATE THE NEXT MORNING, I awoke feeling scrambled and out of sorts. I gazed at the familiar surroundings of Peter's bedroom, his desk, his recliner that no longer reclined. His guitar resting against the red brick and board bookcase. Reassured, my hand felt the empty space where he'd been last night, but sleep refused to return. I pulled the end of the chenille bedspread around my middle, my fingers skittering across the frayed ridges. I swung my legs to the floor and sat up. I dug my toes into the faded hooked mat and scanned the clothes-strewn room for my purse. Spotting it crumpled in the corner, I stood and began rummaging for my cigarettes. Instead, I dislodged a letter stuck to discarded Kleenex.

The script was in my mother's tight hand. I imagined the kitchen lamp illuminating those sloped eyes as they squeezed into angry slits, the pen clenched between the buffed nails grinding words into this paper.

> *Dear Beth,*
>
> *I have accepted you are an adult, now you must accept it and take the responsibility of your actions. Either you are going to start to grow to be a mature person who has morals, ethics, a sense of responsibility, self-worth, and is independent, or you are going to remain an emotional cripple who violates every tenet of moral decency. The decision is yours, but as long as you remain on your present course there is no point in you expecting any member of your family to want to associate with you.*
>
> *I pray constantly that you will open your heart to God, light, goodness, whatever you wish to call it, and that you will have the patience and courage to make a decent place for yourself in this great country of ours.*
>
> *Love, Mother*

"Yah, right." I folded the smudged notepaper back into a tiny square, my chipped nails squeezing the worn creases as if choking off my mother's words. Morals and ethics belonged to a far-off place.

Above me, marking her territory with a loud drone, I heard Mrs. Stanhope, Peter's mother, start the Electrolux. Distracted, I dropped the letter back into my bag and flopped backwards onto the mattress. Why did I torment myself by saving and reading mother's words? My mind raced in ever-wider circles before finally settling into the disturbing memory of my stay at Calgary General Hospital's Psychiatric Unit.

I recalled the details of 30 June 1972 as if they'd been inked into my mind. After the excitement of the morning, electric shock treatments, the ward was eerily still. Only a few patients lost in a fried fog continued to shuffle aimlessly along the halls. I'd peeked around the door to see a woman with silver hair—standing in static peaks—clutching her head as if it might slide off. Ducking back inside, I glanced at the sleeping form of my roommate, Gladys, another casualty of the day. Her wispy, bleached hair rose and fell, accompanied by soft snores. My fingers knotted in anticipation of my mother's four o'clock visit. At last I heard the distinctive clump of her leather pumps striding confidently over the white-and-black squared linoleum. I smoothed the starched sheets of the hospital bed and straightened my gown.

"Well, how are you today, Beth?" Resignation tinged my mother's voice as she pulled her mouth into a determined line, then positioned herself cautiously on the visitor's chair. She crossed her manicured hands in her lap.

My blue eyes returned the dark brown of my mother's cold stare. I waved my hand around the room. "Fine, if you like being in a nut ward!"

"Not this again. I've told you we can't cope, and at the moment it's your only alternative to jail."

"Bullshit." I turned to face the open window, noting the sun's tilt westward.

"You have your nerve, after all the trouble we had talking Dr. Cohen into having you here. It's been a hard day, and the last thing I need is your ungrateful attitude." Her cream-toned silk suit rippled as she rose to leave.

"Wait! The shrink said I could have a weekend pass."

"Well, he shouldn't have. You're sick and need help, not a reprieve." I could almost hear my mother's high cheekbones lock into place.

"Peter said I'm over eighteen and you can't keep me here. I can sign myself out."

"Peter said. Peter said," my mother mimicked. "You wouldn't be in this mess if you'd sense enough to stay away from him. Just try signing yourself out, missy, and we'll wash our hands of you."

She spoke with such force that I raised my arm as if to ward off a blow. "You just pretend to give a shit," I shrieked.

"At least I visit, unlike your father who's too embarrassed by this ugly incident, and besides . . . bad little girls always get theirs." Her spine held rigid, my mother sailed from the room.

I hurled a small enamel bowl at the retreating figure, enjoying its clatter rattle down the hall.

Two male nurses instantly appeared. "I'm not crazy. I'm not crazy," I raged. I struggled as they forced me on to the bed and wound white canvas straps around my skinny frame. One of the men, his wide mouth sneering, jabbed me in the arm with a needle. The Valium soon ceased my frantic jerking against the restraints.

Remembering those soothing effects, my hand wriggled under the bed to finger the row of bulging plastic bags stashed there. Each was neatly labeled and held hundreds of different coloured pills. Resisting the temptation, I managed to snatch my hand away.

I stared at the poster of Bob Dylan on the wall, then eased myself up and lit a cigarette. The round-faced alarm clock on the bare pine desk showed it was almost noon: another couple of hours to fill before Peter returned from his classes at Mount Royal College. His switch from sometimes oil rig worker to student remained a puzzle he'd never properly explained. Most mornings he stumbled around blurry-eyed and grumpy, if he could get up at all. Our nights of carousing left him little time to study.

I believed we could get something happening for ourselves, maybe even straighten out, if he'd just quit his classes, dump the crime activities, and go back up north to make some real money. Whenever I pressed him he'd parrot, "Business is the way of the future. Might as well learn from the inside." But unless we got our shit together, his classes were a waste of time and money, and I resented both.

◀◦▶

Using the bedspread as a makeshift robe, I tiptoed through the paneled rumpus room and into the windowless bathroom at the foot of the stairs. I hunched over the oval sink and sponged myself with hot soapy water before washing my hair with a bottle of Mrs. Stanhope's Breck Shampoo. I retraced my steps to the bedroom and sat on the old steel trunk at the foot of the bed to towel my hair. I brooded on why some people lost things, and others lost people, but only a few, like me, lost everything.

In that first week after signing myself out of the hospital—or as Peter called it, my leap from crazy to just screwed up with the flick of a pen— I'd returned home for the rest of my things. Under a blazing summer sun, I'd cheerily hailed my youngest sister, Deirdre, from over the hedge and entered the unlocked wrought iron gate. I watched the six-year-old's button mouth twist in fear at the sight of me. Blond pigtails flapped in disarray as Deirdre sprinted for the double garage and disappeared. I stood dazed, studying her abandoned polka-dot thongs angled beside the twisted skipping rope in the freshly cut grass. I didn't think I'd ever be able to erase that image. Or how quickly my mother materialized from behind the safety of the screen to bar my way. I attempted a weak smile as I gripped the silver peace sign that hung from a black cord around my neck.

My mother's face remained fixed, her voice crisp: "Your belongings will be placed by the fence in a green garbage bag. You may pick them up tomorrow. If you don't, they will be offered to the Salvation Army. Under no circumstances are you to come here again."

The door closed, and the damning letter was pushed through the mail slot. Its phrases were still echoing deep within me now: *"An emotional cripple, who violates every tenet of moral decency."*

Yes, I'd made the leap from emotional cripple to amoral, but at least I was back at the start of the alphabet. Weary of thoughts and memories jigging at me like fishhooks, I began chewing on a fingernail. Each day it seemed harder to whittle away at all the empty time, waiting for Peter to take me from this refuge, his parents' home. I suspected they were well aware of my presence over the past month and of our nightly comings and goings, but so far they had said nothing. I still wasn't sure if I'd done the right thing leaving the hospital, but at least I wasn't in the nut ward any longer.

"Jesus." These long hours alone made me edgy. Again, I restlessly reached under the bed. My hand caressed each of the plastic bags, feeling the shapes and sizes of the pills before seizing one brimming with Valium. Reaching in, I helped myself to several of the shiny lemon-coloured pills. I waited impatiently for my anger to drain away. As peace enveloped me, I began to count the black dots on the low ceiling tiles.

─◄o►─

The door opened and I sprang upright as Peter threw his bulging book bag to the floor. He squirmed out of his blue jean jacket, exposing a white T-shirt stained under the arms with sweat. "Happy Birthday!" he boomed.

"It's not my birthday," I protested, but, delighted all the same, tore away the white tissue of the package to find a carved wooden jewelry box. "Made in India" was stamped on the bottom.

Peter smiled, his dark face creasing in pleasure, his blunt features softening. As I admired my prize, he threw himself on the bed and pushed me down beneath him. "Someday babe . . . I'll fill that with diamonds. I'll kick over a jewelry store, just for you."

His tongue flicked into my ear and I laughed. Peter held a firm finger to my lips. My mouth closed and I began tapping my fingers along the dagger tattoo on his left arm before mischievously whispering, "I'll hold you to the diamonds." Then I rammed my nose under one of his armpits. "Mmm . . . I like that."

He gave me a squeeze and rolled away. "You are a sick one, my sweet. I'm going to have to shower."

I plucked at his shirt as he stood. "Thanks, even if my birthday was two months ago. It was a psychiatric shindig and I got nothing, of course."

"Ah . . . Jesus . . . you've been reading that damn letter again, haven't you?" He paced the length of the bed. "Your mother is a cold-hearted bitch. No one can change that. Forget about her and try to look on the bright side . . . at least you're out of the psych ward, and you only got probation on the junk beef."

"Umph."

"Being bummed ain't gonna help you or me none." He picked up the battered guitar and his long chestnut hair tumbled over his face as his fingers nimbly plucked the strings.

"You don't take anything seriously."

He made a wry face, crooning a fair imitation of Roy Obison. He belted out the chorus for the third time, "Pretty woman walk on by. Pretty woman, yah, yah yah."

Catching my melancholy mood, he put the guitar aside, gathered me onto his lap, and stroked my face.

"It'll be fine. As for your parents, fuck them. Hang on . . . in a couple of weeks my student loan will come through and we'll have our own place. Now think about getting dressed while I get cleaned up. I'll distract Mum, and you sneak off to the car. You know the drill. It's party time, so let's go do some."

That was our biggest problem. It was always party time.

Chapter Three

"WHAT THE HELL, JUST ONE more time," Peter said, and kicked over another drugstore somewhere on the North Hill. Our party continued as the plastic bags under the bed were replenished once more. This time we sold less and consumed more. With our habits combined with the hundreds of prescription drugs at our disposal, I found consciousness waned into total eclipses. My days and nights fused into a frantic union of fuzzy emptiness; hyperactivity followed drugged silence as I spiraled out of control. Gaps were sliced into my memory, and I stopped trying to make sense of where reality hid in the remaining mist. All that mattered was the sound of a nail tap against the plastic of a waiting needle, and digesting the blues, the yellows, the reds, and the black-and-whites, my rainbow of pills.

The Volkswagen Beetle was jerking back and forth as Peter tried to stay within our lane. We zigzagged erratically to the outlying suburbs. Bombed on downers, I did not recognize where we were, nor did I care when we abruptly skidded to a stop. To help focus, I squinted and made out a deserted strip mall, where two stores, a flower shop and a dry-cleaners, flagged either end. I inched my way over to the driver's seat and rested my tired eyes. When I pried my lids apart with my thumbs, I made out Peter's hazy form sprinting along, kicking in the small shop doors. His heavy work boots were swinging like blunt axes. Alarms were sounding and merging in high-pitched wails. Poised to drive the getaway, I struggled to remain alert, but the sludge of the high was too powerful. I drooped lifelessly over the wheel. My face pressed into the horn and joined the chorus of screaming alarms. I had little memory of Peter shoving me aside or driving off, his curses bouncing off the shield of my stupor. All that remained was the sensation of effort, the experience of keeping my eyes open for as briefly as I had.

Disoriented, I wrestled myself into semi-consciousness. Two curious faces were pressing against the car's rear window, and I raised a shaky middle finger towards them. The boys vanished, their shrill laughter retreating down the street. Stiff and sore, I tried to move but wasn't even sure which limbs were mine. My legs were locked together with Peter's, as if we'd tried to weave ourselves into one pair of jeans in the back seat of the Volkswagen. I made a feeble attempt to free myself and sat up. What day was it? Even that question seemed beyond my grasp. The best I could figure was that it was a week, maybe two, after my failed attempt as a getaway driver. To warm myself, I lit a cigarette and watched the light frost recede under the sun's rays, trying to remember what we'd done where last night.

Peter groaned and coughed the phlegm from his lungs. "We gotta slow down. Have to mellow out, then head for BC," he mumbled. He seemed to look to me for approval, but I saw that his jaw was set: he'd already made up his mind.

Mulling over his thick words, I announced the first thought that came to my sluggish brain—"I don't wanta be sick."

"Junkies don't like being sick, that's why they're junkies." His laugh stirred another round of hacking. Feeling he was making fun of me, I angled away from him. But Peter rubbed his face thoughtfully and persisted. "Gotta come down, Beth. Ain't having no life doing this shit all the time. We're asking for trouble and if we don't cool it, we're gonna get it."

I sniffed, "I know all that but. . . ."

"C'mon now." He lightly elbowed me in my middle, as he chose his words. "They're coming . . . the heat. I smell them getting closer. I gotta get home to the folks' place to get my head straight. I thought of you coming, but we're bad for each other. We gotta do this alone." As I started to pout he grabbed my knee for emphasis. "We'll drag each other down. It's the truth, and I think you know it too."

I had wanted to slow down too, but not by him sending me away. "What about your classes? All that stuff about business being the way and the future?"

"They just told me I ain't gonna get a student loan—made too much money on the rigs. I haven't been doing the work or going to classes. At least I know when it's time to cut my losses." He studied his matted hair and the weedy stubble on his chin in the rearview mirror. "So anyways, I phoned Tina and she says you can stay there a few days."

"Well . . . you certainly have thought of everything. . . . Except I ain't going. I can't think of a worse person to be coming down around." I kicked the back of the seat with my platform boot.

"You got a better idea? 'Cause if you do, I'd like to hear it." Peter climbed over the seat and eased himself behind the steering wheel. "It will only be for three or four days. Just long enough for us to pull it together." He turned around and ruffled my hair. "You'll see, things will be better. We'll rent a little farm, live off the land. No one to hassle us. We'll grow our own smoke, maybe even sell some. Only we have to get over the sickness."

My idea of better times did not include living off the land, or growing weed for that matter, but I was willing to try anything once, especially with him. I grudgingly nodded, knowing I had little choice in the matter. Peter gave the horn a little beep of victory as we headed to his parents' place. There, while his mother was in the living room watching the *Galloping Gourmet* on the television, we ate, dressed, and prepared for our brief separation.

I heard my mother's words mocking me: "Actions have consequences." I wrapped my arms over my ears to silence the voice.

"What?" Peter demanded, as we parked in front of Tina's apartment in the East End. She rented the downstairs of a ramshackle, two-story house a few blocks from Princess Island Park, where the old wartime housing was slated for demolition.

"Nothing." I slammed the car door and ran past the brown, uncut grass and the old push mower abandoned in the middle of the unfenced yard. Tina swung wide the yellowing front door. Several small panes of glass that had once arched gracefully along the top were smashed and papered over with cardboard. I saw Peter slip Tina a twenty dollar bill.

"Whose girl are ya?" he asked, as he shuffled on his black canvas running shoes.

Aware now that I was a charity case, I crossed my arms defensively. "Ain't no one else around at the moment—you'll have to do. But the next bad boy that comes along, I'm gone."

"I'll make sure I'm not gone long then." He slipped a large vial full of the familiar blue-and-black pills, yellow Valiums, and ten dollars into the side pocket of my fringed purse. He managed to squeezed my ass at the same time, completing the transaction fast enough to escape Tina's eagle eye.

"There's a cap in there; use a little at a time to take the edge off. The pills will help you sleep," he whispered. "Don't use the money to score 'cause that'll just piss me off." His hand balled into a mock fist and he waved it under my nose.

"I won't . . . I won't." I bobbed out of his reach, thankful this might not be all that painful after all.

"Ha . . . if that's all the thanks I get." He grabbed me and placed his full mouth over my little one.

I tugged on his arm. "Just . . . stay tonight."

"You know I hate clinging vines. Everything's settled." His brown eyes flashed a warning. "See ya in a couple of days." He tweaked my cheek. "Take good care of her for me, eh?"

"Don't worry about nothing," Tina replied. He winked and closed the door.

"My, wasn't that touching! Considering he wanted to get rid of you." Tina's high forehead wrinkled in rippling waves. She was tall, too thin, and her joints protruded. Her face was pushed in on either side, making her pinched nose look more pronounced and her large round eyes froglike. Her one beauty was the long black hair cascading down her back.

"Her backside is her best side," I thought. "Jealous?" I offered, as I lit one of my Players and took a deep drag. It was beyond belief that I would end up here, but where else was I welcome?

Tina now tried a more conciliatory tone. "I'd make you supper, Beth, but I don't have enough," she said, thumping down a cast iron pot of rice onto the old gas range.

Noting that there was plenty, I feigned disinterest. "I ate already."

As the small kitchen filled with the smell of brown rice and a slight odor of gas, Tina sat across from me at the recently painted white wooden table. She helped herself to one of my cigarettes, peered briefly under the table, then put her head in her hands and studied my black silk Chinese smock embroidered with red and blue threads in a radiating sunburst design.

"A new top?"

"Yah: Peter traded some downers for it." I nearly laughed as Tina looked more acidic than before. With a flourish she finished her cigarette, and a wall of curling smoke billowed between us.

Once the rice cooked, Tina brought her plate back over and sat beside me. "He leave you any pills?" She twirled her fork in the centre of the rice, pouring soya sauce into the hole she'd created.

I took the clear plastic vial from the folds of my purse and held it just high enough for Tina to catch a glimpse of it clamped between my thumb and middle finger. I tucked it out of sight again and returned her forced smile.

"Umm . . . enough." Tina sounded impressed. Her small teeth seemed to gleam with anticipation.

She began her customary whine: "Ross and I ain't so lucky as you, having dope and money and all. I mean we work hard for what we got."

Unimpressed, I blew a puff of smoke towards the water-stained ceiling tiles. "At least you have some place to stay . . . and let's just say Ross works hard."

"That ain't fair . . . I'm looking for a job. You should talk," Tina filled her mouth with a spoonful of rice.

I scooped the vial into my palm and turned my back. I didn't want Tina to see the tantalizing white capsule lying on the top, or how many or what kind of pills I had.

I shook out two of the blue and black, and rolled the caps over the uneven surface of the table towards her.

"Only two?"

"For now."

Taking that as a sign of more goodies to come, Tina gulped down the remains of her supper. Before she popped one of the magic Mandrax she asked, "He leave you some stuff?"

I shook my head and studied my nails. That I would not share. I pulled out my nail file and began reshaping each nail as I waited for Tina's pill to take effect. In ten minutes, Tina began smiling with the first real warmth of the evening.

"Come on, let's go in the living room." We moved to a shabbily comfortable room. The orange sofa was soiled, but well stuffed. There were three other chairs—a green, a yellow, and a brown—all discoloured by age, but still in good condition. The only light was overhead and failed to brighten all the corners of the room.

The coffee table was a board held up with blue-stained cement blocks. At each end of the sofa were two scratched pressboard end tables, one of which held a turntable with a pile of records stacked neatly beneath it. Tina sat in the yellow chair while I chose the sofa. We each lit a cigarette and settled down as our earlier tensions evaporated.

"I've known Peter a long time. He's had a lot of ladies. They come and go pretty regular."

"You bitch," I thought.

"You're only presuming Peter's dalliances." With a sidelong glance I said, "Besides you wouldn't want to get me going now, would you?"

"There you go with those big words of yours. *Presume* and *dalliances*, whatever. . . . You just want to rub it in that you've had more education than me."

I spread my arms and put my socked feet up on the coffee table, enjoying the sensation of having rattled Tina's cage with only a volley of words.

"Some teacher you'd make when ya won't even explain some words to me."

"Shit . . . I didn't want to be a teacher. . . . Remember I dropped out after the folks refused to foot the bill any longer."

To my relief, Tina did not respond. Perhaps she knew that soon we'd go at each other physically if this sniping continued. I waited silently, hoping Tina would doze off.

I still remembered the morning school ended. I'd awakened on my front porch with a dust of snow covering me. Surprised that I'd made it home at all after the all-night kegger, I opened my eyes to see my father's leather Italian shoes by my nose. The black tassels on each shoe were vibrating. I moved my gaze up his gray pants, over his double-breasted winter coat, and up to his icy blue eyes.

"Get up," he roared, glancing around to make sure that the neighbours hadn't seen me laying there. His long arm jerked me to my feet and pitched me inside. I landed hard in front of the Chippendale hall table.

An antique porcelain vase belonging to my great-grandmother rocked slightly as I hit and bounced off the hardwood floor.

My head throbbed as my father continued ranting. "I won't have it. I won't have it, and I Goddamn well won't bankroll it."

He leaned to give me a cuff on the head. "You're a disgrace. Now get yourself cleaned up." He pushed me with his foot. "I said get moving!"

I hoisted myself and lumbered towards the stairs. "I won't have it. I won't," he howled behind me. He slammed the door to punctuate my eviction from my home and the end of my education. But I wanted to forget.

I always wanted to forget. To do that, I needed a fix. I lit another cigarette. Tina remained immobile. I slipped off the sofa and tiptoed down the narrow hallway to the washroom. I locked the door and searched my purse for the small aspirin tin, matches, and fit.

I filled the fit halfway with tap water and left it on the edge of the sink, found the vial, and lifted the white treasure from it. I pulled apart the capsule, tapping it lightly to pour some white powder from one of the halves into the empty aspirin tin.

I wanted to get high. Mandrax was fine, but it lacked heroin's rush of gratification. I squirted the water from the fit into the aspirin tin, then I lit a match and held the flame beneath the tin. As the white powder bubbled and dissolved in the water, the smell of the sulphur and ether excited me. Eager now, I threw the match into the toilet. I reached for the fit, flicked my nail against it several times—watching the tiny bubbles disappear—and then pulled the plunger and sucked the watery substance in the tin up into it.

I took a silk scarf from the bottom of my purse, tied it tightly around my right arm, and then pumped my forearm up and down. When the blue vein surfaced, I gripped the fit with my left hand, ran my fingers across the vein, and plunged the point of the needle into it. Beads of perspiration broke on my forehead as I missed the rolling vein twice.

As if on cue, Tina bashed on the door. Startled, I missed again. Tina wailed on the other side, "I knew it. He left you some. You didn't even share, and I took ya in."

"Shut up! You can have the wash," I unlocked the door, allowing Tina to blunder in.

"You fix me first." Now I wouldn't have to continue to prick myself needlessly. Taking the fit from me, Tina agreed. Thoughts of a free fix kept her quiet. On her first try she hit the vein. I flopped on the toilet seat, welcoming the rush roaring through my body.

Just as I slumped backwards in the throes of a deep nod, Tina shook me. "Christ's sakes, you gotta fix me." I struggled to open my eyes and plucked blindly at the scarf. Tina snatched it away and quickly tied it around her own.

Still surfing my way out of the nod, I waved the fit under the running tap and then released the water into the tin. I managed to repeat the burning ritual, with Tina hanging over my shoulder.

"Hurry up."

This time I gently swirled the water around to get the dregs that remained there and tried at the same time not to drop it.

Finally, the fit was ready, but my eyes were fluttering shut again. I couldn't resist the powerful urge to close them.

"Shit!" Tina yelled.

I studied Tina's arm for the best vein before stroking my index finger over the most promising prospect. Then I stabbed the needle into it and promptly nodded off again.

Appeased, Tina pulled the needle from her arm. "I didn't think you'd be able to hit the side of a barn door." This time there was no malice in her words.

We helped each other back to the living room. I settled into the sofa hoping to drift with the currents of the high.

"Why did ya lie to me? I figured he'd leave ya some," Tina whined.

"'Cause you piss me off."

"You piss me off too. I never had no opportunities. Like getting an education and having a doctor for a father."

"There you go again . . . C'mon, Tina. A semester at university is not an education. Don't you realize that well-off folks have their problems? No one can have a say in the way they're brought up. My family's pretty fucked."

"Well, you didn't have an alcoholic mother that ran off leaving ya. It was hard. . . . I dropped out in grade ten, ya know."

"So you've told me. My life only looks good from the outside. One of my earliest memories is of my father waving a knife under my mother's nose and threatening to kill her. Shit . . . I couldn't have been any more than two or three. And my mother . . . don't even get me started on her. That's crap thinking I'm somehow better off than you. At least your Mum ran off and things settled down."

Tina lit another smoke and changed the subject. "Do ya remember that house where we were roommates over on Fourteenth Street . . . you know, with Bella and Mick?"

"Yes . . . but I wasn't there all that long . . . a couple of months after the folks kicked me out . . . why?"

Tina's hooded eyes narrowed. "I didn't like ya then and I don't like ya now."

"The feeling is mutual . . . so how come you let me crash here?"

"I didn't do it for you."

"The obvious of course . . . just trying to worm your way into Peter's life. . . . Well I can tell you . . . you're not his type. Besides, as you told me, they come and go pretty regular." I was tired of the whole conversation but the effects of the drug mopped away any feelings of resentment. Heroin made the ugly realities of life inconsequential. If only I'd found this crutch to help me through high school, everything might not have seemed so in-my-face and inescapable.

"Well, you owe me big time for introducing the both of ya. Couldn't keep your eyes off him. Remember?"

I did. It had been a Friday night and I'd just returned from an afternoon shift at the Dairy Queen on Tenth Street. The music became more deafening as I climbed the flight of stairs to our three-bedroom apartment. The front door was ajar, and the whole place was rocking to Johnny Winters. I pushed myself through the crowd, breathing in the haze of cigarette and reefer smoke that filled the place. I'd pulled a beer from the fridge and sat on the counter beside a sink full of dirty dishes.

Tina stumbled through the beaded curtains laughing, holding the arm of a good-looking, young guy. He was dressed differently than the rest of the crowd. A white T-shirt was tucked under a flannel shirt; his blue jeans were straight-legged instead of bell-bottomed. His rich-coloured brown hair was parted in the middle and hung straight past his shoulders. He'd squinted at me, noticing the striped uniform. My peaked hat was still pinned on my head, so I grabbed it off and shook my wavy hair free from the hairnet. I felt smug seeing his smile of appreciation. Tina continued to talk loudly in his ear, but he gestured for her to make an introduction. She waved her bony hands from one to the other of us as if the matter was beneath her consideration. "Oh . . . my roommate, Beth. Peter."

She'd yanked him back into the living room. "Look who's here. Let's go meet Mark."

I had almost half finished a beer when Peter sidled over to me, leaned close and whispered, "Anyone ever tell ya how irresistible a woman is in stripes?"

But Tina's voice interrupted the memory. "That very night I warned ya he was bad news. Been in and out of trouble since he was sixteen. But did you listen to me? Of course not, and just look where you're at now."

"I don't need you to remind me where I'm at, so cut the shit and put some music on."

"My, aren't we getting bitchy." Tina sorted through the stack of albums before finally deciding on Janis Joplin. We played music until eleven, when Tina stumbled into the bedroom just off the living room.

I heard Tina turn on the portable radio that stood on the night table; then the bed creaked as she settled into sleep.

Slipping into my nightgown, I nodded off with Mick Jagger crooning in the background—"Can't get no satisfaction." Only the radio played softly on. The one thing to worry about now was coming down. I peered at the gold-painted Timex Peter had given me from some B&E job. It was 2 AM.

I might as well finish up the last of my junk. There would be no Tina this time to interrupt. Why be sick tonight, if I could put if off till tomorrow? I gathered up my purse and repeated my previous performance in secret this time. Not a bad start on a new life.

◄○►

Cradled gently by the rising swell of drugs and slumber, I drifted until a loud pounding jolted me awake. Adding to the persistent racket was the rising chorus of Tina's cry, "Get the fucking door." I cursed the sofa springs that jabbed me. Lurching blindly towards the kitchen, I groped for the string to the light bulb. My bare feet stuck to the linoleum while my fingers fumbled with the bolt. The door's hinges groaned as Peter shouldered past. Cold rushed in with him. I stifled a yawn and shivered.

"Hi . . . what's happening?" It couldn't be any more than five in the morning.

He pulled me towards him. "It's over."

"What's over?" The fog in my head seemed to thicken. The faint lines around his mouth added a sense of hardness to his jaw. He felt tightly coiled, but his eyes looked dead.

What had happened? I stood rooted to the floor as a confusion of thoughts swirled in my head. "Why?"

His shoulders sagged and he lit a cigarette. My agitation increased. Peter was always sure. His confidence was infectious, but now so was his indecision.

"I got popped."

"What!" I reached for the kitchen counter to steady myself. Fear chased the mist from my mind.

He straightened to lean against the refrigerator. "Got me on the Chicken joint job."

"Bullshit, you were with me . . . I'm your alibi."

He glanced at me, then looked away. "They picked up Fast Eddy . . . he ratted . . . they know everything . . . end of story." He shrugged, his right palm up as if it were an apology.

I slapped his hand away. "It's his word against ours. It is . . . isn't it?"

A trace of a smile played at the corners of his mouth for a second. "I already copped to it."

"What? Why would you do that? Why would you do that?" I stifled an urge to throw up.

His large, chapped hand steadied me. "Beth, they were gonna bust you too. . . . I done time before and can handle it, but I ain't that sure about you."

"What do you mean ain't that sure about me . . . I can look after myself!" I dipped into his pocket and helped myself to one of his cigarettes. My hand trembled as I flicked the Bic, and I turned away so he wouldn't see.

"Sure you can—the one who can't even drive a getaway car is gonna take on every butch in the joint? Shit . . . you even let that bitchy wimp Tina push you around." He tapped the top of my head lightly. My mind seemed insulated in wet cement.

"With you being on probation and all . . . they'll throw the book at ya." Just for a moment he lightened, "C'mon now . . . think about it." He tapped my head again.

"Fuck that! I don't get it . . . everything was airtight." I toppled into his chest, as if to hide there.

"Nothing's for sure. You know that."

A tear dribbled out of the corner of one eye, and I wiped at it, ashamed of my weakness. "If you go down, then I fall too."

"Don't be stupid. One of us falling is enough. Now I don't have much time, so listen. I wouldn't do this for no one else, remember that, and always remember that I did care for ya. Now pay attention." He tilted my face towards his. "I go up at eleven and I want ya there for me . . . understand?"

I nodded dumbly and tried to avert my watering eyes. He took a wadded Kleenex from the back pocket of his jeans. As he wiped my face his blunt words offset his actions. "No point in crying . . . ya knew as well as I did that it was bound to happen."

I snatched the tissue and dabbed at the tears, as his thumb brushed along the ridge of my nose. "I gotta go. I ain't that good at goodbyes and the pigs are waiting outside. It's okay, I bargained that before I'd cop the guilty plea, that I'd get to say goodbye to you."

Confused, not wanting him to go, I pushed his long, dark hair back behind his ears. I wanted to see his face. In the past when I'd done this, he'd teased me that the other girls might find out how handsome he was. But this time he endured my gesture in silence.

"I really gotta go." His voice cracked. "Think about going back home to your folks, and don't forget to be there at eleven."

I refused to release him. Finally he pushed my arms to my sides. He kissed each of my red, watering eyes. As his lips grazed mine, he whispered, "So long, Baby."

As I fell to the dirty floor I remembered that day at the picnic table, when we were two young people sharing an old cloth coat and surveying the unfolding drama of spring.

"Do you love me?"

"What's love, Beth?" He offered his hand and we'd walked along the muddy bank listening to the roar of the river's retreat south. He pointed across to George's Island on the other side, where we could glimpse the swelling buds of the cottonwood trees.

"See all this . . . it's just like love. Every spring the water rises and washes away the winter. It clears the way for the sizzle of summer. Like love, it changes, floods and dries with the heat, or lies frozen in your heart. I feel it ain't right to tell someone you love them because it's like the seasons. What I feel this year may not be what I feel next. But I can say I care for ya now, think you're beautiful . . . and ya should be grateful for such a good looking old man as me."

Wrenching my hand free of his, I had run off.

"Ah shit. . . . You're not mad again . . . are you? . . . Beth? I'll throw myself in the river—anything for you."

I had stopped, laughing to see him standing on one leg, teetering on the edge of the water.

He swayed so uncertainly that I'd run back to him.

He'd lifted me off my feet and swung me in the air. "Don't ever ask me again if I love ya . . . you think I'd spend as much time with ya if I didn't? Someday this will all pass, but if it makes you happy to hear it, then just this once: I love you."

I'd felt such happiness. I tried to remember those feelings now because he never again told me that he loved me.

"Stop that blubbering!" Tina bellowed from the bedroom.

Chapter Four

TINA POURED THE HOT WATER into a cracked mug and smiled, as she tapped her spoon against its sides stirring her instant coffee. "You know, Ross thinks you're a bad influence on me . . . I mean you're always feeding me dope and . . ."

"Right . . . I just force it down your fucking throat." I went to the can and splashed some tepid water on my face. I grabbed my cigarettes off the coffee table and confronted Tina. "You take my drugs, my old man's money, and then say I'm a bad influence. What bullshit!"

As Tina went for a fistful of my hair, I shoved her. His double shift finished, dull, solid Ross stepped into the middle of the melee. Tina flew into his arms wailing, "She's so mean after all I've tried to do for her, she's yelling and pushing me around."

Brushing past the two of them, I walloped the door with my boot on the way out. I stomped along towards the court house, shivering in the growing grip of fall, my words rising in foggy clouds.

"That bitch . . . that bitch." The mantra caught some of my frustrations, and gave me something to focus on. Each step brought me closer to having to confront my aloneness. I did not notice the blue sky and the sun's attempt at warmth. I only felt the push of the November wind against the unlined suede jacket as I dug my hands deep into its pockets. The black glass and concrete blocks of the city's core approached, and I found myself caring little about where my life would bottom out.

In front of the squat blue building, I gritted my teeth and marched inside. The hallway was jammed with people. The place smelled like an overcrowded hospital waiting room. Uniformed policemen milled about, gathering in small clumps as if drawn together by magnets. I observed the lawyers with their expensive suits and briefcases, engaged in a perpetual state of backslapping while the accused waited, pacing and smoking with jerky movements that highlighted their anxieties. No one noticed me standing alone, eyes fixed and mouth drooping. I claimed an empty bench over by the main door. Crossing my legs, I jigged my left foot back and forth.

Finally a voice penetrated my gloom. "Hey, Beth . . . Beth . . . what are you doing here?" A young, freckle-faced, Twiggy-thin woman stood before me. It was Sue—Snaky Sue, as she was known on the streets. Why the label stuck I never knew, because her bobbed, dark blonde hair, fine features, and sea-green eyes seemed to match a pleasing personality.

"My God, girl . . . what's the matter? You look as if you just lost your best friend." Sue smoothed the back of her crimson miniskirt under her open ankle-length coat. "Your old man?"

"Can't talk about it," I snuffled, turning my head to hide the tears.

Sue nodded and placed her hand on my shoulder. I could see that my pale cheeks, lifeless eyes, and wild hair shocked her. No doubt she noticed my enlarged pupils and the beginnings of a sweat breaking on my forehead.

"What time does he go up?"

"Eleven."

"You don't have much time. Come to the can with me, I'll freshen you up. Wouldn't want him to remember you looking like this would you?"

Sue reached down and helped me to my feet. "Robin goes up today. You remember him? We go back a long way. Got busted for trafficking. You must of heard that on the street?"

She did not stop for my answer. "I've come to see him off. But of course we were just friends, not like you and yours. With Robin gone, I'll have to get another supplier. I just might be able to cheer you up yet!"

Once safely in the washroom, Sue inspected all the stalls. Satisfied we were alone, she pulled a balloon full of knobby caps from her leather bag and began to scout around for hiding spots for her illicit treasure. I sat on the sink counter and watched with more than just a passing interest.

"I'll give ya a good deal, later," Sue said, stuffing her bundle into the middle of a spare toilet paper roll. As Sue replaced the roll behind the toilet, I scowled thinking it would have to be a hell of a deal before I could afford it.

Sue whipped out an orange hairbrush and extended it. I set to work to untangle the long bushy mess while Sue watched the painful process. Next, she waved a pretty cherry lipstick under my nose, but I shook my head. "Peter doesn't like me to wear makeup."

"Well, just use some rouge then; you need colour in those cheeks." I took the blue case, and brushed the blush in well, hoping he wouldn't notice. Afterwards, I had to admit I looked much better. Sue glanced at her watch again. "Better go, it's almost time, kid."

"Thanks." As I left, Sue was curling her thick brown eyelashes with her metal contraption.

I drifted through the crowd to Courtroom Two. Opening the heavy dark door I spotted him, sitting in the first bench with a burly dick on either side of him.

Glancing behind him, Peter saw my hesitation and began waving me toward him. He seemed relaxed as if the men who sat with him were minor inconveniences in an otherwise pleasant experience.

The solemn dick on Peter's left moved down the bench to make room, and I stepped warily around him. Instantly, Peter's arm pulled me close and I landed on his lap.

One of the dicks immediately yanked me off and onto the bench. "No close contact."

"There ain't much we can do squeezed between you two," Peter said, putting his arm around my shoulder. He ignored the warning and nuzzled my ear, muttering, "Could I ever use some stuff now."

Casting a quick sidelong glance at the gray-suited cop to my left, I whispereded, "Sue stashed some in the can."

A tremor of anticipation shook Peter. "Get it."

"No!" I was appalled.

He pressed harder. "Please, baby . . . I'm going for a long time. . . . Give me a little good-bye present . . . just something to take the edge off . . . c'mon." Sensing me melt, he gave me a slight shove. "You know, I'm going up in a few minutes . . . it's like my last request."

I crossed my arms. This was not why I had come.

"Please do this . . . help me out a little here."

"All right . . . all right." In his haste to get me going, he elbowed me off the bench.

My exit had again aroused the suspicions of the dicks, who reacted like distrustful dogs with noses and hackles raised. I could feel their alert stares burning into my back as I left.

I started briskly down and across to the washroom. Finding the toilet paper roll, I quickly removed the bulging balloon. I ripped the tight knot with my teeth and I withdrew two of the white capsules, and then replaced the rest of the bundle. I scanned the washroom for something to wrap my stolen treasure in. I could find nothing. My heart pounding with fear that Sue could be watching, I placed the capsules into my mouth, shoving them along the right gum.

The dicks stared as I sat down. Peter asked in a voice intended for the dicks, "Christ, couldn't you have gone before?"

"Sorry." Then as the gelatin slowly dissolved in my mouth and began spilling its bitter load, it was hard to keep my face still. I moved my mouth close to Peter's ear. "It's melting."

"You didn't wrap it?" he asked incredulously. I made another sour face. The dicks moved closer to us. "I love you too," Peter said rather too loudly, kissing me passionately on the mouth.

Instantly, his tongue ran along the edge of my gums, eager to transfer the bitter cargo. As the dicks moved to separate us, Sue burst into the courtroom cursing loudly. "You bitch . . . I'm gonna lay a licking on you that you ain't never gonna forget. You cunt."

Sue's wrath blinded her to the gray-suited men surrounding the two of us. She stopped a couple of feet away and shook her fist at me. I smiled from within the fortress of heavy men.

"I'll see you later," Sue said as she whirled and stormed out.

"The people this place attracts," I murmured. The dicks passed a knowing look between them.

Gently stroking my inner thigh, Peter said, "You gotta be the tough one now . . . you're going to have to have it out with her. . . . Just make sure that you give as good as you get."

"All rise," the bailiff intoned as the judge entered. "The court of the honorable Judge Ciconne is now in session. The court calls Peter Stanhope." Peter gave me a last peck on the forehead and trudged to the box. As the charge was formally read, I noted with some amusement the slight twitching of his mouth.

The rest of the court proceedings were a quick blur. The sentence, "Three years," stuck in my mind like a dart.

Peter was lead away. Three years . . . three years . . . three years. My silent grief seemed to touch the serious dick to my right, and he asked, almost considerately, "Would you like to see him upstairs?"

"Yes, oh yes," I said, raising my red-rimmed eyes, and noticing for the first time his square, honest face.

As we turned towards the elevators, I spied Sue down the hall and quickly looked away. For the second time that day I was grateful for the security my escort afforded, and I smiled at him as we stepped into the elevator that would take us to lockup.

On the third floor, the dick left me alone to speak to the guard in the wire cage behind a heavy steel and glass door. The beefy guard gave a rude stare, then pressed a button to swing the door open into the visitor's room.

A thick sheet of glass divided the room in half. Four stools stood bolted to the floor on each side. My escort moved to go. "Thanks," I murmured. He blinked an acknowledgment and the heavy door closed behind him. The unreality of the day swirled around this concrete room.

Peter sauntered to the other side of the glass, giving me one of his wide smiles. He picked up the phone on the counter in front of his stool and gestured to me to do the same. "Jesus, you should have wrapped it. That stuff tastes awful."

"I left my purse on the bench . . . there really was nothing to wrap it with." I quickly changed the subject. "I still don't see why you pleaded guilty. It just doesn't make any sense."

"You don't need to know nothing more than what I told you." An angry glint in his eye warned me to drop it. At the same time he pointed to the phones to suggest our conversation might be bugged.

Frustrated that there could be no honesty between us, I rubbed a thumb along my cheekbone. Against my best intentions I began to cry again.

"Stop that . . . I don't want to remember ya like this. Listen, Beth . . . I've been thinking you gotta get on with your own life . . . forget me . . . find someone else . . . I think it would be better for both of us."

"What?" Surprise replaced grief. "You can't be serious!"

"Afraid so . . . three years is a long time and I don't write much. So the way I see, it the best thing for you would be to go home and start over. We obviously weren't that good for each other anyways."

He nodded as if he expected me to agree with him, but the rest of him remained inscrutable.

My response was more tears. "Beth, you just gotta stop crying."

"You're just cutting your losses again. You think you can throw me away! . . . You can't . . . I won't let you . . . ."

"Are you threatening me? You don't know what three years will bring."

I really felt sorry for myself now. "Tina kicked me out, you're gonna drop me, and Sue's gonna kill me. Thanks a lot!"

"Quit being a baby. Of course, Sue has to at least lay a licking on ya. You really gotta toughen up." He shrugged; he couldn't protect me anymore.

"Shit, the pen . . . you're going to the pen."

"I know where I'm headed." He placed his large hand over the glass. I stretched out my smaller one, wanting to smash my knuckles through the cold barrier.

The guard shouted from the other room, and the visit was over.

"Go home, Beth," Peter said, before hanging up the phone.

He withdrew his hand from the glass, touched his heart, and followed the guard from the room.

The same dick I'd come in with re-entered. His face was emotionless as he greeted me. "Interesting report of a girl that night, couldn't have been you now, could it?"

Feeling like a small animal caught in the teeth of a steel trap, I blinked back my tears and shook my head. "Good. Run along then before we investigate further."

Chapter Five

ONCE OUTSIDE, I WIPED AT the sweat on my brow as I scanned the street for Sue. I began jogging west towards the York Hotel. As the distance between myself and the Courthouse grew, my stride became more confident. I began to dwell on the task of scoring and the hope that something would turn in my favour.

"You gonna get it now, you bitch."

I pivoted, and confronted flint-green eyes. Sue's face was twisted with anger. "No dicks here . . . no Peter to hide behind."

Laughing with glee, Sue mocked me, "I followed you . . . don't see so good do ya?"

I tensed for the physical onslaught, knowing it was part of the code. Sue lunged, swinging her fist into my face, hissing, "Too bad about Peter."

Before I could recover from the first blow, a second landed on my right eye. The pain made me hit back blindly. Another rapid punch to my midsection connected, winding me. I doubled over groaning.

"Rip me off," Sue snarled, grabbing a handful of my sweat-drenched hair and throwing me to my knees. I clawed at her but missed. Sue delivered a heavy clout to the side of my head and I rolled along the pavement, my hands covering my face.

Sue repeatedly kicked me as she screamed threats. "You owe me fifty bucks . . . bitch . . . I should kill you! You're marked . . . do you hear me? Marked." After a few more well-aimed boots to my head, she turned as if bored by her superior performance. She marched off without a backward glance.

I got to my feet and charged after her. Catching her off guard, I landed a well placed kick on her rear-end and sent her flying into a startled afternoon shopper. Then, aiming my purse with precision, I bounced it off her stomach like a wrecking ball. She backed up, surprised, and smiled with slight admiration. "You got guts . . . too bad that you're going to have to pay for them now."

She swung wide, faking a blow to my head, and as I moved to cover, she ploughed her fist into my midsection. She used my long hair as a rope to spin me into a light post. Stunned, I shook my head to clear it, but, already, Sue's deadly feet were striking me while I curled into a tight ball.

"If you got any sense, don't get up this time." Blood seeped from my nose and dripped slowly onto the sidewalk as I lay gulping for air.

One of the bystanders walked up and stared down at me. It was the whore Big Marie, the one I'd seen in jail the first time I'd been busted. I hated those heavily mascaraed, black beady eyes as they studied my shameful predicament. Then Big Marie opened her bright red lips, exposing uneven teeth, and spat on me.

"Hippie trash," she snorted, stepped over me, and continued her strut along the drag.

I crawled to my feet and staggered to the pay phones in the foyer of the Regis Hotel. With my eyes puffing up, impairing what vision I had, I hunted through my purse for a dime. My nose was squirting red spurts and I could feel a clot of blood coagulating beneath the corner of my left brow. I pressed a bruised arm across my face to catch the seeping blood.

My trembling fingers dislodged a dime from my wallet. Ashamed at the beating Sue had laid on me, and at a loss without Peter, I wanted my mother.

I felt the bumps of the rotary dial. I dragged each number to the top and I waited as the phone started to ring. Relieved, I heard my mother's "Hello."

"Mum . . . it's me."

"What do you want?"

"Can I come home?" I rushed on desperately—"I only left because I couldn't take the psych ward any longer and Peter looked out for me. . . . And now . . . and now . . . he's in jail." I could not control my breaking voice.

"What a surprise!" My mother's voice resonated with sarcasm.

"Mum . . . oh . . . Mum, I'm out here all alone. Let me come home . . . I promise I'll straighten out . . . this time I won't let you down. I mean it . . . I do!" I'd promise anything, do anything, to get away from what I had just lived though.

"We told you when you walked away from the hospital that was it.

We're tired of having you disrupt our lives. You remember the story of the little boy who cried wolf too often? You're that little boy as far as we're concerned. Your promises mean nothing."

"But I have nowhere to go."

"That's your problem—one you should have thought of before."

"God damn it, I want to come home." Anger replaced hurt.

"And I said no."

"How can you turn . . . your own daughter away? It's not human . . . you're no mother."

"You're no great shakes as a daughter, either."

"I want to come home . . . I want to come home, . . . Do you hear me . . . I want to come home." Hysteria was not helping, but I couldn't control myself.

"And I've had enough of this!"

"Mum, please don't hang up . . . please."

It was already too late. I held on to the receiver, then hurled it against the wall. If that wasn't just like my fucking mother, to turn away when I really needed her.

I stormed off through the bar to the washroom, where I held cold wet paper towels to my face and tried to wash off the blood. I went into one of the stalls, locked the door, and sat on the toilet. It was too early yet for any action at the Summit, and here it was safe and warm. I leaned back, rested my battered head against the streaked wall, and tried to ignore the pain.

Later, I wandered to the stroll, in the direction of the Summit Hotel. Through the condensing fog hovering over the city, I could make out the round tower rising above the squat sandstone and cement buildings of the downtown. Oblivious to the curious stares of other pedestrians, I shuffled along. When I finally mounted the rounded steps of the gathering spot, I was overcome with nostalgia. I'd spent happy nights in the pursuit of my pleasures here.

As I entered the bustling beer barn, the rock band near the back was singing, "Those were the days, my friend. We thought they'd never end. We'd sing and dance . . . forever. . . ." I sank into a chair at the first empty table I saw. The young barmaid, just starting her shift, gave my battered face a disapproving look. "Wat'll it be?"

"A draft." I hunched closer to the table as if to make myself invisible. She slapped a tall glass of foaming beer in front of me, and I tossed a couple of quarters on the table.

"Keep the change." I puckered my lips at the beer's yeasty tartness and took a look at Junkie Corner. There sprawled the kids who considered themselves hippie junkies, proud not to be part of the east-end scene or the Rounders, whom they dealt with only when absolutely necessary. They were far more familiar to me than the rough Rounders, who lived and worked Calgary's Seventh Avenue east of Centre Street. I noted that Sue was deep in a nod in the corner along the wall, her strawberry blond head almost touching the table. Sue had saved face and I doubted there would be any more physical retaliation. However, just to be on the safe side, I stayed where I was. Goose pimples began breaking on out my skin, as another round of chills set in. As wave after wave of nausea took over, I shuddered.

"God, you look awful." I gazed into the cherub face of Sandi, a hippie junkie I knew slightly. Surprised that I had not seen her approach, I looked around to assure myself that no one else, especially Sue, was headed my way.

"God, you really do look awful!" Sandi repeated, working her jaw up and down and crackling her gum. Her light auburn hair was tied into side ponytails and gave her a childish appearance. "Your eyes look like cream puffs." Her deep voice was both mannish and seductive. "I heard about your scrap."

"I suppose everyone on the street has heard about it by now. My wonderful showing and all." I wiped my nose on the back of my hand.

"Fuck . . . you should have been able to take Sue." Sandi propped her elbows on the table and studied my damaged face.

I shook my head, "Heart just wasn't in it."

Sandi's voice softened, "Yah, I heard about your old man." The working mouth opened, exposing tiny threads of saliva as she leaned closer to whisper, "Want to score?"

"You have some?" My mind clicked into the never-changing game. I sought a position to bargain from, "I'll trade ya thirty odd Mandrax and ten bucks for a cap." Seeing Sandi's skeptical look, I rushed on—"They're worth a dollar a pop. It's a good deal." My tone was too high and whiny.

Suddenly losing confidence I rubbed my scraped thumb across my cheek.

"I dunno . . . blues would be better. No one knows much about Mandrax." Sandi paused with an air of importance, before adding, "I'll hafta ask Blade. I'm supposed to see who wants, collect the money, then bring the stuff back."

"I can't wait. Look at me, I've been sick since this morning. I have to know now." I was beginning to feel both hostile and hopeless.

Sandi hung back, moving her lips and popping her gum. "Okay, I'll ask . . . just for you, mind, but don't expect nothing." She hurried down across the bar and out the side door to the parking lot.

Trying to open the slits of my swollen eyes wider, I watched for Sandi's return. Soon her laced-up canvas runners strutted back across the floor. Blade must be hiding out somewhere close by. Searching the angelic face for a positive sign, I was rewarded by a slight nod. For the first time that day, I had something to smile about.

Grinning widely, I took the large vial of blue-and-black pills from the bottom of my purse, I wrapped the ten dollar bill around it, then swiftly offered it to her beneath the table.

Sandi cast a watchful eye around and snatched it from me. She examined the vial. "You sure there's thirty of these babies?"

"Peter gave me forty yesterday. There's at least thirty-seven left. I've already been in one scrap today, I ain't going to rip you off."

Nodding, Sandi popped a foil-covered capsule from her mouth and slipped it into my hand. "Got a fit?" I asked, clutching the treasure in my balled fist.

"Yah. You want to fix in the can?"

"Let's go," I urged. The two of us abandoned the lone beer and sauntered to the ladies' washroom. We waited until the two girls primping before the mirrored wall finally left, then we both headed into one of the vacant stalls.

My brain screamed with the euphoria. I did not notice as the dulled point was jerked from my arm. Nothing mattered any more, I was high . . . high.

I tilted forward, almost tumbling off the seat, but Sandi caught me and steadied my weight against her hard body. While I swayed unsteadily back and forth, she stuck the fit down to the water between my legs to rinse it out.

Tucking the needle back into her sock, Sandi watched my teetering body. "Ain't you never done a whole cap before?"

"Nope."

"Well, I ain't staying here with you. You'll attract too much heat."

Sandi's face showed a small trace of concern as she struggled to avoid any further responsibility.

"I'm okay."

"Yah, sure you are," Sandi said. "Just lock the door after I'm gone. People'll think you're having a shit." Opening the door, she turned before leaving, "I'm real sorry about Peter."

"That bastard," I chewed the words, my tongue as thick and bloated as my face. "Think he done me some great favour . . . leaving me with no one or nothing."

"Well, he did leave ya the Mandrax. . . . Just the same, I'm sorry."

I fumbled for the lock and succeeded in pushing the bolt in. I sank deep within myself—gone to the sweet land of nod, my secret place of nothingness. I didn't care how long I stayed there. I was exploring the honeyed emptiness that floated in and around me.

◄o►

A loud rap on the door jarred me. "What?"

"I want to talk to you. It's Sue."

"I've got nothing to say to you now or ever." I tried to rally my wits to face the next bout of unpleasantness.

"C'mon Beth, I ain't gonna fight you no more."

"Yah . . . right."

"All I want is to talk."

"Then tell me from there."

"I need your help," Sue whispered through the door.

I laughed. "You're out of your mind. . . . What are you high on?"

"Let me talk to you."

"What the hell." I slid back the bolt, and Sue locked the door behind her after she stepped in. We stared at one another warily.

Sue's finger traced the swollen flesh around my eyes. "You had that coming."

Brushing away her probing finger, I scowled. "I have to see my probation officer in a couple of days and I'll look like shit. How's he going to believe that I'm on the straight and narrow looking like this?"

"I had to, you know that. I would have fronted you, if you had asked. But you ripped me off instead. You deserved it."

Annoyed at being lectured on etiquette junkie style, I hit back. "What do you want? To gloat? Then do it and fuck off. I'll probably be breached, thanks to you."

"You forget . . . you still owe me and I figured a way for you to be square."

I pointed to my damaged face and ribs. "I figure we're even."

Sue squatted down. "You don't understand . . . all I want is for you to book a room for the both of us."

I studied her face for some secret twist to this simple request. "Why?"

"Because when Robin went down, I figured the bundle he fronted me was mine. So I did three caps, you took two, I sold four, and I kept the rest. Now the Man wants his money."

The irony was too much. "You mean you beat me for dope you already ripped off?"

"You could put it that way, I guess."

"You guess . . . you guess!"

Sue held up a finger to her copper-coloured lips. "What I need is a place to stay till the heat's off. No one would think we'd be together after what happened between us today."

I turned this proposal around a bit. It was pretty good: Sue had lots of dope, and I, too, needed a place to stay. "I suppose . . . I suppose."

A smile from Sue sealed the agreement. "Get a cab and wait till I come. 'Cause we can't be seen leaving together."

Rising unsteadily to my feet, not quite believing this latest turn of events, I pushed past Sue as she held open the door. I staggered outside to the line of waiting yellow cabs. Functioning better in the coldness of the frosty air, I stumbled into the first car. "Where to?" the driver asked, eyeing me in the rear view mirror.

"Nowhere yet. Just wait till my friend comes." I forced myself to sound normal, but didn't fool the young cab driver. He watched my head bob as I drifted back into the nod.

He flipped the meter on and, fidgeting with his radio, waited for about ten minutes before Sue darted in. "Alexandra Hotel."

The engine roared to life, and we were off. I opened my heavy-lidded eyes as Sue was paying the fare. Rousing myself, I yanked on the handle and stood relishing the cool air for a minute.

Sue and I walked the few steps to the heavy carved doors of the Alex. Once one of the finest establishments in Calgary, it was now a has-been— though its brick facing showed no trace of the creeping decay within.

Sue's eyes flashed, and I moved into the faded splendour of the lobby. The boards beneath the shabby blue and red carpet creaked as I limped to the desk.

The elderly clerk blended in with the decomposing surroundings. His tired face looked up from his game of solitaire.

"How's it going?" I asked, leaning over the piles of white cards that contrasted with the dark, peeling varnish of the oak desk. The old man waved me off. "I'd like a room," I said, managing to keep my swollen eyes open and to stand upright.

"Double or single?" He frowned as he scrutinized my dirty torn jacket, stained flared pants, wild hair, and swollen eyes. "Where's your luggage?"

"I just flew in tonight, and Air Canada managed to misplace my bags." I made a wouldn't-you-know sort of face. "It's the least of my worries as I'm trying to escape a very bad domestic situation. As you can see, things at home got a little out of hand."

"Oh." He sounded dubious, but pushed over the register for me to sign. I grasped the pen and scribbled: Barbara Hanson, Kelowna.

His spidery fingers plucked key 210 off the hook and placed it on the desk. I smiled through my teeth and seized it. I headed towards the stairs just as Sue strode past the reception desk.

"Hey you, where do you think you're going?" the old geezer yelled as the elevator clanged and started its upward chug with Sue inside. I continued my climb up the stairs. The clerk's curses echoed across the lobby. "Jesus Christ, some people have their bloody nerve."

As I hustled down the second-floor hallway to meet the elevator, I could still hear his distant rumblings. The door clunked open and Sue stepped off, having already pressed the button for the other floors. We hurried to room 210, where I fit the key into the sturdy wooden door.

I breathed in the room's homey smell of antiquity. Inside was an old brass bed and a pine dresser, run down but not altogether neglected; someone had just polished them. The gilded mirror above the bureau sparkled in spite of the age spots that marred its surface. A small clean bathroom adjoined the spacious room.

I flopped on the tan quilted bedspread. Sue plopped down beside me and suddenly we were laughing, our mirth sweeping away the bitterness of the day.

Chapter Six

MY TANNED PROBATION OFFICER SAT securely behind his steel desk. His dark eyes stared me down.

"What is this troubling news I hear about your boyfriend?" He glanced at the report in front of him. His slight European accent made each word a question and the query a singsong.

"Mr. Slavitch, I didn't know. Do you think that I would have approved of such activities?" I hoped I sounded self-righteous enough as I adjusted the black suede miniskirt Sue had loaned me.

"You know, under the terms of your probation you're not to associate with criminal types." He tapped his pen angrily on the desk.

"I didn't just associate with him. He was my old man and . . . honest, he never told me what he was doing," I twisted my hands together and tried to look earnest.

The little man leaned forward. "Did you have sex with him?" One of his bushy eyebrows arched up.

"Well . . . yah. I told you he was my old man." I wondered what this question had to do with anything.

"Yes but did you enjoy it?" His tongue moistened his upper lip.

I shifted again and crossed my legs. "That's none of your business. I'm over 18." I began rummaging in my bag. Before he could get the jump on me and continue, I looked up quickly and lit the end of a Players. "I'd like your permission to visit him."

"Oh!" He leaned back in his chair, then announced with mock surprise, "I thought you knew. He doesn't want to see you."

"Impossible." The cigarette fell from my hand.

"My dear, I assure you it's true." He was watching my reactions intently.

"Never . . . he'd never say that." I bent to pick up the smoldering fag from the carpet.

"Well now, if you choose not to believe me, perhaps you'll believe his probation officer."

"Yes, maybe I would."

He pushed a button on his intercom. "Mrs. Emerson, would you please ask Mr. Woods to come to my office."

I began pacing around the perimeter of the small office.

For this interview I had washed and brushed my hair, and tied it back with a yellow ribbon. Thick beige concealer covered my blackened eyes, so that from a distance it only looked as if I suffered from a lack of sleep. However, Mr. Slavitch seemed more interested in my breasts under the low-cut blouse.

A young man in his early thirties, dressed in an expensive blue suit, knocked. "You wished to see me?"

"Mr. Woods, I was hoping you'd tell Miss Hudson here what Mr. Stanhope had to say in respect to her visiting him."

"Stanhope stated he doesn't want to see you. If you try, you will not be granted access." His face betrayed no expression as he recited the words in a bored fashion.

"But why?" I sat down again.

"That's all I can tell you," he said, closing the door.

I shrunk into the chair, a hand to my mouth. Before I could compose myself, Mr. Slavitch began again.

"Now, where were we? Ah . . . yes. . . . Did you enjoy sex with him?" He placed his glasses on the desk.

I wanted to find a place to run and hide. I twisted my purse strap around my thumbs. "Why do you want to know?"

"It's most important that I know how well adjusted you are sexually." He was moving his wheeled chair and inching closer to me.

"I don't know why." I was becoming apprehensive and rubbed my thumb along my cheekbone.

"How often did you have sex with him, then?"

"I don't have to answer that."

"This report—he reached over and pulled the report off his cluttered desk, held it up, and read slowly—"known associate of Peter Stanhope, suspected accomplice." He tossed the paper back to his desk. "Don't you see? I can put you in jail for that, revoke your suspended sentence. But if I knew that you were well adjusted sexually . . . and, well, shall we say . . .

open to suggestion . . . then I just might be inclined to disregard this breach." He smiled invitingly.

Fearful of the power at his disposal I smiled back seductively, "Mr. Slavitch—of course, you should know I'm always open to suggestions . . . especially yours."

"Such a pretty girl." He reached for me with his sweaty hand and squeezed my knee. I tried not to show how repulsive I found him.

"Thank you." I stifled an urge to kick him in the nuts.

"Yes . . . yes." Mr. Slavitch clasped his hands thoughtfully to his face. "You must visit me at my home. We have such important matters to discuss. Don't we?" He nudged my thigh suggestively.

"We most certainly do." I played along. He searched for a pad of paper, hastily scribbled down an address, and handed me the paper. "Next Thursday at eight?"

"Eight would be just fine. How very thoughtful of you." I hoped he wouldn't notice the acrimony behind the remark.

"Very good. See you then." He dismissed me with an affectionate rub on my shoulder.

"See you Thursday." I tried to look cheerful and ignore his greedy hands as I escaped.

I walked past the receptionist's desk, vowing I would never go back to that odious man's office. I'd rather be breached. I ripped up the piece of paper he had given me and tossed the fragments down the carpeted hallway.

◄O►

Sue and I cemented our tenuous friendship with an orgy of greed. I confided in her about the pain of Peter's loss, and talking helped lift the burden of my guilt. Sue turned out to be an avid listener but spoke little of herself. I did not push, content with having my words echo off her instead of empty walls.

Because Sue was reluctant to risk being seen, once a day I went to the Chinese corner grocery store, to load up on Twinkies, chocolate bars, cigarettes and milk, which we devoured on my return.

After a few days, Sue asked if I would go to the Summit Hotel and find out what the word was on the street. I agreed, but was loath to leave the protection of our room.

I slowly pulled on my jeans and located a soiled cotton top among the piles of clothes and garbage that littered the floor. The room smelled stale, a combination of old sweat and moldy food, but neither Sue or I cared.

Sue, dozing contentedly on the unmade bed, was oblivious to my departure. Shocked alert by the night air, I walked the nine blocks to the Summit Hotel. The uniformed security guard and his dope-sniffing German Shepherd were on duty, so I skirted the inquisitive beast. I wondered why the management bothered with this charade; it was well known that the dog's shift began at eight o'clock, so anyone who was packing came before then or just slipped through the side doors.

Smoke sheathed the crowded bar as I approached Junkie Corner. Its three or four tables at the far right, clustered close to the wall, offered a good vantage-point for spotting heat and was usually avoided by the rest of the bar's patrons. I saw the group's packed, inert bodies draped over the chairs and tables, and realized too late I'd picked a bad night to be here. Only a panic would bring them all together: the chippies, the hippies, the Rounders, the old and the young. The shivering huddled mass advertised their shared misery.

I squeezed into a space beside Jacob, an acquaintance of Peter's, and was instantly surrounded by the sea of suffering. The eyes in Jacob's large head peered into my eyes and became more alert—"You got?"

I shook my head. "Looking myself."

The big head quivered. "Panic. The man split." His round eyes studied me. "You're not sick." His discomfort made him appear more comical than usual. His huge head was tacked onto a thin, short body, with arms and legs ridiculously out of proportion. No wonder his nickname was Goofus.

Just then, a tall, gaunt man rose from a table at the far end of the corner and headed towards me. A shiver of fear ran down my spine. It was Rick. On his own turf in the east end he was considered king of the Rounders. Here, too, he was treated with respect, and the drooping bodies pulled back from him as if clearing a path.

His pockmarked face loomed over the table. "Where'd you get your stuff?"

"My old man left me some." I met his stare but then lowered my tell-tale eyes.

"Bullshit." His slicked back hair was almost bristling.

"Ain't like he can do the stuff where he's at."

His eyes compressed, showing thin, yellowing lids. "You wouldn't hold out on me now, would you?"

"No one would hold out on you." I felt agitated by his manner, on top of all the pairs of eyes watching us.

"They don't if they know what's good for them." He gave me a penetrating look and left.

Jacob shifted closer. I began sipping one of the many drafts sitting on the table. I hoped a thoughtful expression covered my anxiety. How was I going to get back safely to Sue?

"Tell me honestly, have you got?" Jacob pressed again. I ignored his question and all of the dilated eyes from the other tables that seemed glued to me. I tried to suppress my mounting paranoia. Instead, I turned to my sweat-drenched companion and asked, "Why'd the man split?"

"No one knows, probably too much heat."

This was what I'd come to hear. As I rose to leave, my movement set up a ripple of unease among the other tables.

Jacob clutched at my wrist. "Please, Beth, just a jimmy. You're the only one I've seen high tonight. You got a connection . . . don't hold out on me too!"

I shook off his clammy hands. "I don't have," I said, loudly enough for the others to hear. After all, it was Sue's I'd been feeding on. "Honest, if I did, I'd jimmy ya." As I walked away from the corner, four others began following me and one of them was Rick.

I hurried out the exit and hopped into one of the waiting cabs. "Carlton Hotel." I glanced over my shoulder as the four others also piled into a cab.

"Try to lose them." I pointed out the back window. The driver looked into the mirror and sped up.

We turned down Sixth Street and then onto Ninth Avenue with the other cab still in pursuit. I searched for a five dollar bill and tossed it into the front seat as the cab slowed with our approach to the Carlton. Without waiting for a full stop, I leapt out. I dashed into the hotel, heading for the back door and the alley behind. I sprinted through it until I emerged onto Centre Street, where I was forced to slow to dodge the traffic. Again, my pace picked up as I turned into another darkened alley, coming out on First Street. Here I slowed into a practised jog, drawing on my track and field days. Still watching for a sign of the pursuing yellow cab, I ducked into another lane. This led to the rear entrance of Alex's bar where I cut across to the main lobby. I walked past the dozing desk clerk, and, once out of sight, I mounted the stairs two at a time. I knocked on the door, and, breathless, called out, "It's me . . . hurry." The door swung open.

"What's up?"

"Panic . . . only one high . . . followed."

"Shit!"

"Lost them . . . ran from the Carlton." I fell on the bed, still winded. Then I remembered why I had gone. "The man's split . . . you're safe."

Sue's freckled face beamed and she gave a long sigh of relief. "Let's fix and celebrate." She stretched out a shapely leg to admire her pink toenails.

"Sounds good to me."

After the ritual of the fix, we lay back, lost in our nods. "We're almost out of money, and we have yet to pay the hotel bill," Sue drawled.

"I know."

"We're running low on dope, too."

I was too tired to think of those things. "Let's worry about that tomorrow." I closed my eyes. Beautiful visions of happiness appeared: heroin falling from the heavens while I frolicked making snow angels.

◄○►

As if seeking to sweep the darkness from the room, the sun burned through the green mottled curtains. I yawned, filling my lungs with the accumulation of sour body odours trapped in the fibers among the chaos of clothes on the floor. Then I climbed into the tight jeans that were bunched under the bed. Noticing the unraveling of the threads of the embroidered sunburst on my smock top, I began snapping off the hanging strands with my teeth.

Sue was sitting on the floor. "Your cap's on the table."

I was quickly filled with purpose and sprang to scoop the cap into my hand. The process of converting the white flakes into liquid was rewarding. Amazed at the success of injecting myself, I relished the savoury wave of the rush. I tipped back on the bed. My brain was swimming with euphoric feelings. As these sensations receded, I rose listlessly and wandered into the washroom. I glanced, then stood staring intently into the cracked, slightly blackened mirror. I drew back, startled by the sallow skin tones I saw. I closed my eyes for a moment, ran the water, and used the diminished bar of hotel soap scrubbing vigourously, as if that action would rid me of the reflection.

Once more I searched the reflective surface. The mute, sickly image returned my stare.

I plunked myself on the floor beside Sue and closed the open pack of Players lying next to my companion. "We have to go boosting . . . today."

Without opening her eyes, Sue replied, "Have to get by the front desk first."

I thumbed my nose thoughtfully as I remembered the unpaid hotel bill. As if expecting an answer, I looked to Sue, but she'd retreated further into the nod. Her head rolled lifelessly on her breast. I continued to puff my cigarette, pondering the matter for a few minutes, then threw the butt into the waste basket, and stood up. "You know it has to be done . . . so let's do it."

Sue stared resentfully before struggling up from the floor. I lifted her sheepskin coat off the adjoining hook and handed it to her.

Sue slipped it on but kept fumbling with the buttons. When she succeeded, she smiled innocently.

I puzzled over how it was that Sue could be that much higher than me. Suspicious she'd skimmed some from my cap, I frowned. "C'mon." I grabbed her elbow and escorted her into the hallway. Instead of catching the elevator, we went through the exit door and crept down the stairs to the ground floor. Here we peered around the corner and both of us smiled broadly. The clerk was absent. We ran across the lobby and escaped out the main door.

I started to shiver as my unlined jacket let in the cold. The sunlight hurt my eyes. I held a hand up to shade them while my other arm wrapped itself around my body in an attempt to hold in my fleeing body heat.

"You should get a proper coat," Sue said, as she pulled matching brown leather gloves from her pocket.

"I need a lot of things." I didn't bother to tell her that most of my possessions were stored in a corner of Peter's closet, and I did not think I could face his parents' silent accusations.

We hiked energetically along Eighth Avenue until First Street, where we crossed over and stuck out our thumbs. A man, his hair glinting with silver strands, slowed and pulled his Volvo over to the curb. "Thank God," I muttered, thankful for the quick pickup. Sue climbed into the back and I scrambled in after her.

"Where you headed?"

I gave him a wide smile. "Chinook Centre?"

This request was greeted by a grunt and the car started forward. Happy that he seemed more interested in listening to his radio, some classical station, than initiating conversation, I nervously licked my lips while Sue again retreated into the nod.

Soon the car was stopped in front of the sprawling shopping complex on Macleod Trail. Sue struggled out after me and, in unison, we called our thanks to the driver who waved as his car re-entered the traffic.

Before entering the mall's main doors, I announced the game plan— "I'll boost, you return."

Sue's mossy eyes blinked with relief; "I'll get the bags, meet me in front of Ricky's."

I gave a slight nod of my head and we separated. With confidence I did not actually feel, I walked towards the south end of the mall to Woodwards Department Store and made my way to the men's section. With a look of what I hoped was total absorption on my face, I began slowly browsing through the cellophane-wrapped shirts. I checked to ensure all the clerks were busy with shoppers searching for the pre-Christmas specials.

I felt there was a certain grace to my movements, with every muscle fiber concentrated on not drawing any attention. But I was not impressed with the shirt's prices, so I moved to a display table of men's sweaters. Despite my pounding heart, here I spotted a suitable boost, a forty-five dollar camel cashmere sweater. Again, with a few darting glances around, I stretched out my smock top and pushed the sweater beneath it.

I paused to zip up my jacket and then began edging towards the open glass doors and the mall beyond. Once past them, I peered nervously behind to be sure I hadn't been followed, then became a part of the aimless movement of the crowd.

Sue stood, as arranged, outside Ricky's, a bored expression on her peaked face. I winked as I strutted by. She ambled about ten feet behind while I led the way to the elevators just off the food court on the second floor. Sue opened the Woodwards bag held loosely by her side and I dropped the sweater into the waiting bag. As Sue moved to go, she muttered, "Ticket wicket."

I spotted a bench in front of the ticket wicket, sat down, pulled a package of cigarettes from my back pocket, and lit up.

Fifteen long minutes and two cigarettes later, I picked out her willowy form making her way towards me. Sue grinned as she closed the gap between us. I squashed my cigarette under my boot, gestured to the bench, and headed this time to the north end of the mall. I hoped that my clenched teeth were the only outward sign of my mounting tension.

The bright lights were welcoming as the red banners proclaimed "Sale . . . Sale." I made for the escalators, which took me up to Sears housewares department. Here I strolled between the aisles of kitchen appliances, took a cunning look about as I bent low over a ten dollar kitchen knife.

"Can I help you?"

I resentfully eyed the salesclerk, whose stoop seemed to add to the weight of her years. "No," I said, now pretending interest in the electric kettles but maneuvering my way back towards the escalators. Once safely down, I sauntered over to women's accessories, where I began studying a brown leather shoulder bag with a tempting thirty-five dollar price tag. Unnerved by the encounter with the sales clerk, I scanned the department, then ripped off the tags and stuffed them into my pocket. I plucked the shoulder bag off the shelf, clasped it under my arm to make it look like my own, and walked away.

Sue was circling around the ticket wicket. With an unspoken cue, she trailed me down a hallway to the exit doors by the Bamboo Inn. I stopped and thrust the purse and torn tags at her. These Sue neatly deposited into the Sears shopping bag.

From my tight mouth, a long sigh of relief escaped. "I'll wait here." I watched my companion amble out of sight. I leaned against the smooth lime green bricks that lined the hall and tried to calm down. I wished I'd managed to snatch household items since they were easier to return as bridal shower doubles. I began rubbing my cheek as my tension mounted.

Sue drifted back into view and I dropped the pretense of not knowing her. "No hassles?"

"Easy exchanges," Sue said, thrusting two twenties at me. These I pushed into the front pocket of my jeans. "I gotta get me some clothes, give me the bag."

Sue's slanted eyes opened wider, "We should split."

"Shit . . . I can't stand these smelly rags." I pointed down at my offending clothes and plucked the empty bag from Sue, who stood firmly shaking her head.

"I'd forget it. It's best to pull out when ahead."

"Don't sweat it . . . I'll be back shortly." With my teeth clenched again, I hiked off towards Dalmy's. The hip styles and cool music of the chain made it a happening store, one I frequented often. Greeted by the wailing sounds of Led Zepplin's "Stairway to Heaven," I moved to the far wall, lured by the pants lined up neatly on their hangers. In the size tens I spied a lovely shade of cinnamon brown cords. I did a quick check: the nearest sales clerk was a good ten feet away with her back turned, talking quietly to the cashier at the desk. I released the cords from the hanger pins. As I was about to deposit them in my bag, a familiar but demanding voice got the attention of the gossiping sales clerk.

"Would you help me please . . . I need a V-necked sweater," Sue's voice rang out loudly.

I smiled, feeling reassured with this added backup. "God no! Not that colour . . . don't you have lemon yellow!"

More confident, my hand deftly pinched another pair of light blue cords from their hanger. Again I stuffed them into the oversized plastic Sears bag.

The irritating voice continued barking at the cashier behind the counter, "That's lime . . . it's not what I want!"

I suppressed a giggle and re-entered the mall. "No . . . no . . . I said V-necked not turtle-necked. . . ."

With fear receding, a persistent thought kept bouncing around my head. I changed direction and headed back towards Woodwards. This time I entered through the toy section and caught the escalator up to women's wear. In the coat department I stopped by a display of Wood's ski jackets. As I whipped a size twelve off the rack, I remembered pleading with my parents for one of these when I was still in high school. Well, I'd get one now, I thought, as I shed my tattered suede jacket and wedged it into my bag. I slipped into the new one, ripped away the telltale tags, and discarded them on the carpeted floor.

I advanced towards the door. Only when I seemed safely outside did my apprehension increase, and I found myself running across the parking lot. I halted and looked behind: as I'd suspected, a heavy-set man charged past the door, then weaved through the parked cars. I increased my speed. The man's coat flapped against his legs as he started to jog after me. I flew across the last twenty feet of the parking lot and up the hill to Fuller Avenue. Afraid to glance back, I sprinted along Fifty-eighth Street. Terrified to lose even a second's advantage, I plowed blindly on, knowing that the man who followed was gaining. A few more blocks to Elbow Drive—if only I could reach it! Panicked, I rallied and continued the gruelling pace.

My breath rasped painfully in and out, filling the air above me with steam. I stumbled past the park that butted onto Elbow Drive. Made it . . . Elbow Drive . . . at last. Now what?

I ran into the traffic and miraculously saw a Checker Cab making its way along the wide highway. I ran towards it, waving my arms; afraid it would pass, I darted in front of it. The cab lurched to a halt, and I scrambled into the passenger side. The young driver seemed stunned as I croaked out, "Bay . . . downtown . . . hurry." I saw the man running onto the street and towards the cab. "Oh . . . hurry."

As if sensing my panic, if not my plight, the driver pulled over to the left lane and roared off.

"What's your problem lady?" the driver asked, as I stared out the back window at the man standing in the middle of the road, holding his knees, and staring after the speeding cab.

"Oh . . . nothing I can't handle now."

Chapter Seven

As I pulled the fit from my arm, a sense of peace soothed my thoughts and brought contentment for a few hours.

I became aware of the sudden movements about me. Prying open an eye, I observed Sue's careful application of lipstick as she preened in front of the oval mirror.

My eye slammed shut. I tried to float again, down inside myself, but the feelings of euphoria had vanished. Instead, a disturbing memory chased and caught me.

My sandals were slapping over the concrete as my silhouette darted between the street lights.

A brown half-ton truck was trailing me, the driver's face indistinguishable, a voice called from the open window, "Come here. Hey. I want to talk to you." My steps quickened, followed by the laughter of the man. "You can't out-walk me, honey." At the insistence of the voice my breath came in fast gulps. "Just hear me out . . . I won't hurt you."

Ignoring his pleas, I concentrated instead on each stride forward, all too aware of my vulnerability.

"Listen to me . . . all I want to know is, do you go out?" I showed no sign of having heard him.

"It's worth twenty-five bucks." He waved some bills towards me and I slowed to venture a sidelong glance at the money held so temptingly close. The man, encouraged by my curiosity, again prodded, "Just talk to me about it. C'mon."

I chewed my lip, then approached the truck and parted my hair, which had spread across my face like straw curtains, to examine him more intently.

"Well, what do you say?" He grinned, and his gleaming teeth clacked together. I searched his face, though for what I did not know. I saw only a middle-aged, balding man with swollen pouches under his eyes, and pudgy red-stained cheeks.

"I'm not sure what you want."

"Don't play dumb, honey." He gestured to his crotch.

"Oh!" I stepped back.

He flashed the bills again, but I did not see them—instead I saw only a small white cap. I willed myself to stop thinking about anything else as I walked around and jumped into the passenger side.

The man chuckled. "Knew you'd come around. Don't worry none, it won't hurt . . . if you relax."

My mind sank into neutral, as if it were a sponge unable to absorb any more. I couldn't remember the drive, or where we went or by what route. But the images of lying against the leather seat and the man's palms sweaty with eagerness removing my jeans and underwear were starkly clear. I offered no resistance and yet was unwilling to help. Wincing under his gyrating thrust, my head turned away and my mouth clamped shut trying to avoid his slick tongue. His words beat against my ear drums—"if you relax."

When he finished he heaved himself off. With my eyes averted I dressed, afraid to look as the man placed the crisp bills in my hand.

I flung open the door and ran blindly with the man's calls booming into the night, "Hey what's the matter? Don't you want a ride somewhere?"

I moaned, struggling to come out of the nod. I couldn't stand seeing any more.

◄O►

"What's your problem?" Sue was momentarily distracted from the careful application of liquid black eyeliner to enhance her green eyes.

I gave her a mutinous look. "I can't do it . . . I just can't."

Sue gritted her teeth. "What the hell are you going to do . . . be sick? I ain't gonna fix ya . . . I'm done with that."

I glanced up, surprised at the contemptuous way Sue snipped her words. "But, it's so . . . I don't know, disgusting. Strange men poking you and all . . . don't you think?" I jumped off the bed and helped myself to one of her cigarettes in an attempt to focus on something else. Lighting it, I orbited around the room.

"Relax," Sue snapped. "It ain't that bad and it beats being sick. . . . Besides, the time you'll get if you're popped isn't much compared to, say, what your old man just got." Then, with cynicism, she prodded, "You ain't gonna tell me you never done it before. Just about anyone who gets this far has . . . I do it between my deals and have for some time."

Eyeing me brightly, she pointed her finger, "You probably done it between boyfriends."

"Don't take it so bad. We all have to dabble in it. It's not as if we all have old men plotting rip-offs, doing ARs, and rolling over drugstores to keep us supplied. If we do . . . well, you know how that can work out."

I crouched back down on the edge of the bed and confessed, "I guess so . . . I've done it twice."

"Well, there you go . . . see."

"But . . . I hated it. The first time was the worst." Seeing Sue's interest, I continued. "I had this fight with Peter at the York about the way he divided the cap. Two thirds for himself, a third for me," I snorted. "Well anyway, I stormed out. On the way home this guy in a truck propositioned me. I thought what the hell. I'll get my own cap and show that prick. But I still can't believe I actually did it." I shook my head.

Sue smiled knowingly. "The other?"

"Oh . . . that, Peter was fronted a couple of bundles from this guy from Van. Great dope. Well, he came up short both times. So the guy cut him off. We were sick . . . so, I know the dealer digs me . . . he was always drooling when we was there. So naturally I thought maybe he'll front me a cap and then Peter would figure some way to be square with him. But the dealer laughed when I propositioned him and said no way he'd front me, but if I fucked him he'd give me one."

I began butting my smoke in the ashtray again and again, destroying all traces of the red cinders. I looked up, "I've never told this to any one."

Laughter greeted my confession. "I don't see no problem. You're broke in already. . . . Shit, quit acting so virginal. Most housewives are no better than us. Eh? We do it for dope. They do it for a roof over their heads."

"Maybe you're right." I dropped my chin to my chest before protesting again. "Shit. All those strange men fucking you . . . AGH!" A housewife only has to do one guy, but us. . . ."

"You can be so morbid." Sue clicked open her Max Factor face powder case. "Now either get yourself ready or figure some other way to get your fix." She straightened the spaghetti strap on her shoulder and adjusted the silver dress that barely covered her crotch. With a move that ended the conversation, she applied the finishing touches to her cheeks, and then stood by the door tapping her foot—"Well . . . come on."

"Okay, then." I ran a brush through my hair, put on my jacket, burrowed deep into the warmth of the goose down, and tagged along.

"Jesus, I wish you'd stop looking like we're going to a funeral."

"I feel like I am . . . my own." Other than brushing my hair, I'd made no other preparations. But I still felt that in my face there was still a touch of wholesome appeal that the made-up Sue lacked.

As we walked over to the strip, fine white snow fell softly on our heads. The cold wind of the afternoon had died down, replaced by a gentler breeze from the west. Sue kept rattling off all the things she felt I must remember. "Never let a trick kiss you or touch your breasts: you're a lay . . . not a lover. Insist on a condom, but don't push it, as most johns don't like them . . . and it's nothing a shot of penicillin won't cure. Free checkups are at the Health Clinic in the Municipal Building—go once a month whether you need to or not. If you get the first trick, get him to book a room . . . preferably at the Calgarian or Regis, 'cause they're right on the strip and it'll cut down on the amount of walking we have to do. Now, if you're longer than ten minutes, I'll check on you. Do the same for me. . . . Are you listening?"

Without waiting for an answer she babbled on: "Always give the desk clerk three dollars, that way they'll let you go in and out freely. Remember the rates are twenty-five dollars for a lay and forty dollars for a blow. A lay is based on the price of a cap. That's why you'll find the lay and the dope are both cheaper in Vancouver. Don't ever undercut these prices or the other girls will find out and lay a licking on ya. Always be aware that the vice squad goes undercover pretending to be johns, so never mention price. That's soliciting. We can prostitute ourselves—we just can't say for how much."

"Yah . . . yah."

The strip, the block on Seventh Avenue between First Street Southeast and Centre Street South, was anchored by the York Hotel on the Centre Street end and the Beverage Block Apartments on the First Southeast end. In between lay the York Hotel's parking lot, The Legion, The Calgarian Hotel, and The Regis Hotel. Like a house that expresses the character of its inhabitants, so, too, this one stretch of pavement has a living presence. It came from the bar patrons who went in and stumbled out, from the cars that jammed and clogged it with their gassy fumes, from the women who lined the street shading the backdrop of the rundown buildings behind them, and from the johns who ambled amongst them searching to have some need fulfilled.

We stood together at the east end of the strip, just outside of the Beverage Block Apartments' front doors. From the more valued position, a few feet away from the Regis Hotel, a clutch of hookers looked us over and whispered amongst themselves.

We ignored them and huddled closer together. Sue offered a cigarette and I accepted, relieved to have something to do while we waited.

Big Marie broke from a larger group further down and began heading towards us screaming, "Get the fuck off my turf !" Her spiked, pointed leather boots made her appear to be well over six feet. The most frightening effect of her charge came from her hair, which was wound into a beehive and piled high on her head.

I turned to flee, while Sue yelled at the advancing giant—"It's a free country."

Another hooker—a slight, rather plain one, who was older—raced after Big Marie, laid a hand on her shoulder and said something. Marie turned and went back to her group.

"Who was that?" I was amazed at the woman's retreat.

"Vie."

"Why'd she help us?"

"Who knows?" Sue swung around and gave me a hard shake. "You were going to run. Down here that's the last thing you can do. If they"—she gestured to the other hookers—"know you're chicken, they'll run you off every time. If Big Marie decides to give ya a licking, you fight back. No matter what! She'll respect you more for it and won't bother you for a while. More important, you'll earn the respect of the other hookers and they'll leave you alone too. Don't ever run!" She shook me again and then let go.

I shuffled my feet wondering why Sue had such a knack for making me feel so stupid. While I pondered this, a dark-skinned man, his hair greased into a shining ducktail, stepped up to us. He looked directly at me. "You go out?" I lowered my head and hid behind Sue, who quickly sidestepped out of the way.

"Yes." I said, without looking up.

"Good," he said, and the deal was sealed, "Where to?"

"You have to get us a room in there," I pointed up the street to the Calgarian Hotel.

"Well . . . let's go." He started off, and Sue gave me a little shove.

In the small cramped quarters of room 103, I felt secure. It was well lit and clean and had a good feeling to it. I stood there and was surprised at the sight of the naked man standing before me. I remembered why I was there, but I was watching from somewhere else as I shed my clothes and folded them neatly at the foot of the wood-framed bed. I climbed between the laundered sheets, trying not to think or feel anything. It was the beginning of learning to split into two people—one who lay with strange men, and one who watched.

The man rushed over and lay down on top of me. I helped him insert his erect penis and we performed the loveless mating. He came quickly, rolled off, and began dressing. I pulled the covers over myself. The man laughed unpleasantly, as if he knew it was my first night on the job, then threw ten dollars and the room key on the bed.

I touched the money, then drew my hand away. Unable to understand the acute loss I felt, I pushed it out of my thoughts. In a tidal wave of soap and water I tried to rid myself of the unwanted cloudy sperm. I closed my eyes for a moment and let the memory of my last fix with Sue in the Alex sweep away all feelings. I knew then that the work and the smack were a matched set. I could not do one without the other.

I placed three dollars on the clerk's desk on the way out. He covered the bills with his dimpled hand and slid them off the reception desk into his vest pocket, but, he never once looked at me. With a new understanding of my place in this world, I rejoined Sue.

"Well . . . was that so bad?"

"I guess not." I shoved my thumbs through the belt loops of my jeans.

"The rest is easy, now that we got us a trick room," Sue beamed approval. "Did you remember to give the clerk the money?"

"Yah . . . yah."

A tall man stepped between us, tapped Sue lightly on the shoulder and she smiled seductively. "Give me the key." Sue winked mischievously and sauntered off with the man in tow. We were on the very edge of the stroll, a respectful distance from our nearest competitors. As I scanned the avenue, I felt very much alone. I slunk close under the overhang of the Beverage building and watched suspiciously the continuous parade of passersby.

An elderly man of about sixty stood by my side. "You go out?"

"Yes," I did not smile, yet I did not step away.

"Twenty-five good enough?"

"Yes . . . but you'll have to wait a moment till my friend finishes with our room."

"Oh, I'll just wait over there," he gestured to the Saan Store. "When you wave, I'll follow you." He crossed the street and looked engrossed with the store window displays.

In about ten minutes Sue was back. I signaled for the key. I motioned to the waiting man and slowed for him to catch up. He was already puffing as he followed me up the hotel stairs. Once in the room, I repeated my earlier experience. Although the old gent was eager, he was less than competent.

No sooner had I returned to the street than a lanky man slobbered, "You go out?" Reluctantly, I returned to the room. This time, when I'd finished with the john, I found Sue waiting in the hallway with a short stocky man. I hurried past, slipping her the key.

The wind outside was colder now, as it shifted again to the north and drove the scattered flakes before it. I stomped my feet for warmth, and winter nipped at my toes despite my boots.

A well-dressed man in a wool jacket approached. "Twenty-five, right?" I nodded indifferently and led him too to room 103.

—◀○▶—

After another couple of tricks I'd had enough and stood facing into the wind. "But I got the cash for three caps and my share of the hotel bill, and I want to quit."

"No, not yet," Sue insisted. "We gotta make more, for food, smokes, and some clothes."

"Ah shit," I bitched, unable to hide my disappointment.

A balding man with a beer belly sidled up to me. Again, in 103, I spread my legs for the money that came after. This time, when I returned, I announced, "That's it for me!"

"Suit yourself. But please just wait till I finish off my quota," Sue said, leaving with a rotund egg-shaped male.

I leaned against the stone of the building behind me, thankful for the warmth of the smoke that filled my lungs.

"You go out?" This time a young uniformed army officer asked.

"Oh . . . what the hell." He offered me his arm and I marched him off to the room.

Afterwards, I loitered in the hallway for Sue to finish with the frail man she'd propositioned. It was warmer here, and I had no desire to turn another trick. At last I was rewarded when Sue finally emerged with a grin. "Let's go score," I said.

We raced away to the other end of the street, to the York Bar, ignoring the grumbles of the scattered groupings of women who huddled together along the busy promenade. Old Jimmy was there, oblivious and nodding above his untouched beer. A closed wooden matchbox sat on the table in front of him.

I poked him playfully in the ribs. The weary eyes opened and squinted at us, "How many?"

"Twelve," I chimed happily.

"Good, that will clean me out, and I can go home," he croaked through cracked lips. He cupped his veined hand for the money, counted it, and, assured that we had not shorted him, flicked the matchbox towards us. I placed it on my lap, where I opened it and counted the caps. Satisfied, I smiled and we rose to leave.

I hid the little box in my change purse and the two of us walked back to our room. I stopped briefly at the reception desk to pay the overdue hotel bill, listening to the complaints of the wizened clerk. After agreeing to pay the balance every day at noon, I skipped off. After Sue and I fixed the first of the white caps, we lay down together on the bed side by side.

"Sure had a good night . . . and it's only ten thirty," Sue chuckled. "We got ourselves enough dope . . . so we don't have to go out till it's gone."

"UGH!"

"C'mon . . . it ain't that bad."

I rolled a Lifesaver around my mouth, clicking the sides of my teeth with it. "I'm fucking sore and I want to forget it."

"Ah . . . you'll get used to it."

Chapter Eight

As usual, the bedspread was half on the bed and half in a heap on the floor. Cigarette butts stuffed into pop bottles and milk cartons filled the room with the stinking odor of stale smoke. Chicken and pizza boxes with food still splattered inside covered the top of the dresser. Our pants and T-shirts were tossed in a corner as if they'd been regurgitated there.

Sue and I opened the door and stepped in, oblivious to the chaos about us. Then, each jockeying the other for position, we raced to the medicine cabinet for the fits. Silently, we left another red prick mark on our punctured arms. Aware only of the waves of pleasure our brains emitted, we slid slowly to the floor. The rush subsided, leaving us afloat in a world of padded reality, and the Teflon of the high held us there.

"What a bitch of a night," Sue muttered.

My voice, equally flat, complained, "Had a hell of a time with the last drunk. They're the worst . . . take forever."

"Took in a good two hundred dollars each, though," Sue's head bobbed forward, as if her neck could no longer support it.

I closed my eyes and rubbed my nose. For the first time that night my entire body was relaxed. I stroked my throbbing twat beneath my brown cords, as if to comfort it. The quiet of the moment brought its own sense of contentment.

A loud rap sounded on the door and both of us snapped upright. "Who is it?" Sue asked crossly.

"Don't worry now. It's Bruce," a commanding masculine voice boomed back.

"He's okay," Sue whispered, and scanned the room to make sure no evidence of dope might be lying around. Tossing the fits into a dresser drawer, her tone became more confident as she answered, "Just a minute." Then, standing shakily on wobbly legs, she opened the door.

I sucked in my breath in terror: an enormous cop filled the doorway. He was about six feet six, with a broad chest that made him look heavy in spite of his height. His eyes seemed to twinkle under his hat. "Ah, shucks, you shouldn't have cleaned the place just for me," he said. Behind him, almost dwarfed by the huge man, stood a younger, slighter officer whose face was full of curiosity, although he looked ill at ease. Still able to feel a twinge of embarrassment, I blushed over the slovenly room.

"We don't get much company," Sue said.

"I can see why," the big man laughed. "Since Sue hasn't introduced us, I'm Bruce; this is Alex."

"And you are?" He stared directly at me. I was poised for flight, although at the moment I could see no way to escape.

"Beth." Aware of the stiffening of my shoulders and spine, I began weaving my hands together.

He abruptly turned his attention to Sue. "See, Alex here, he's a rookie and is going to be working with me. He's never met a junkie, so I thought, we'll pop in on Sue. She can answer his questions better than me . . . eh! . . . Alex?" He slapped the younger man affectionately on the back.

Sue smiled, as if she'd been called on to do this before. She slid her bare feet into a pair of knee-high boots. "How about we go to the coffee shop downstairs?"

"Sounds fine," the young cop said, trying to sound casual.

Plucking her matching purse off the bed-post, Sue led the rookie away, leaving me to stare after the departing figures. What was expected in this situation? Bruce didn't look like he was going anywhere. He brushed an empty cigarette package from the wooden chair, then moved it closer to the bed. He sat down, ignoring the dirty pair of pantihose draped over the chair's back. He patted the rumpled bed and seeing me recoil, he asked, "You afraid of this uniform?" I nodded.

"I'm human underneath . . . honest . . . just relax and tell me about yourself." He smiled, as if to reassure me.

I moved to sit across from him. "What do you want to know?" I was unable to think of anything except the fits tossed so carelessly in the drawer only an arm's reach away.

"Well, for instance, how'd you end up like this?" His arm arched through the air, indicating the rest of the room and, rubbing against the dresser drawer in the process.

"Well, this room ain't bad when it's clean. The Alex even has its own bathroom. It's an awfully boring trip down memory lane."

Only later, with Sue, would I question my trust in the man. How could I have overlooked his uniform? Was my grip on reality breaking that thin? What was it about Bruce that made me believe in him? Perhaps I did belong in the psych ward. The only thing I could think of was that he seemed to want to know me. Maybe that was all—it was someone who cared. This thought frightened me more than anything. Could my need be that great? Or was I so high at the time that it affected my judgment?

"I got time." He stretched his long legs out in front of him, took a package from inside his navy jacket, and offered me a cigarette.

We puffed together for a few minutes. "I got kicked out of home and dropped out of university . . . the two kind of went hand in hand. One superimposing on the other, if you know what I mean."

"Getting kicked out or dropping out?"

"Both, but it all got carried away and I got caught in the ride." Seeing his earnest interest, I continued. "After the parents evicted me, I moved in with some friends. They were into the hippie thing . . . you know, peace, love, and all that crap. I was wild before—drinking, pot, and lots of parties. Don't get me wrong, I was no angel." A twinge of bitterness crept into my voice.

"And?"

I snorted unpleasantly. "All I did there was drugs. Hard, soft, you name it, we did it—pot, hash, MDA, acid, mesc, coke. So, instead of partying over the weekend or through the week a few times, which is what pissed my parents off so bad in the first place, this party didn't end."

"Didn't you work?"

"For a while I did, at the Dairy Queen. But it didn't last long, what with all the dope I was doing." I giggled self-consciously, then paused as the memories crowded together.

"But how did you get hooked on heroin?" I thought his eyes held the same kind of pain I'd seen in my father's, but his face remained hard.

I glanced away, my voice distant as I recounted the beginning. "One day this guy came to visit Tina at one of our parties . . . she was one of my roommates, a real winner that one. Anyway, he was wild—been in trouble since he was sixteen. That aura of the good looking, bad-boy thing, I guess. He must have felt the same about me because we hit it off instantly. He was trying to straighten his life out, had a job on the rigs. When he'd come home for his ten days down time, we'd go crazy. Well, one night we went over to Ivan's place to hang out. He was a big-time dealer and usually had smack. Peter seemed to know everybody."

I paused to consider how to proceed and moved my thumb across the bridge of my nose. The cigarette in my hand singed the ends of my hair, but I barely noticed. The web that was my life was tangled, each strand difficult for even me to understand, let alone to try to explain to someone else.

Bruce cleared his throat, which flushed me from my silence. "Well, ever since I can remember I heard about the evils of drugs . . . Mum and Dad were really down on them." I shrugged, tapped my socked foot on the floor, and sighed. "But who likes to listen to their parents?"

"You thought you were still just playing?"

"Yah, I really thought I was," I agreed. "I said, sure what the hell, I'm not going to get wired after just one fix, but it was the best high I'd ever had. Sure, I threw up lots but, like, inside I quit hurting." I inhaled and exhaled slowly before confessing more. The cop scowled, but before he could say anything I warned him. "It starts to get confused now."

"Go on . . . I can follow."

I wavered and moved further down the bed away from him. "I'm not sure I can go on." The cop said nothing and, almost defensively, I charged in again to fill the silence. "I mean, it's really fucked. Even I have a hard time believing it, let alone make any sense of it . . . but I'll try. . . . When Peter was away on the rigs I started hanging out at Ivan's and he'd fix me real good, usually for free. We became close—I admit there was also the pull of the drugs, but he was a good friend."

Bruce cleared his throat, as if to show his doubts.

"It's true," I said, and ran my tongue over my teeth. "Then one night the horsemen came and busted us. . . . Fuck, charged both of us with trafficking. It wasn't my dope but still. . . ." My voice trembled. "Mum and Dad freaked . . . put me away in the psych ward at the General Hospital. I couldn't believe it . . . I wasn't crazy!"

My voice rose steadily. "I hated it there . . . being in with those cracked people, worse than if they'd left me in jail. . . . I came down there, through. I really didn't think I was wired, but I was so sick. A few weeks later, I signed myself out. I moved in with Peter at his folks' place. Shit! None of my goody-two-shoes friends from school would have fuck all to do with me, even my hippie friends turned their backs on me."

Another long sigh, as I butted my cigarette. "Peter quit his job up north so he could be around more. Do you believe in karma?"

"No."

"Well I do . . . Peter and me were meant for each other—as if I'd known him all my life." Tears threatened to erupt and I longed to lay my tired head on the big man's lap.

Instead, the grief steeled me. "My parents, Mr. and Mrs. Middle Class, cut me off." I sneered, then my eyes grew wider, and for a brief moment, I felt cheered. "But Peter looked out for me. You know, when I went up for the possession beef—thankfully they dropped the trafficking charge— he was the only one there for me."

I recalled how he had sat behind me—brushing my hair as it fell over the back of the bench in the courtroom—his whispered words of encouragement, and how my tight body took in only the soft lulling sounds from Peter as I waited to be called.

The big policeman broke in on the vivid memory, "If he went with you, I'm surprised they didn't throw the book at you."

"Oh . . . he figured that, he sat behind me."

The cop laughed. "What was the sentence?"

"A year's probation. Unbelievable! Probably got off so easy 'cause my dad works with the police sometimes—causes of death and corpse identification," I said, "and it was my first beef. Ivan got eight years . . . some justice system."

"What happened to Peter?"

I winced and tried to hold my voice steady. "Got three years . . . AR, although his specialty was drug stores. It's funny in a way; we were trying to straighten ourselves out when the shit hit the fan. It's like he was the best thing that ever happened to me and yet together we fucked up royally."

I turned away to hide the pain, only to turn back, a biting edge twisting my words. "What the fuck . . . what would I do now anyway, be a teacher? That's as stupid as Peter thinking he could get an education and feed our habits at the same time."

"You could get help."

"Where? . . . there's nowhere . . . we're the new lepers, only they've got no island to maroon us on." I glanced at him—"Why are you so interested anyway?"

He stood up, towering above me. "I took one look at you and knew you had some class, just like Sue did when I first met her a year ago. You don't belong in this world. It'll eat you alive, burn you out before you're twenty-five. You won't even recognize yourself."

"I don't now . . . so what's the difference?" I stared at his polished black boots. The door swung open and Sue returned with Alex. Bruce motioned to me: "Well, I hope something works out for you."

"Yah, it sure has so far."

"And you," he looked at Sue sternly, "you should go home." He signalled for the younger cop, who followed him out and closed the door.

Sue's penciled lips were rigid, and her bobbed head bounced energetically. "We gotta get out of here."

Still perched on the edge of the bed, I was busy mulling over all I had just told so freely. "Why?"

"Because his coming here was a warning . . . he let us know that he knew we were here . . . so the narcs do too!" Sue insisted as she cleaned out the illicit contents of the drawer and dropped them into her wide-mouthed purse.

Instantly alert, I repeated fearfully, "Narcs!"

"Yes, narcs," Sue replied. "Get moving . . . now!" She began rooting through the heap of clothes, wrinkling her nose in disgust before throwing a short skirt and two tube tops on the bed. "C'mon Beth . . . we don't have that much time."

"Now . . . right now?" I remained unmoved by Sue's dramatic urgency.

"Now . . . trust me . . . now." Sue darted into the bathroom.

I followed and watched as Sue's precious jars, tubes, and containers of makeup were pitched into the folds of her bulging purse. Around Sue's flurry, I reached and plucked my toothbrush off the sink and returned to the room. I placed it in the front pocket of my jacket, then laced up my Grannie boots. "C'mon already."

Sue emerged from the bathroom and squawked. "Is that all you're taking?"

"Yep, everything else is dirty."

Sue glanced briefly at the skirt and tube tops she'd shoved aside. "I suppose you're right. What the hell . . . eh? We'll buy some more clothes tomorrow."

"Fucking right we will and even a small suitcase, so if we ever have anything clean we'll be able to pack it."

We chuckled in unison as Sue agreed, "Yah . . . it wouldn't look good if we arrived at the Imperial Hotel with dirty clothes over our arms."

"Got the fits and dope?"

"Of course."

"What else do we need?"

We linked arms and walked away. As we waited for the elevator, I suggested, "Let's get a room with a TV this time."

My eyes opened just as the first drop formed on the end of my nose, and I wiped at it with my thumb. There was no morning fix waiting, and the race was on to outrun the sickness that pursued me.

The warmth beneath the covers made me linger for a moment. I glanced around at the confusion and disorder of the room. Piles of clothing were strewn about, lying rumpled where they had been discarded. White Spot steaks, the gnawed remains of last night's late feast, were scattered about and a few dried-out french fries littered the floor. Beside the bed smoldered an ashtray loaded down by a mountain of butts. It was just another in a succession of dirty hotel rooms in which we rarely stayed more than a couple of days.

It was an effort to force myself into a sitting position; as I arched my back, a loud fart escaped. My long hair was matted from the drugged slumber. I picked at the sleep curds stuck in my eyes. An opened pack of Players lay on the bedside table and my yellowing fingers fumbled for one. I struck a match and sucked, watching the red glow brighten. Then I hobbled to the desk chair. I sat shivering in the morning coolness, kicking at a heap of garments at my feet. I succeeded in uncovering a T-shirt, which I pulled free from the tangled mess and dragged it easily over the grubby bra I wore continuously.

An unmoving form was curled in the double bed. "Sue, Sue," I called.

She stirred and moss-coloured eyes opened. "What time is it? I hope the bar's open. Find out will ya?" She hoisted herself free from the embalming covers and began sorting through the strewn clothes to find something of her own to wear. She unearthed a printed pink blouse and a polyester silver miniskirt, then made for the washroom.

Picking up the black desk phone, I dialed the memorized number: 144-9999. "The time at the tone will be . . . 11:32," said a recorded female voice.

"It's eleven thirty." I walked around the crummy room in search of my pants.

"I hope Young Jimmy's there already," Sue exclaimed loudly over the sounds of the toilet emptying.

I found a wrinkled pair of blue jeans under the bed, waded into them, and lit another cigarette, which made my dry tongue stick to the roof of my mouth. Wishing now I'd bought some gum last night, I tumbled down on the bed and listened, irked, by Sue's energetic gargling. Feelings of irritation were the first signs the sickness was building.

A few minutes later, Sue appeared, her face well scrubbed and made up. "Aren't you going to wash up?" Her motherly tone annoyed me more.

I crackled with resistance, "No . . . when I'm fixed."

"Really, at least you could do something with your hair," Sue insisted as I pushed past.

After I'd finished emptying my balky bowels, I discovered Sue outside the door thrusting out her well-used orange brush.

"God, a person can't get any privacy around here," I bitched. I returned to the bed to begin the time-consuming task of forcing out the knots. Closing my eyes, I grimaced at the painful pull on my scalp. After a few minutes I threw the brush down angrily.

"Jesus," Sue said, retrieving it off the floor. Feeling foolish, I ignored her and slipped my feet into a pair of suede boots. Throwing my leather bag and ski jacket over my arm I stalked out, leaving Sue to lock up. I was still waiting for the clank of the approaching elevator as Sue sped down the hall to catch up. Together we entered the lobby and hurried past the overly attentive desk clerk.

We marched along the street, matching each other stride for stride to the York Hotel. With each step I felt more cranky. Sensing my sour mood, Sue made no effort at conversation. We wanted to reach the York quickly; neither of us noticed the sun push away the clouds to shine warmly down on this chilly December day.

Five minutes later we entered the dark, cheerless bar and scanned the late morning crowd for Young Jimmy. We were in luck: he sat alone in a corner, sipping a tall glass of tomato juice. Scurrying to him, we sat one on each side.

Young Jimmy was only nineteen, with soft features and shiny light coloured hair. A tweed jacket covered his blue shirt. A pipe lay smoldering in the ashtray. Jimmy's father owned a successful chain of hardware stores, and he always looked every bit the part of a millionaire's son. Young Jimmy only made sporadic appearances on the street. He worked up north on a gas line and, on his leave, invested his money in junk; it provided a nice profit for him as well as some recreation.

"Got?" I asked, my face flushed with excitement.

"Of course." That was all the reassurance we needed. We thrust our money at him under the table.

He hastily folded the rumpled bills into his money clip. I noticed his heavy sliver clip already held a sizable wad of money. We were not the first to have found him this morning. Shielded by the table, he squeezed two white caps from a yellow balloon hidden between his legs and placed one in each of our outstretched palms.

I was deftly rolling mine in the foil I'd torn from my package of cigarettes when a surly middle-aged barmaid approached. "You two going to order?"

"Just leaving," Sue smiled at the sullen woman.

"You going to be around for a while, Young Jimmy?" I asked.

"Yah, for the next couple of days. Then I'm heading north for another three months. That's good, 'cause I don't want to get too wired . . . might get taken for Old Jimmy then." He laughed lightly, and put the pipe stem between his teeth.

"Have to be down a long time to look like Old Jimmy," I smirked. "We'll see ya later then." We bustled past the mostly empty tables, eager to return to the security of our room.

I held the cap tightly in my hand, and hummed happily to myself. "Not so grumpy?" Sue remarked, stopping for a moment to admire herself in the reflection from Sterling Furniture's showroom window.

A soft whistle replaced the hum as I walked on and then I confessed, over my shoulder, "Things are looking better."

Suddenly a hand latched onto my arm. "Calgary City Police," the voice skewered me.

"Oh God," I thought, instantly turning and shoving the big man away while at the same time bringing my hand to my mouth and attempting to swallow the dope. It only went halfway down before he tackled me; I crashed to the hard sidewalk, knocking my head in the fall. The burly cop sat on my chest, his hand clamped firmly across my neck, squeezing with deadly precision. I could feel the cap propelled up my throat.

I kept trying to gulp, driving it, willing it down. Dimly I was aware of another cop who hovered over us, shouting excitedly, "Can you see it?"

I was suffocating, my lungs screaming for air, and still the iron grip clenched tighter. I wet myself, felt urine trickling down my legs.

The cop forced his hand into my mouth, poked at the sliver speck now visible to him.

The empty juices of my stomach churned violently in reaction to the stubby fingers that probed my throat. "Spit it up!" he yelled "Spit it up!" and again tightened the deadly grip, "Spit!"

Blackness began closing in. No longer did I have the will to push down the lump. A greater need surfaced: survival. Just as I was about to cough it up, the cop above us ordered, "Enough." The choking hold released.

Swallowing hard, I finally delivered the fought-for lump to my stomach. Then, blowing and gasping, I curled into the fetal position.

I was roughly yanked to my feet and catapulted into a waiting patrol car. Squirming with discomfort, I sat in my soiled jeans, breathing hard.

"What the hell do you think you're doing?" I rasped, massaging my bruised neck.

"Come on, we know you swallowed some stuff," said the heavy cop, whose fingers were still imprinted on my neck.

"You almost killed me!"

"It sure was tempting." He laughed, and the other cop joined in.

"Where are you taking us?"

"Down to the station."

"Ah . . . shit!" I wheezed angrily, already feeling the dope being digested by my queasy insides. The ride ended as the officers braked neatly between two other cherry-topped cruisers in the police parkade.

I felt my face settle into a grim mask as I was handcuffed and hustled by my captors into the cop shop. I observed for the first time how quiet Sue was as we shuffled down a sterile hallway to the dicks' offices.

I averted my head, hoping none of the drab-suited men would recognize me and pass the information along to my father. No one paid much attention to the scruffy pair Sue and I made. We were separated and placed in adjoining interrogation rooms.

The big cop who had inflicted the pain and humiliation accompanied me. I sat on one of the wooden chairs and watched as the uniformed man straddled a matching chair. He crossed his arms across his chest and studied me. It made me realize what a wretched sight I must be with my clammy face, the T-shirt stained with steak sauce, the salt-stained black suede boots, and the wet blue jeans whose unmistakable smell permeated the room. I refused to meet his searching eyes.

I fumbled in my leather purse for a smoke and concentrated on the curling clouds that I brought forth from my lungs.

"I'm gonna report this to your probation officer." This statement startled me as much as the static silence being broken.

I tried not to show any visible sign of apprehension. "Go ahead," I wanted to shout, but my jaws locked together and my tongue once again beached itself on the roof of my mouth as another puff of smoke filled the airless room.

"We got your number and we'll bust you yet." He moved his chair closer, his knees almost touching mine underneath the small table that set us apart.

"Keep trying."

"You're a smart mouthed little bitch and I don't like you." His face, the colour and texture of stone, seemed suspended as it paralleled mine.

I shrugged, keeping my eyes downcast and my voice strong. "No one's asked you to."

Now, shifting, he was almost on top of me and I could smell his minty breath. "Who'd you score from?"

"I have nothing to say." I began clicking my nails like castanets. Peter had taught me the fine art of clamming, and they'd get nothing from me but the irritating noise from my fingernails.

"You heard me, who did you score from?" he shouted as he pounded the table.

The cop heaved his burly body from the chair. "I'll give you some time to think over the question."

"You can't keep me here." I dug my fingernails into my palms in frustration.

"I'll keep you as long as I want," he replied, pulling the door shut behind him.

"I want a lawyer!" I screamed, "I want a lawyer!" The soundproof room began to close in. Alone, except for the two chairs and a wooden table, I found the dead stillness unbearable. These rooms never seemed to change, I thought, so small, so boring. I dropped my pounding head on the rough surface of the table. I noticed it had been defaced; "B.R. was here" was carved into it. I traced a finger over the etching, wondering who B.R. was.

The sickness was worsening and a drip kept forming on my nose, forcing me to keep snuffling. Beads of sweat flowed off my face. I realized that a bump had formed at the back of my head where I had hit the pavement. Closing my eyes, I tried to shut out the bleak surroundings.

Days seemed to have gone by, instead of just a couple of hours, before a desk clerk unlocked the door. "You can go."

"About bloody time," I grumbled rising, my body creaking with the effort. The jeans had dried, leaving just the outline of a stain that was not too noticeable. Clutching my purse and cigarettes, I held my head high as I paraded again past the line of dicks' desks, back into the main reception area.

I saw Sue positioned against the glass doors waiting. Her enormous pupils told the story of withdrawal pain and her face, too, was covered in sweat and snot.

"Why the hell didn't they choke you?"

"They were so busy with you I just popped mine in and down she went before they noticed me." Her freckled face looked slightly superior.

"Why do I take all the shit?" I complained. "What did you tell them?"

"Nothing."

"Me neither," I said, stressing the second syllable as we began hiking West along Seventh Avenue. I was grateful for each step we moved away from that building. A cold wind whipped my hair and yet it felt good after the confinement.

"I suppose no point in up chucking?" I asked sourly.

"Doubt it, they kept us too long."

"Bastards," I shouted, gently touching the bruises that were forming on my neck. "We'll have to ask Young Jimmy for a front . . . but you'll have to ask him! I'm such a mess. I pissed myself you know."

"No wonder. I thought that pig would snap your neck," Sue said, trying to be consoling as she touched my hand.

We reached the York Hotel and parted. I remained outside keeping watch for the dreaded blue and white cars, hoping Sue would be able to suck-hole well enough to get a front. I paced up and down until a new misgiving began to darken my thoughts. I moved over to the other side of the building for a better view of the back lot in case Sue decided to keep both caps for herself.

A few minutes later, Sue bounded out the front door smiling broadly and I ran to catch her.

Chapter Nine

MUCUS DRIPPED FROM MY NOSE, spotting the pillowcase; goose pimples crested in wave after wave, making me feel as if I was wrapped in ice instead of wool blankets. My teeth clicked together making strange, sporadic sounds. I hugged the covers tighter.

Across from me, Sue paced as though our spacious room was a prison cell. A wooden dresser at the far wall had a framed mirror tacked above it. Off to the left a varnished desk and chair sat beside the bathroom door. Two side-by-side windows looked down onto Ninth Avenue. A small black and white television on a portable steel stand stood between the two double beds. The place was clean, except for the overflowing ashtrays and a pile of clothes tossed across the beige winged chair in the corner.

"I can't stand this much longer," Sue snuffled as she pushed herself into restless action.

With my tongue tumbling against chattering teeth, I tried to raise my pounding head from the pillow. "Ole Jimmy will be back from Van soon."

"Could be a day or two . . . no one knows anything!" Sue continued gliding aimlessly between the two walls.

"But if some stuff comes in tonight . . . we might miss it," I said, and pressed the wet pillow over my face in an effort to smother the sickness.

"We sat in the bloody bar almost till ten. If you want to sit there the rest of the night . . . go ahead, but I'm telling ya, if there was some, it would have been in. No one's got any!" Sue kicked the wastebasket and sent its contents spilling across the carpet.

Surprised at the sound, I lifted the pillow off my face. I couldn't see her, only heard the sounds of her retching from the bathroom. I grabbed a cigarette and tried to smoke it. But the smoke burned my mouth and started my unsettled stomach churning. About to butt it out, I heard a soft knock on the door. "Who is it?"

"It's Mike."

"Tell him to fuck off . . . he ripped me off last time there was a panic," Sue snapped before vomiting again.

"Just fuck off," I barked at the man, only too happy to comply with Sue's order—for the mere idea of seeing this late-night creep made me uneasy. I couldn't help recalling that his front teeth were missing, and the rest were in various stages of rot. A long white scar ran from the corner of his mouth to the edge of one of his narrow-set eyes. His nose had been broken and was twisted over, flat against his face. His black hair was filthy and curling up at the ends with grease. He was not only ugly, but I felt he represented all that was wrong with the world I now found myself in.

Undeterred, he whispered, "I got some good news."

A wad of toilet paper held to her mouth, Sue staggered from the bathroom and opened the door a crack. "Well? . . . I suppose it's the same good news from the last panic."

"The man just come into town, so if ya want, I can get. If you're going to hold a grudge then I'd say you'll be the one missing out," Mike explained.

My eyes widened, while Sue's tightened. "What man? You can forget it! You don't look fixed to me." She held the door ajar with her foot.

"Just give him a chance, Susie."

Sue retreated to the windows where she watched the street below, while tapping her nails across the glass a rapid drill-like sound.

Mike raced in and sat on the edge of my bed. "Nice place."

"It was, until you showed up," Sue retorted, her back still turned to him.

"Jesus, gimme a break." He turned to me. "I wouldn't rip you off . . . honest."

"Like hell," Sue sneered, distracted from her drumming against the window pane.

I searched his face for some redeeming quality and found none, although his blue eyes held steady. "How'd ya know we were here? We only moved in last night."

"I have my ways." He smiled, keeping his protruding lips pressed together. "Well do you want? Or do ya just want to shoot the shit?"

"Of course we want . . . you idiot!" Enraged, Sue charged over to him, her fists clenched and raised.

He lifted a palm to calm her. "Then all you gots to do is give me the money." He paused and, eyeing Sue warily, added, "Just take it easy." I stalled half way into a sitting position on the bed, unsure of what to do while Sue stood over him glaring.

He began staring at his torn and scabbed cuticles. "Well, I thought I was doing you a favour . . . but if you don't want." He shrugged, and stood to go.

"Wait." I withdrew a pile of bills from under the pillow. I peeled off two tens and a five and threw them down on the bed .

"You fool, you'll never see him again," Sue cautioned. "Look, he ain't even fixed himself."

"I ain't fixed yet cause I have to sell eight caps first for the man," he answered easily, as if expecting that observation. He scooped the money into his oily palms and tucked it in his frayed pants pocket.

"Mike, if you rip me off . . . you better pray you never go to the pen." I ran a finger swiftly across my neck. He winced and I smiled, knowing that the message was clear. Peter was known for his temper.

"You got nothing to worry about . . . so neither do I."

Sue's fists relaxed, rounding into claws.

"You'll see, Sue . . . she'll get fixed and you won't." Mike gloated and patted his pocket.

Sue seemed to consider his words for a minute before pulling out a twenty and a five dollar bill from her bra. Her lip curling, she extended it to him. "If you rip me off . . . I'll kill you myself."

He smirked and plucked the bills from her hand. "Quit worrying . . . I'll be back in thirty minutes," he said, and, moving to the door, he glided out.

"You better be back!" Sue hollered down the hall after him. Then she stomped over to her bed and threw herself down. "I know he's gonna rip us off . . . just watch . . . it's the oldest trick in the book . . . I can't believe I got sucked in again . . . and after last time too."

"Settle down . . . either he comes through or he doesn't . . . your bitching isn't going to help."

"Shut up!"

"Fuck off!" We glowered at each other as the tension in the room mounted. After what seemed like hours of unbearable quiet, Sue leaped up and trotted to the phone. She dialed, listened, and then slammed the phone back down. "According to time, he's only got seven minutes and forty-one seconds to get here."

"So . . . he's got seven minutes and forty-one seconds left." I moaned with the effort of speech as chills in mini-convulsions racked my body.

"I've had enough of this shit," Sue said, returning to the phone. "Give me the number for Air Canada," she ordered the operator unpleasantly.

I peeked over the covers, watching as Sue dialed another number, "Yes . . . when is the next flight to Vancouver?" A fleeting smile then, " Thank you."

She pulled a the small suitcase she'd purchased that week from under the bed and began stuffing her belongings into it.

I sat up and demanded, "What are you doing?"

"Just what it looks like . . . I'm going to Van," Sue replied stiffly, without looking my way.

"What!"

"We got took . . . and I'm tired of being sick," was her explanation, but seeing my angry face she added, "You can come too . . . if you want."

"No way."

"It's been six hours since our last fix. Just think . . . the last plane leaves at 1 AM. We could be in Van in two hours and fixed by three thirty." She again picked up the phone. "This is room 523 . . . I would like a cab. . . . Yes, I'll be right down." She put on her coat, leaving it open as she swung her purse over her shoulder, grabbed onto the suitcase and dashed to the door, where she hesitated. "Sure you won't come?"

"No." Vancouver was a strange world, a world I did not yet know. Fear kept me as immobile as the sickness on the bed.

"Well, I guess I'll see ya around sometime."

"Yah . . . sure." I glumly watched the door close.

◄○►

My stomach was rumbling and twisting. I leaned over and vomited a yellow-green bile into the waste basket. I wiped at my mouth, my thoughts now plaguing me as much as the discomfort I was feeling. I lay limp on the damp sheet trying to float above both the sickness and the notion that the events of my life followed a pattern of connection, desertion, connection, desertion. At last I felt myself drained of all emotion. I cared for nothing, nothing at all. Mike's rip-off and Sue's desertion rated no more than a blip on my memory screen. Both were part of this life. I digested this fact, grappling with the reality that I was truly alone and there was nothing I could do except get used to it.

The sickness brought a sense of not caring, released me from the confusion of guilt and sorrow that troubled me when I wasn't high. But it also denied comfort and peace and that was what I craved most.

The hours slipped by and stretched on; when the morning light eased through the blinds, it found me curled into a ball, rolling gently back and forth. All my strength was sapped and I'd made no attempt to move off the bed. Then I thought I heard a faint knock, and so I stayed very still, listening. "Beth . . . Beth?" a voice whispered through the door.

"Who is it?" I croaked.

"It's Mike."

Somehow I managed to stumble to the door. "You bastard," I hissed, but swung the door wide.

He unclenched his fist revealing a small white cap.

I ran to the bathroom, my hand trembling so I could hardly hold the spoon. I was in ecstasy as the needle plunged into my arm. My body stopped fighting itself. When I opened my eyes I felt the peace and comfort I'd been denied. But I also began to smell, for the first time, the sweat that covered me and the sickness that had streamed from my mouth. I scrubbed my teeth, washed my face, combed my hair, and then returned to the bedroom.

Mike was seated comfortably on Sue's bed. He wore the same clothes from the night before. However, he did not seem quite so repugnant.

I parked my rear end on the dresser. "Some twenty minutes," I remarked, lighting a cigarette and relishing the sweet smell.

"Yah . . . I wasn't going to come back, but I checked the register this morning and saw that the bitch had gone." He laughed. "I don't have nothing against you."

"That's nice." I could feel my eyes narrowing. "Where did you get the stuff?"

"Do you care?" he smiled, as if we shared some secret together.

"Not really, but I'll need more."

"I know." He suggested shrewdly, "We could be a good team, you and me."

I laughed, appalled at the thought. "I've been a team before. It didn't work out so well."

"That was then . . . this is now."

I flung my butt into the ashtray. "Who are you kidding? You want me to support your habit."

"I won't deny it. You'll get lonely and this is no life for a woman alone."

"I think I'd like it better this way." I couldn't believe his nerve.

"You'll be sick again in a few hours . . . what then?"

"I'm going down to the bar to wait with the rest of them. Wherever you got it . . . it will come sooner or later." I moved to the door, opened it, and stood waiting impatiently for him to leave.

He lunged and gave me a hard push. "I should have ripped you off."

"Maybe," I inclined my head and smiled as if taunting him to do it again.

"You don't like me . . . do you?"

"As a matter of fact, I can't stand the sight of you."

He stood with his thick lips pulled together. "You bitch . . . you'll be sorry," he warned, brushing roughly past.

"I doubt it," I countered, slamming shut the door. Anxious to have a purging bath I began singing, "Happy days are here again."

Chapter Ten

I HAD TO HIT THE street earlier and work longer hours as my need for heroin increased. I was on a treadmill of fucking and fixing. My legs were muscled from the constant streetwalking, and I could feel the hollows in my stomach and once-full cheeks.

The other whores accepted my presence; despite grumblings of resentment, I had passed probation. I claimed my own little square of pavement, just outside the Regis Hotel. The other girls' spots butted against its rough outlines but never overlapped. Everyone had their place. I was not bullied, although Big Marie always made it her business to glare, mumble threats, and bump into me. I became adept at stepping out of the big woman's way. Compared to what damage Big Marie could do, it was nothing. I did not question why the others allowed me to stay; I just showed up and stood alongside them.

The only part of the routine that I came to enjoy was the solitude of my room, where, for a few hours, I did not have to share any part of myself. My junk was the only company I craved or needed.

I huddled with four working girls behind the glass doors inside the Calgarian Hotel lobby. My reddened hands were shoved deep inside my jacket pockets. I gulped in the warm air, dreading the next time the desk clerk would force us back out into the cold. These evictions seemed to be timed in one-hour intervals, unlike the Regis where we were constantly shooed back onto the street.

I noticed Vie eyeing me. Only thirty-one, she was one of the oldest prostitutes. Her face was sanded by street wear; her skin was almost transparent, stretched over a shrinking skull. She resembled a matronly school marm with her black laced-up Hush Puppies, beige skirt and coat. Wire rimmed glasses perched on her thin nose; with her brown eyes, she exuded an air of confidence.

"Would you like to know why I stopped Big Marie from running you off the strip that first night you showed up with Snaky Sue?" she asked.

"I suppose." I felt apprehension about the older woman's directness.

"Because you were Ivan's old lady till he got popped . . . and he's an old friend of mine." She laughed, as I stepped back in surprise.

"You knew Ivan?"

Her mouth turned up at the corners. "Sure did . . . how about we meet, say eleven thirty, at the York lounge for a rap."

I seized the invitation. It had been weeks since Sue's departure and sometimes my isolation hit me hard.

"It's settled." Just then a small foreign-made car honked. Vie turned. "One of my johns . . . see ya later."

I turned to Gloria, who was leaning against the other door in apparent boredom. At twenty-nine, Gloria was beautiful in spite of the tiny lines that had set in around her eyes. For some reason I admired her: her blond hair fell in wisps around the worn splendour of her face.

Gloria's Madonna profile belonged in a carved cameo, not staring through smudged glass from a seedy hotel lobby. I tried to imagine how stunning she must have been in her youth. I held an uneasy hand up to my own face.

"Isn't it dangerous to trick in a car?" I asked.

"Sure . . . but it's cheaper than getting a room."

"Of course . . . of course." I remembered my first time had been in a truck.

The older woman looked over. "A lot you haven't thought about."

Before I could think up a retort, an old man, his white hair unable to hide the pink of his scalp, tapped on the glass and pointed to me. I dragged myself out of the lobby.

It was eleven thirty when I finished tricking my last john and made my way to the York lounge. My cold toes curled around the wad of bills hidden in my left boot. I calculated the night's take. Over two hundred dollars: it was enough to keep me going for another day.

I spotted Vie sitting in the corner of the dark lounge sipping on a tall glass of something pink. "So . . . you were Ivan's old lady?"

"*Were*, or *was*, are definitely not the right words."

The eyes studied me as if I'd become an opponent. "First let me tell ya why I wanted to meet with you. Then we can go score together . . . eh?"

The waitress tapped her order pad. "What would you like?"

"Brown cow." I slipped out of my jacket, and we waited until the waitress left.

Vie whistled under her breath. "I never thought I'd see the day when one of Ivan's old ladies would be working the street."

"First, I'm not or ever was his old lady. Second, I got a habit to support . . . a habit, I might add, he helped along."

"My, you are a touchy little thing. Now sit down . . . I ain't finished."

I sank slowly back into the red leather chair.

"That's better. What I really want to know is why you haven't written him?" Her hands gripped the edge of the table, and I saw a glint of malice in her face.

"I don't think it's any of your business." I hoped I sounded braver than I felt.

"But I do, as I told you . . . he's an old friend and I don't like to see my friends hurting."

"But I got nothing to say to him."

The woman stretched in her chair and lit a cigarette. "The guy's in for eight years . . . I figure you could think up something. There ain't a letter I get from him he don't ask about you."

I sucked on my drink, relishing the chocolate taste. "I'll write him if only to tell him I don't know where he got the idea we were more than friends and that that ended the day we got popped."

"I don't give a shit what you say, that's up to you . . . I just want him to hear something from ya."

"You really care for him?"

The older prostitute crossed her legs. "Yes, and it's lucky for you I do . . . or I'd help the other whores kick the shit out of you. You seem to forget that you're in Rounder territory. We're not chippie hippies, and we certainly don't believe in free love."

I looked at her with new understanding: "You mean to tell me Ivan's the only reason I ain't been run off the strip?"

"You forget, this is a very competitive field. Us older ones band together to get rid of the younger faces. In your case, I made an exception 'cause Ivan asked me to look out for you. Don't look so surprised, there are only so many johns to go around."

"I must say, though, that after talking to you I'll be damned if I can figure out why he seems to care so much for you."

I lowered my eyes, unable to answer.

"I might as well warn you since you're here. Watch your step. I hear you're fast becoming a good money maker and there's lots of jealousies out there."

"How'd they know what I make . . . I don't see or talk to hardly anybody."

"First law of the street, everybody knows everything . . . you got no secrets. And the second law is, never trust no one."

For the first time a smile softened her tight lips. "Ya know . . . I came here determined I wouldn't like you. No disrespect, but there must be something about being young and stupid." She shook her head, reached over and patted one of my hands. "Now . . . let's go score."

"We could fix up in my room . . . I don't get much company."

Vie nodded in agreement and threw five dollars on the table. "My treat."

Back out in the freezing cold, I marvelled that Ivan had reached out from behind bars to offer an umbrella of protection.

◄○►

An arrangement of white lilies filled a crystal vase and packed my nose with their smell. My grandmother had called them the death flower, and their placement in one of The Palliser Hotel rooms made me uneasy.

I watched behind lowered lids as the trick unbuttoned his coat, then tossed two one hundred dollar bills onto the bureau. I tucked the bills into the side of my left boot and waited for instructions: it was obvious he wanted more than a lay.

I observed the roundness of his stomach as he folded his pants over a chair. I studied his flecked gold eyes as he handed me his charcoal belt. I covered my naivete with a smile and fingered the buckle as he slipped out of his briefs. He leaned over the bed exposing his buttocks and, with his teeth, began pulling his leather gloves from his hands.

"Leave only your boots on. Remember, I want to feel the pain. Name is Dan."

As if I had been born for this, I planted my feet and swung the belt. I enjoyed the sound of the leather against his flesh. "You're bad . . . a bad boy Dan." I swung again and found my rhythm: "Danny's a bad boy . . . a bad boy."

The man had a rhythm of his own, as he took up a pleading chant: "Yes . . . yes . . . sooo sorry . . . sooo sorry."

With each swing, I felt a thrill of satisfaction. As the belt whizzed through the air I could hear my mother's voice. "The sight of you makes me want to puke." I readied to swing again, feeling as if my mother was in the room with us—"You're like a dog in heat." This tumbled out of my mouth as, "You're a dog, Dan, a filthy dirty dog." The belt was a living thing as it flew through the air to embrace Dan's backside.

"You're more trouble than you're worth," became, "Bad boy . . . you're more trouble than you're worth."

To each of my swings, the man's mantra continued. "Sorry . . . sorry . . . sooo sorry."

Both of us were in a high state of arousal as Dan turned on his back and began wiggling up the bed, masturbating. I continued to lash him between his legs, my voice reflecting my anger. "Wicked, lazy, no good, worthless, bad boy."

Dan's voice had speeded up with the movement of his hand. "Get over here and piss on my face."

I was enjoying this much more than I should. I dropped the belt, kicked the pillows away, and planted my heels on either side of his head. I emptied my bladder over his eager features and then watched as he reached orgasm.

As I was zipping up my jacket Dan tucked an extra fifty dollars into my palm, saying, "For your enthusiasm."

I ignored the cold and the falling snow as I walked slowly back to the strip. I was unable to rid myself of the disturbing scene: I could never again do a kinky trick—I had enjoyed it too much.

◄○►

Vie began dropping in after work. In anticipation of her visits, I bought an extra cap for my new-found friend.

Too old to be a good money-maker, Vie made enough to scrape by. I turned johns away and money came easy. As if it was her due, Vie took the fixes and continued her good words with the other whores.

In the middle of a sentence, Vie would nod or drift off, neck stretching to tip her head to her chest, her hands curled under her chin. Even awake Vie showed no emotion.

I saw a hint of feeling only when Vie spoke of her the children she'd abandoned along with her husband, six years before. She never saw them, but she wrote to them once a month.

I began to think of her as an older sister who told me where the cheapest trick rooms were to be found, what shifts the obliging desk clerks worked, and where to go to trick a john in a car.

I also discovered that Vie had gone to school with Ivan. As long as she could remember, they'd been friends. Finally, I did sit down one night, using the hotel's stationery, to write Ivan. I found it difficult to put words on the unlined paper. The violence of our bust was still fresh in my mind: the night I'd fallen into a nightmare and burned my life into fragmented pieces. His free fixes and the nights spent in his company while Peter was away on the rigs sentenced us both. I'd yet to forgive myself. Instead, I filled the letter with anecdotes about my life on the street, and thanked him for his concern. As I dropped it in the red mailbox, I felt confused by my lack of honesty. Afraid of losing Vie's protection, I had not confronted him about his crazy notion that I was his old lady.

◄○►

A persistent car horn broke the silence of the street. I glanced up the deserted strip like a dreamer waking. I moved warily to the cop car and the officer who was impatiently waving me over with one hand while his other hand continued to lean on the horn. I glimpsed only the tilt of his head through the half-opened window as he ordered, "get in."

I opened the passenger door and sat primly on the seat, secure in the knowledge that I was not packing and my last trick had been at least a half-hour ago. This would be a round of "see if there are any outstanding warrants." But this officer did not turn on the car lights and remained a shadowy silhouette. His blue-rimmed cap almost touched the top of the car's roof, so he must be tall.

"I didn't do nothing."

"I don't give a shit about you. What I want is info on Frankie," the male voice thundered back.

I jumped and twisted my eternally itchy nose between my fingertips. Frankie was the black pimp who ran a string of girls who rarely worked the strip. Mostly, Frankie only joined us hypes to score at a meet. Since Frankie was no dealer, this cop's demand seemed a ruse.

"Don't know no Frankie."

"Bullshit! Everyone knows Frankie."

"Well, I don't." I rested my hand against the steel of the door handle just as the click of the lock sounded. Suddenly, my head was pushed down to him.

"You blow, bitch."

I tried to twist free, but the grip around my head remained steady, pushing me closer to the rigid cock poking through his undone zipper.

"Open wide," the cop laughed, thrusting his penis into my mouth where it butted against my teeth. I could taste him and I tried to jerk away.

"Open wide or else I'll make your life a misery by dragging you in every night."

His hold on my head remained steady until I parted my teeth. Then the cop began using my ears as grips to lift my head up and down, up and down. I hated men who used my head as a battering ram to push deeper down my throat. It took away the only form of control I had.

His hands stretched my neck to eye-level. "Let me feel you swallow."

I willed the salty load down, managing to swallow my anger and rage. The door clicked open and I stumbled back onto the empty street.

I waited to vomit until I had walked up the block to the old fire hall behind the Beverage Block Apartments.

I wiped my mouth with the back of my hand. Vie had been right: never trust no one.

Chapter Eleven

I WONDERED IF THE STREET light tinted my eyes lemon as I stared at the pavement beneath my chilled feet. If that was so, then perhaps the lines around my mouth and eyes would not be so noticeable. At nineteen I'd stopped examining myself, terrified to see proof I was growing old down on Seventh Avenue.

I watched the big flakes of snow fall down the length of the street, then melted back into the shadows. I coughed and spit out some phlegm. In disgust, I threw away the cigarette. The emptiness of the strip made me feel I was working a *Twilight Zone* episode. Tonight, even the homeless and unwanted had found refuge. I leaned against the brick of the Beverage Block Apartments, my head sagged forward.

The City of Calgary had dressed the downtown streets and lit the strip with seasonal cheer, but for me Christmas Eve was just another night to fill my veins and quiet the loneliness.

I had felt a deep connection with Snakey Sue; now there was only the emptiness of my room. Tonight I'd visit Jacob at his apartment, the one he'd promised to look after for his girlfriend who was currently doing time. Here he welcomed hypes off the street in return for a fix. It had become a regular shooting gallery, a junkie drop-in centre.

I heard the engine of an approaching car, and stepped quickly out to the curb. Seeing the blue-and-white vehicle, I spun around and began walking along the sidewalk in the opposite direction.

The cop slowed to a stop, honked, and waved me over.

Cops did a lot of waving. I obeyed by edging around to the driver's side. With relief, I recognized Bruce.

He rolled down the window, "For God's sake Beth, what are you doing out tonight? Don't you know it's Christmas Eve?"

There was something about the way he smiled that made me want to wish him a happy holiday, but, remembering his question, I mumbled, "No place to go."

"You must have somewhere . . . for Christ's sake, it's Christmas Eve."

He sounded angry. I brushed the snow off my boots. "Lost some pounds you didn't need to since I saw you last."

"Yah . . . I guess."

"It's not healthy. What you need is some good home-cooked food. Why don't you come over to my house . . . I get off my shift in fifteen minutes . . . C'mon, hop in."

I ran a hand through my hair, feeling as if I held a mirror and saw myself clearly for the first time in months. Tight cords, high-heeled boots, T-shirt underneath my fur jacket, all screamed of my trade. The too-red lipstick and rouge on my face probably looked clownish. Thoughts of a family setting made me want to flee, as if I might have something that was contagious.

"I can't . . . but, um . . . thanks anyway."

The cop persisted, "Aw . . . what you afraid of ? No one will say anything to make you feel bad, and I'll bring you back after you've had something to eat and the kids have opened some presents."

Seeing that I still hung back, he cajoled, "The wife wouldn't mind . . . in fact I'm sure the whole family would be happy to share our holiday with you this evening."

He was not afraid to bring me into the midst of his family, a place cops guarded jealously. I rubbed my hands together like kindling sticks. "Why ya doing this?"

"'Cause I want to, and that's all there is to it . . . honest. You could say that I'm filled with the spirit of Christmas."

Satisfied that he had no hidden motive, I smiled. "Thanks, Bruce, but I got some friends I gotta meet later. Besides, don't you think your family would want you all to themselves tonight . . . not have to share you with something you dragged in off the street? Give them a break." Surprised at how brittle I sounded, I placed one of my hands on the cop's jacket.

"Well, my little urchin, if you won't come home with me, how about I take you out? I'm sure we could still find some place that's open to get a bite to eat. What'ya say?"

I shook my head. "I can't be seen with you . . . people will think I'm a rat or something." I withdrew my hand. "Thanks anyway."

"Well, just remember if there's anything I can do, let me know."

He was disappointed, and I, too, felt regret.

Then I moved in closer, trying to hide my excitement. "Yes, I do need something . . . and you just might be able to help."

"Shoot then."

"I have to find out why they won't let me see my old man . . . or if it's true that he doesn't want to see me."

"What's his name?"

"I told you before."

"Oh, yeah . . . Peter wasn't it? You know, after our last talk I had him checked out. He's bad news . . . you're better off not seeing him."

"You ask if there's anything you can do and I tell ya . . . and then you go acting all cop."

"Okay, okay, don't go huffy on me. I won't promise much, but I'll look into it out for you, eh . . . my Christmas present to you, let's say."

Seeing my smile, he raised his hand again in caution. "I think you should know that there's a guy out here right now biting off hookers' nipples. So far he has contained himself to a few call girls, but you never know when a pervert like that might strike down on the street."

"Merry Christmas." I backed away from the car, annoyed he had to bring up reality.

"Same to you kid." He grinned and cruised away.

I sat down on the steps of the Regis Hotel. A part of me was grateful for his invitation, the rest of me was unsettled. My only offer of Christmas cheer came from a cop. To be such a charity case, to be so friendless and disconnected, was galling. I spotted another car travelling down the empty street.

I held out my thumb to the passing silver Oldsmobile. It braked to a stop and I climbed in, happy for the distraction.

"Know where a guy can find a little action?" asked a man, dressed in jeans and a bulky jacket.

"Right here." I swallowed hard and flashed an obliging smile.

The trick paid two hundred dollars for an hour of my time—something I had plenty of tonight. It had been a fair exchange. Christmas Eve was as empty for him as it was for me. Funny thing, this hooking business, that he should pay when I was as lonely as he was. I accepted his offer for a lift back to the strip, though I'd hoped that I might stay away longer.

I paced along the deserted strip, moving between the York and the Beverage Apartments like some kind of zoo animal. I was about to give up when a mini-wagon idled alongside.

A kid in his teens unlocked the passenger side. "Merry Christmas. . . . Are you what I think you are?"

"And what's that?"

"You know . . . umm . . . a lady of the evening."

"What's it to you?" I tried to stretch my legs in the cramped space.

"Got some money from the folks to get a sweater for Christmas. They're back in Moose Jaw, and I got to thinking I ain't never had a hooker . . . so I just took it in my head to go looking for one. Hey, they must take Christmas off, 'cause you're the first I've seen." His face reddened.

"This one's still working . . . answer your question?" Something about the kid was irritating.

"Twenty-five, and you do it in the car. I gotta get over to my cousin's place. I'm late already . . . know a place?"

I directed him down by the river just off Ninth Avenue. Our mechanical act was quick, and I pushed his Christmas money into my pocket.

Minutes later, I was taking the stairs up to Jacob's place. I banged on the second apartment door on the top floor.

"Who is it?"

"Beth." The door swung open. I joked with the ungainly man who towered over me. "Think narcs knock, you goofus?"

"Merry Christmas." He bowed down and planted a wet kiss on my cheek, making me wipe at my face with my sleeve.

Linking his arm through mine, he led me down a brightly lit hallway to the living room. It was crammed with people. Three female bodies crowded together on a love seat. A man with transparent blue eyes sat at their feet, blond hair styled in a crude Rod Stewart cut. On a recliner sprawled Rick, and my spine tingled with unease. "Hi . . . babe," he drawled, doing a fair imitation of a Texas accent.

"Hi yourself . . . you got?" Jacob and I settled down on the shag carpet near his feet.

I could not understand how Rick, who resembled a greaser from the fifties, commanded so much respect. His black hair was slicked back, his white T-shirt with a pack of cigarettes rolled up in the sleeve, his pointed black leather boots—all out of a Jimmy Dean movie. "Fuck, not another front," he growled.

"No, cash," I said, clutching my purse closer.

A red-haired woman on the love seat snarled, "Ain't no one got money 'cause there ain't no tricks."

"Did you look for any?"

"No point in that. I knows there ain't, so why bother?"

"That's why you ain't got no money." I eased myself over to Rick, who gestured for me to sit on the arm of his chair.

"You lazy good for nothing . . . here comes my idea of a hard-working whore." He patted my arm. His touch reeked of ownership, and I fought an urge to slap his hand away.

I glanced around the room and saw they were all fixed. I knew then they'd been fronted. None dared to speak because as long as Rick had the stuff, he was king. The bushy red-headed one whined, "Aw, she must have ripped off someone 'cause no one gets tricks on fucking Christmas Eve."

"Shut up . . . at least I don't have to play Santa Claus to all of ya." He hauled up his long body, and I followed him to the bedroom, just off the small kitchen. It was the most exotic room I'd ever seen. On a round bed a frilled red bedspread was covered with white lace. Tapestries lining the walls depicted men and women in various stages of fornication. A blind with the naked body of a woman outlined in red covered the window, and several sheepskin rugs were scattered over the floor. A faint odor of perfume filled my nose. A small Pomeranian ignored us from a heart-shaped basket in the corner.

"Pretty wild . . . eh?" Rick counted the two hundred dollars I'd given him. Into my outstretched palm he placed eight caps. I tore open one and tasted it. Satisfied with the bitter taste, I wrapped them in some cigarette foil and stuck them in my purse.

"I wouldn't rip you off," Rick said, noting the tasting ritual.

"That's what they all say."

We left to join the others in the living room. Someone had turned on the radio and "Silent Night" was playing. I stood and watched the unnaturally still bodies.

I closed my eyes, trying to dispel my unwanted memories: I could picture the fireplace blazing and my grandmother playing carols on her old Steinway piano.

"C'mon sit here," Jacob patted the floor beside him.

"Naw . . . I'm going to use the can and then I best be going." I had no intention of spending any more time in Rick's company. I didn't need to be any more creeped out.

"Aw . . . Beth you could help me liven up this party," Jacob said.

"That would take a miracle," I said.

As I was cleaning up, I heard one of the women growl, "She makes me want to puke . . . thinks she's so fucking good."

"She's okay," Jacob said.

"Ain't nothing but a two-bit whore, like the rest of us," another female's voice joined in.

"She's the best two-bit whore on the strip—makes more money than the three of ya put together," Rick said.

The man from the floor joked, "Then she'd make someone a hell of a good old lady . . . ain't bad looking either."

"Leave her alone, Lanny, you wouldn't want to mess with her old man," Jacob warned.

I pushed my ear against the door, I was beginning to enjoy this conversation.

"Shit, he's inside—and I heard that he don't even want to see her."

"That's so," the one they called Lanny said.

Vie had warned: everyone knows everything about everybody down here. I flung open the door and sat next to Jacob. I leaned against him, and, as if he understood, he put his arm around me.

The unnatural silence in the room was broken when the red-haired woman stood up and announced, "I gotta get some smokes before the Chink closes down that dump he passes off as a store. I'll be seeing you around, Beth, honey."

"Don't pay no attention to Debbie . . . she's just naturally a bitch," Jacob said, his awkward features crinkling sympathetically. The toned blond man sprawled across the floor was eyeing me. His stare made me nervous. First Rick, now this stranger's blanched eyes blasting me like a welder's torch. I ducked my head into Jacob's armpit, but, when I looked up again, the watery bluish eyes still held me in their sights. Agitated, I lit a smoke. After a few hurried puffs, I declared, "I'll be rolling along now."

"Aw, stay just a little longer," Jacob said.

"No, I gotta go to my cousins'. But thanks for saying I could come over anytime, 'cause I had to score. Oh . . . is Rick gonna be around tomorrow?"

"Yah, all day." Jacob squeezed my knuckles and I winced.

I shook free, then clutched my purse to my chest. Jacob protested, "Why you being so unsociable? I know you don't have nowhere to go."

"Just shut up and I'll see ya around." With a sense of busting free, I went down the dimly lit hall to the fire exit. The rickety steel stairs zigzagged their way down into the darkness of the alley. I was flustered by my need to get away, and wounded by the return of my loneliness. A few steps from the bottom, I paused to admire how clean the tiny snow flakes made everything.

Just as I was about to emerge from the alley into the lights of First Street, a figure moved in behind me. An arm hooked around my neck, and I felt the steel point of a knife under my ear.

"Give me the dope." I recognized the voice of the red-haired woman. I raised the heel of my boot and brought it down on her shoe. As the blade sliced through the air, I spun and slammed my metal-framed purse into the woman's gut. The redhead doubled over and I raised my knee and brought it up under her chin, knocking her upright again.

I clutched the woman's thick hair, then flung her to the ground. The penknife fell from the woman's hand onto a cushion of snow. I scooped it up and aimed another kick at her backside. She struggled to get up and my next blow sent her sprawling again.

"Bitch . . . bitch," I stormed at the woman, who was scurrying away on all fours, as I continued to aim well placed kicks at her backside.

"NO . . . no," the woman tried to raise herself off the ground, only to have me kick her down. It was as if she had become a focal point for all my pain and anger. As my kicks continued, the woman struggled to protect her face with her hands.

"I ain't such an easy mark"—I was reveling in my victory as I ran the small blade smoothly across one of her shielding hands. Blood spurted out, accompanied by the woman's piercing screams. Frightened by the sight of the blood, I ran, the knife still in my hand. As I entered the lobby of the Alexandria hotel, I tossed the knife in my purse. The night desk was staffed by Duncan, whose glasses were perched lopsided on his nose. He looked up from the pile of receipts scattered across the register book.

"Lord of Mercy . . . you've got blood on your clothes and hair." He started around the desk for a closer inspection, but I waved him away.

"It's nothing, just a family disagreement. Duncan, if anyone asks, could you say I've been here most of the night, say, since eight?"

The apple face wrinkled in thought, as he rubbed his silver stubble. "Sure. Go take care of yourself. Don't worry, I'll cover for you."

"Thanks." I flew towards the stairs.

"Hey, aren't you even going to wish me a Merry Christmas?"

"Merry Christmas," I whispered to myself.

Chapater Twelve

I'D BEEN ASLEEP FOR ABOUT three hours when there was a pounding on the door.

"Hurry. Open the door. It's Vie."

"Oh, Jesus! Hold on." I pulled the blanket along, using it as a wrap as I unlocked the door. Vie stalked in.

"What time is it?"

"About five thirty." Vie half-smiled as she produced a wad of bills from her coat pocket. My eyes widened as she flipped the money revealing fifty and one hundred dollar bills.

"What the hell did you do, rob a bank?" I shook my groggy head and bolted the door.

"Nope, I rolled a john." Vie balanced on the edge of the bed and lit a cigarette. Her hiked up brown-toned skirt hiked up exposed a hole on the knee of one of her nylons.

"You did what?"

"Piece of cake . . . he was staying in the same hotel as me. You know the Carlton . . . and on the way to my room last night . . . I see this guy sleeping, his door wide open . . . his wallet on the bedside table. So I tiptoed in and helped myself . . . and now I'm $2,400 richer."

She fanned herself with the money. "Well . . . how'd ya like to come to Van with me?" Vie stroked her exposed calf, dropping a couple of the bills to the floor in the process.

"Really?"

"Yah . . . really!" Vie mimicked. "I can't stick around here . . . When that guy wakes up, the cops will be crawling all over the strip . . . and I was even registered in the same joint. No, I got to clear out till the heat's off. Anyway, this'll be a holiday for us . . . eh? The best hotels, food, and lots of dope. I was gonna go by myself, but that wouldn't be no fun. And I got to thinking . . . you fixed me quite a few times lately. No one does that for old Vie no more . . . so, kid, you're it. Sound good to ya?"

I dropped the blanket and ran around the room, hunting for something to wear. I found a pair of jeans and a T-shirt on the threadbare carpet. Throwing cosmetics into my purse, I began to open drawers, tossing my clothes onto the bed.

For the first time I heard Vie laugh. It was soft, like raindrops against glass. "Ya know . . . I was going to ask how soon you could get ready . . . 'cause I got a cab waiting. But skip the suitcase, 'cause we're going light."

—◄○►—

I felt like a kid on a trip to Disneyland. I peeped out the window of the plane admiring the masses of clouds. Vie sat looking serene, picking at the pancakes and sausages on her breakfast tray. I felt too elated to eat and had asked the stewardess for a chocolate milk. Driven by a junkie's sugar craving, I usually ate Turkish Delight and Nelsons Four Flavored to accompany this choice beverage. I began digging through my purse, but I found only a Coffee Crisp bar. I tossed it back into my bag.

"By the time they get around to taking this tray we'll almost be there, so I'm going to catch some shuteye," Vie said.

I finished the last of the chocolate milk and settled into my seat. Soon, I too drifted, until the pilot awoke us. "We are now approaching Vancouver International Airport. Please fasten your seat belts."

I edged closer to my window and watched as the plane eased down over the water. We landed with a bump on the paved runway. When it was our turn to disembark, Vie hurried us through a confusion of hallways, escalators, and many airline booths to a fleet of waiting taxis.

We took the first cab in the long line. "Hastings Street . . . hurry," Vie ordered the driver. She wriggled her bony ass into the plush seat and promptly dozed off again. My eyes almost danced as the great city began rolling past in a maze of interlocking streets.

I rolled the window halfway down to let the fresh sea air blow in. I'd forgotten how much I loved the sea—longed for it as much as I yearned for the child who had once felt safe along its shores. As we approached the centre of the city, with its usual muddle of industrial smells, I sighed and rolled the window up again.

The cab let us off at a place that looked as if it once held the city's heart, but concrete branches that extended in all directions had sucked the life from it. A couple of cars passed on this early Sunday morning, their tires rumbling eerily down the street. Most of the people I saw were slumped figures in doorways. Framed under a gloomy sky that threatened rain, they added to the bleakness of the decayed street. We stepped over a drunk sprawled in the middle of the sidewalk, vomit still drying around his lips. His tongue lay exposed in the bottom of his open mouth. A cold Pacific wind blew loose pages of a newspaper along the sidewalk. This street was a world away from Calgary's Seventh Avenue. I was glad that I was not walking it alone.

We had gone about two blocks when a young man with hair clinging to his shoulders stepped from the shadows of a sooty apartment building. "You looking?"

"How much?" Vie glanced nervously up and down the barren street.

"Twelve."

"Make it ten and I'll take what ya got left." Vie's eyes were darting in all directions.

"Done," the young man smiled, exposing a broken front tooth.

"Tell ya what . . . I'll get a room there," Vie pointed across the street to a chipped sign that read Champs Hotel—"and I'll fix ya too," she offered, almost as an afterthought.

"Sure." He followed as we darted across to the hotel.

I stood in the lobby, appalled that it dared to call itself a hotel. The smell of the place was horrific, a stew of body odor and human waste. The desk clerk, his face chalky white, took the three dollars Vie put on the battered desk and handed over a rusted key with an indistinct number scratched into it.

We scaled a flight of creaking stairs and ambled down a dim hallway. I tried to hold my breath in an effort not to gag at the putrid odors. We stopped in front of a door that had a faded ten outlined on its surface.

"I guess I don't need this." Vie threw the key in her pocket when she saw the lock had been broken off. She pushed the door open to reveal a floor with dirt oozing from between splintering boards. A stained mattress on a metal frame was shoved under the window. The place was bare except for a free-standing sink that had been pulled away from the wall.

"We ain't staying here . . . are we?" I asked.

"Of course not," snapped Vie. "We're only going to fix here . . . so get behind the door and keep it closed so we can get this over with."

I freed the fit from my sock and tossed it to Vie. Then I stood, keeping the door shut with the weight of my body.

The dealer's raven-coloured hair must have come from a bottle, for I could see brown roots close to his scalp. He popped a small green balloon from his mouth and I watched as he wiped it on his oily jeans and squeezed three caps from it.

Vie turned one of the grainy taps on and waited as it sputtered forth with a trickle of brownish water.

Relieved of door duty, I waited for the water to run clear to clean the fit. I didn't mind a dirty fit, but a bloodied one was something else. I completed the burning ritual and attempted to hit my vein.

My head toppled to my chest and my eyes banged shut while an apparition shifted into reptilian forms. I watched with uneven curiosity the evolving shapes my brain conjured.

As if from far away, I heard Vie explaining—or maybe she was complaining to the man—"She ain't used to this good Van dope. That shit they send out to Calgary is headed and cut down with icing sugar."

I thought he mumbled something in return, but what it was I wasn't sure and didn't care.

The lizard's head dissipated as Vie began shaking me. "C'mon, snap out of it . . . or I'll leave ya here. So help me God I will." She hauled me to my feet and then held on firmly.

I was trying not to lose my balance and was quite happy to have Vie anchor me as my knees buckled like ships on a choppy sea.

"Great dope," I said, but Vie attempted to ignore me and get back to business. "How many you got left?" Vie asked.

"Ten . . . the money."

"Just a minute." As she fumbled in her purse, she let me fall again onto the smelly mattress. The springs moaned as I bounced but I did see Vie gesturing and holding some money tight in her hand.

"You're thirty short."

"Ah shit . . . Beth, have you thirty dollars?"

"Un-huh." I tried to open my eyes again—"In my bag."

Vie seized the brown pouch dangling from my shoulder and found a ten and a twenty in the inside pocket.

The man spit the balloon into her hand and Vie wiped off the spittle on her plaid skirt. She popped the treasure into her own mouth and then extended the money to him.

Everything seemed to be happening in slow motion when Vie suddenly hoisted me to my feet and began pushing me towards the door. But the man blocked our way and, even in my stupor, I noticed the dangerous glint in his eyes.

"What's the hurry?"

"We have to meet some friends," Vie crackled importantly.

"I thought you might want to talk about scoring some bundles."

"We don't have that kind of money," Vie said and pinched me hard on the arm. I understood and remained silent, although my fingers could not help rubbing the tip of my nose.

A look of indecision spread over his face as Vie stared him down.

"You could have fooled me," he said and stepped aside. Vie lugged me along by the arm, wasting no time in hustling the two of us into the grease-smeared hallway.

We were in full retreat with the man jogging after us. As we entered the lobby he overtook us, trying to be friendly again. We paid no attention as we matched our steps towards the street. Outside we were met by drops of rain, and in the distance, I could hear the faint drumming of thunder.

"Hey, if you change your minds . . . you can find me at the Gastown Bar. Just ask for Chris . . . eh?"

"Fine." Vie was rigid with tension as she flailed her arms at a passing cab.

The guy called Chris stayed uncomfortably close behind us. "Where did you say you're staying?"

"We didn't." An audible sigh of relief escaped from Vie as a cab's brakes screeched. She opened the door and, catching my arm, hauled me in.

"Where to?" the cabby asked.

"Any nice motel away from here . . . yah, somewhere in the suburbs," Vie said, watching the man still standing on the curb staring at us. The rain pasted his black hair to his skull. As he began walking away, Vie slumped in the back seat.

The cabby repeated, "Any motel?"

"That's what I said . . . any place as long as it's nice."

"Whatever you say, lady."

As I felt the apprehension evaporating from my companion, I succumbed to the lure of the high and nodded off.

The driver took us to a white building where a neon sign flashed "Paradise Motel." Vie and I looked out of place in the lobby full of potted palm trees and climbing vines. Vie's stockings were sagging around her ankles and my tight jeans and high boots were pinching me. The wallpaper's rain forest scene blended into the emerald of the carpet on which we shuffled uncomfortably. A clerk wearing a safari hat showed us to our room, which was bright and spacious with two double beds.

"Vie . . . a colour TV. With cable!" I began flicking the remote control, trying to contain my chirps of pleasure.

Vie lay down on one of the beds. Her sharp features sagged and she looked old. Her makeup had worn off and I saw that her lipstick had bled into the fine lines around her lips and left her mouth a pale, thin orb.

"Why did you need thirty dollars to make that deal?"

"Because I think that little weasel spotted the money in my wallet . . . tho' I tried to be careful. He didn't want to let us go. Thinking of ripping us off, he was. I figured if he thought I didn't have thirty bucks it might throw him off balance . . . and it worked." Her voice was strained from lack of sleep.

"Oh . . . I sensed something wasn't right." My eyes were glued to the television.

"Never trust no one," murmured Vie.

"You've said that before. I've had a bad run-in with a cop and my probation officer. Well, I don't even want to talk about that."

"See, you're learning already. When I say no one, I mean no one. I'd rip you off without a second thought if you had and I didn't. No one." There was an uneasy silence before she lowered her voice—"Let's get some sleep, then we'll fix and get something to eat. Tomorrow we'll score some bundles, but from people I know."

I checked to make sure that the frail chest rose and fell. Then I drifted into sleep. In the background, Ernie and Bert were singing, "Big and small, little and tall, that's not all, there's short. . . ." I really was in paradise.

-◄○►-

I heard Vie moving around and wondered why she seemed unaffected by this potent smack. "How come you don't get high on this stuff?" My voice was raw and sounded raspy from the effects of the drug.

"You better enjoy it while ya can . . . the day comes when you're so used to it, all it does is straighten ya and you end up doing more and more, hoping for that well-remembered high. Maybe after we eat, I'll do a double."

"I can't eat now." I was holding onto the mattress as if it were a lifeboat.

"Fuck . . . it does piss me off to see you so ripped . . . Maybe I'll fix now and we'll just order in something."

The ether odor of burning smack clogged my nose. I lit a cigarette, held it between my slack fingers, and then dropped it to the plush carpet. "Shit." My uncoordinated fingers finally found the butt which left a black mark on the broadloom.

"By God, that did it," Vie sounded well satisfied for a change as she crashed on her bed.

We slipped into fragile strands of consciousness that buckled under the weight of our high. Parallel curls of smoke rose from the cigarettes in our hands as we let the long ashes drop anywhere. This art of letting a cigarette just burn down after an obligatory drag or two was one I was becoming quite practised at. Amazing that more junkies didn't die in house fires than from overdoses.

My voice limped along: "In Calgary, I met this Van dealer and I went once to see him alone and . . . he fixed nine caps . . . held some back for me . . . I refused . . . shit . . . didn't know what would be in there . . . all I could do was half a cap . . . anyway, he let me do the wash and man did I get wasted . . . the only wash that ever got me off."

"I pity the poor bastard when he came down. Now that would be hell," muttered Vie.

I was chilled at the thought. "But he didn't seem high . . . I mean, I was bombed on the wash and he was just normal . . . hard to imagine."

"Not for me. I just told you how it happens. Now, you take a dealer out here . . . he can get his stuff for five to seven dollars a cap. A Calgary dealer usually can only get his stuff for twenty, so a Van dealer does four to a Calgary dealer's one. Easy to see how the hypes here get their big habits."

I made a sound in my throat, or at least I thought I did, then sank into the dark, scurrying pools of the nod.

◄○►

With the sun already low in a menacing sky, Vie and I returned to Hastings Street. Our destination was the Broadway Hotel, a well-known gathering place for needle freaks. Inside, the battered wooden tables and chairs were grouped along the nicotine-stained wall over which a lone string of Christmas lights was still draped.

An aura of despondency permeated the stench of spilled beer and the rising clouds of cigarette smoke. As I watched the people sitting around the small tables, a ballast of misery pressed against me. I fought off my feelings by setting my features into hard lines and watching everything through suspicious eyes.

Vie sat next to me, waiting patiently for a junkie called Rob to show. She'd known him for several years and felt he would be more trustworthy than an unknown.

I was intrigued by two young men who entered. One was Aboriginal, with a rich complexion. His braided black hair sported an eagle feather, but it was his partner who caught my attention. He was wearing a shirt with the top few buttons undone, and khaki pants. A matching jacket added to his neat appearance. His face was appealing, with plump cheeks topped with reddish hair cut into a long shag. He had a smattering of freckles across his nose.

I leaned closer to Vie. "Do you know him?"

Vie glanced over. "Yah, name's Chuck. Seen him in Calgary . . . don't know what he's doing with Dal, though," she shrugged, then turned and waved at them as the two men started to sit down at a nearby table. The guy named Chuck smiled in recognition and began moving towards us.

"How are you, Vie. . . . Calgary dried up again?" His words were directed to her, but his blue eyes remained on me.

I figured I looked good, with a charcoal half-sized T-shirt that showed off my flat stomach and a wide plastic belt holding up a pair of bell bottomed jeans. My hair was clean and brushed. Beaded earrings dangled from my ears.

"Yah, Calgary's dry again." Seeing that he hadn't heard her, Vie raised her voice sharply—"Forget it, she's taken."

His eyes glistened mischievously. "Such bad manners, Vie!" He extended his hand—"I'm Chuck."

I tossed my hair. "Beth," and as I withdrew my hand from his grip his fingers ran across my knuckles.

"Okay, ya met her—now get lost," Vie ordered.

"Ladies . . . Vie." He gave a curt nod and left to rejoin Dal.

As I stared after him, he caught my gaze and smiled. I blushed and looked away into Vie's frowning face.

"He's such a mother-fucking snob. He thinks he's really something. . . . I'm surprised he even came over."

"I'm not."

"Well . . . I know he didn't come to see me."

Despite Vie's darkening mood, I couldn't let go—"Does he have an old lady?"

"I ain't got nothing else to say about him."

"Suit yourself."

"I've told you that I don't want to hear about no one but Ivan from you," Vie warned, and squinted over the top of her wire-rimmed glasses. Then she rubbed her nose for a moment and changed the subject—"I wish Rob would show . . . five bundles." A man, his face lined from years of abuse, approached.

"Ole Tommy," she called out affectionately, as she indicated the chair beside her. He eased himself down and floundered for her hand.

"I can't get no fix," he whimpered.

She touched his hand sympathetically. "C'mon, you used to be a pretty resourceful fellow."

"I can't hustle so good no more . . . I'm getting too old." Water rolled out of the corner of one his puffy eyes.

"It happens to all of us," she reminded him. "You seen Vernon around?" She glanced over—"One of my ex's."

I was repelled by Tommy's used-up body sagging over his chair and bored by the conversation. I ran my thumb across the sticky table leaving my prints etched in a semi-arc along the dirty rim. Behind me a woman, blood streaming from her nose and mouth, burst from the washroom screaming as two younger women bolted out the rear door. The only person in the bar who appeared concerned was the balding bartender, who wiped the blood off the howling woman's face with paper towels and succeeded in quieting her. When he offered to call the police, the woman refused and rushed out as if in pursuit of the other two. Aside from a few curious looks, the incident didn't seem to register with the other patrons.

"You know I'd help if I could," Vie reassured the old junkie. Her deception was sickening, as his frail voice pleaded, "For old time's sake."

Vie's patience ran out. "I can't . . . sorry Tommy . . . it was good to see ya, but we gotta go." With that she signaled and we rose to leave. "Let go," she urged, as she shook him off and moved towards the door.

"Poor old bugger—turned to mooching a few years back. He . . . Rob, he's come!" We scurried over to a slim man with a gold hoop in his right ear.

I hung back while Vie touched his wrist and began whispering in his ear. He became attentive and waved away the few hopeful junkies who had swarmed around him. He said something to Vie, huddled with her in the doorway, then turned on his heel and made for a table in the back.

"He's going to finish up a little business here, then he'll meet us in the coffee shop across the street," Vie said, brushing some white lint off her jacket.

◄○►

We dodged the traffic and sprinted to the coffee shop. We ordered tea.

"If he comes through for us . . . we'll hole up in the motel . . . and party," Vie said, chewing at the cracked corner of her mouth.

I blew smoke rings across the counter and over the grill. I watched them disappear as easily as the meaning the word *Broadway* had once held for me. My version included New York, lights, actors, theater. Vancouver's Broadway was a purgatory with a Third World flavour.

"Bloody depressing place this street, and that bar is unreal . . . something out of a horror movie!"

"You'll get used to it. When I first came down here, I couldn't get over how dirty and twisted it was. Now it's like a second home."

We both cast expectant glances as Rob lifted up a chair, turned it around, and lowered himself as if on a saddle. "Only you come, Vie. The other can wait in my office."

"Now?" Vie drained the last drops of tea from her cup.

"Now." He stood and lead us out. We walked with Rob wedged between us for about five blocks to a grey stone building. Whether it was north or south east or west, I had no idea. Addresses were as unimportant as directions in this world and best forgotten anyway. Inside, Vie paused to catch her breath while Rob and I began climbing the three flights of stairs. At the end of the dim hallway, Rob thundered, "Move it." Vie hurried to catch us. She was still puffing as he unlocked the door and ushered us in. "You sit there and wait," he told me, pointing to the solitary chair.

Put off by his manner, I reluctantly sat. I was about to object, when he ordered, "Let's go," and left.

Vie tapped me on the shoulder. "You'll be okay . . . if I'm not back in a couple of hours . . . you're on your own." Then, still panting, she dashed after Rob.

This being left alone was becoming too familiar. I took a deep breath and looked at my bare surroundings. Pushed against the far wall was a bed with a dirty quilt on the naked mattress. A dresser was jammed against a sink that squatted low to the floor. All the drawers were empty except for the dust that coated them. I concluded that Rob didn't live here. Restless now, I found the air stuffy. I stepped to the paned window and peeked out. The alleyway was overflowing with trash and another tenement house stared back. With no sunlight to soften the image, it was a dismal picture. I tried to pry open the window, but it had been nailed shut.

I began pacing back and forth, worrying. I was being set up. Vie was never coming back. How would I get back to Calgary? And what the hell was I doing here anyway?

I sat back on the hard chair, counted my money, and clutched my eighty dollars. At least I could get home without having to work these streets. Why hadn't I insisted on going with Vie and Rob? I put my head in my hands and watched the door, suddenly fearful of the habit doors had of crashing down.

A door caving in had exposed my addiction. The images of that night never changed. Their outlines were like razor blades always ready to open the vein of guilt. How I bled rivers of regret over that night. Ivan had been going out for a pickup, leaving me with eight caps to safeguard. Not thinking much about it, I'd placed them in my change purse and forgotten about them. I'd bolted the door after him and sorted through some albums before putting one on the stereo, "The Doors" . . . I could even remember the song I'd played. "People are strange . . . when you're a stranger . . . faces come out of the rain. . . ."

I could see myself on the coffee-stained sofa, one leg hanging over the edge, my foot tapping in time to the music. With a smash, the door hit the wall, and five yelling men exploded through the opening.

My eyes wide, my mind unable to react to the pressure on my throat as the first of the men swooped down. "Hands on knees."

They crowded around—these men who looked ordinary, in jeans and ski jackets. I sat watching as they systematically searched the small apartment, leaving a trail of ruin. They dumped sugar, flour, coffee, tea on the floor. They ripped up the carpet and broke every movable object. As a vase smashed against the wall, I prayed they were Rounders come to steal hippie smack. These wild men didn't look like Eastenders, yet I held on to that fading hope.

The one that the others called Mones was emptying the contents of my purse. "Eureka!" he called, and displayed the eight trophies to the others. "What's this?" he demanded, holding the caps up under my nose.

"Aspirin?"

A voice was saying, "You have the right to remain silent; you have the right . . . ."

"No . . . no!" I'd cried.

A blond man laughed—"You're playing in the big leagues now . . . sweetheart." My tongue stuck to the roof of my dry mouth. I did not know how to respond. This was never supposed to happen in real life, certainly not to me.

"Where's Ivan?"

One cop standing by the door whooped and three others ran with him into the hallway. I was left with the blond man standing over me. "It's over," he said, as we listened to the furious pounding of running feet outside on the stairs. Then Ivan was dragged in across the living room.

I felt sick as I heard his head being slammed into the bedroom wall, again and again, the pounding matching their angry chorus of "Where is it? Where is it? Where is it?"

High and terrified, my scream pierced the air. A large hand clamped over my mouth and nose and I was forced to a waiting ghost car. The ride to police headquarters felt surreal even though the familiar streets seemed normal enough.

I blanked out the rest, except the call, "Mum . . . I'm in trouble."

"What now?"

"I've been arrested . . . for possession . . . for the purpose . . . of trafficking . . . heroin. I'm in jail . . . Mum!"

I heard my mother's hysterical sobs, on the other end, cries that filled my ears and lived there still. Only now I wondered if they were for me, or for her, or for both of us?

—◦—

"Shit." I lit a smoke to evade all the unwanted memories. The quiet grew to a loud buzzing in my head. I finished a sixth cigarette, and decided I could no longer stand this confinement or the roaring silence. I walked through the open door. Down the hall I saw Vie with Rob behind her and the happy look of success on Vie's face. Unable to restrain myself, I flung my arms about her. Vie pushed me roughly away. "Want to do some great dope?"

"Do junkies' noses itch?"

Chapter Thirteen

BACK IN OUR ROOM AT the Paradise, Vie was happy. "We're staying right here till we've shot up a couple of these suckers. Then we'll head home to Calgary and sell the rest." Vie playfully tossed two of the bundles in the air and caught them again. She untied one and squeezed two white caps onto the desk.

I flashed a smile as Vie tucked them into her bra. We left another red prick mark on our never-healing arms, tottered to our beds, and collapsed.

I broke the silence. "How come those chicks beat on that broad at the bar?"

"They're people down there who'll kill ya . . . that broad just didn't have no good sense . . . I've seen an old whore's throat slit in there for a fiver and some loose change." Her words jolted me. I shrunk deeper into my pillow and wrapped my thin arms around myself. "You got an old man, Vie?"

"Why you ask?"

"Dunno, just interested . . . I guess."

"I got one . . . name's Terry." The woman's hesitation made me feel I'd touched a nerve as she scratched her ear. "I done left my husband to go with him . . . not that I minded, 'cause I was never happy with Vernon . . . beat me regular, he did . . . whenever he'd drunk himself silly, which was more often than not."

A rasp rattled from her chest, and the deadened voice deepened. "Terry and I known each other since we was about six or so . . . Ivan too. Shit, I can hardly remember a time we wasn't together. But anyhow, after I got myself hitched we were still close . . . and then Terry started coming over alone when Vernon was at work—he was a welder—anyways, it was no big deal . . . we'd smoke a little weed, listen to music and talk about the old times. I don't know how it happened, really, but one day Terry and I got it on together and it seemed so natural . . . that is till Vernon come home one morning . . . and found us there together. God, what a mess . . . my babies screaming . . . Vernon kicking and punching both Terry and me. Threw me out on the street with only the clothes on my back."

She took a few puffs on her cigarette and began again, "Terry took me home to his parents and they took me in . . . and I've been with him ever since. He weren't really any good at holding a job or nothing . . . he dealt some hash and stuff and one drug led to another. Soon we was shooting up . . . so I was out on the street at twenty hustling to support both our habits."

"Where is he? . . . I ain't never seen him around."

"He's in for theft . . . only about the seventh beef for that, so they locked him up for two less a day . . . been gone about a year now, but he'll get out soon . . . in fact any time now, . . . might even be out when we get back."

I thought I detected a hint of a smile on her stony face. It vanished quickly. "You go back so far and you never talk about him," I said.

"Why talk about things that don't do no good anyhow?"

I closed my eyes trying to picture Vie as a young girl, but my mind went blank and I drifted into a dream. Vie's voice rattled me back to consciousness.

"Ya know what the clincher to my story is? My husband became a junkie . . . it's almost unbelievable . . . that's who I was asking Ole Tommy about . . . that bastard . . . hard as nails, he is . . . made quite a name for himself out here . . . I try to avoid him cause he'll still beat on me if he sees me . . . mostly I feel sorry for my babies . . . my twin girls . . . .Kendra and Kathy." This time there was the unmistakable sound of sorrow in her voice. "They done took my babies away—when Vernon quit his job and left them with his sister . . . put them in foster homes . . . my poor little ones."

"Yah, that must have been hard." I was surprised she was confiding all this and unable to relate, felt I had to say something.

"What the fuck would you know about it?" Vie was stabbing out her cigarette. "You're a dumb little hippie chick. Probably always had everything handed to ya . . . what, didn't daddy bail ya out the last time? . . . Is that why you're down here slumming? . . . Poor little rich girl!"

I raised myself up on an elbow, "What the fuck do you know about me? Nothing . . . the snottiest little bastards in Calgary . . . the Mount Royal elite . . . made my life a misery. Do you know what that's like to live there, when you don't belong to the Glencoe Club, you don't ski, you sure the hell aren't dressed the way they are, and you're picked on every day of your fucking life? When you go to your parents and tell them how miserable you are . . . do you know what they say? 'Life isn't easy. So what if you don't have seal skin boots, alpaca sweaters, or a Wood's ski jacket? If everyone jumped in a lake, would you jump in after them?'"

"And ya know what I wanted to say? Yah, I fucking want to drown in that lake. The shit those rich little bastards put me through. I wished I was dead every day for two years, and by the time I got to high school . . . God, it's no wonder that I turned to drugs." I stopped to catch my breath. "My parents wouldn't bail me out of that hell hole of a school . . . do you really think they'd help me out of the shit I'm into now?" A tear stuck to my eyelash. "No, Vie . . . I don't know what it's like to lose your kids . . . but I sure know the hell of learning to hate yourself."

"Bullshit," Vie's voice boomed from deep in her chest—"Your father was a professional . . . you could have had all that stuff !"

"Could have, but didn't," I said, trying to drive my anger under the umbrella of the drug once more.

"Why ya have to tell me all that stuff and ask me all those fucking stupid questions?"

"I don't know."

"Don't ask . . . don't tell . . . most of us want to forget about who and what we were before. Keep your trap shut . . . or I'll slap ya, so help me." She rolled over, turning her back to me.

The silence hung, confining us to the caverns of the high. Neither of us cared about the other; we were too busy searching for the broken pieces of ourselves.

I awoke with sunlight streaming through the open drapes. For one moment I wished we'd pulled them last night, but as the rays bounced off my face I felt almost happy. I jumped up and stood stretching and yawning. I went to the woman tossing in the next bed.

"No more confessions," I said, placing my hand on Vie's bony shoulder.

Vie's hazel eyes opened with a hint of forgiveness, and she shook her head to clear the remains of sleep. "Forget it . . . I shouldn't have come down on you like that."

Everything was fine—we were even somehow. I gave a small smile and returned to my bed.

Two pillows plumped up behind her, Vie said, "Been thinking . . . we're moving on . . . back to Calgary. I want to make some money on this deal, ya know."

"Fine." The thought of having the holiday end upset me as much as my lack of power over the other woman's decisions.

"We going to fly back?"

"God, no . . . sure way to get busted. We're going Greyhound. Only to Banff, mind . . . then we hitchhike the rest of the way."

"So we leave . . . when?"

"First thing in the morning."

Between fixes we spent the rest of the day watching TV. After Harvey Kirk signed off the news we ordered out for pizza. When the late show ended, we went to bed.

But we slept most of the next day away and the room was already settling into semi-darkness as I awoke. As a drop of snot fell from my nose, I went to wake Vie.

I watched as Vie tied up the bundle and then returned it to the safety of her underwear with an upward push.

"That's where you keep it?"

"You bet . . . safest place I know . . . up there." Vie sounded amazed.

"Why couldn't you get high before?" I changed the subject to discourage any further evidence of my ignorance.

"'Cause I'm shooting up great dope, as much as I want . . . and after all these years I not only get sick, I get where I can't move. It'll happen to you some day . . . sooner or later," Vie said as she began dressing for the trip back.

There was little talk as we gathered our scanty possessions. Vie called for a cab and we left the Paradise, going as we had come, under a canopy of street lights.

—‹o›—

The sootstained bus station in the city's east end was bustling. On wooden benches the passengers were crushed together while the stench of diesel fuel mingled with the sweaty atmosphere of the place. We stood in line and, after Vie purchased the tickets, she took my arm and steered me over to the cafeteria. As we stood before the little smudged windows that held the cakes, cookies, and pies, the smell of grease and fat triggered our appetites.

"Load up with some sandwiches. It's almost supper time, and we got a long trip." Vie pointed to the window that held the cellophane sandwiches. I selected four ham ones, ordered fries and a coke. As I began stuffing my mouth with the fries, Vie tapped her watch. "Don't dawdle or we'll miss the bus."

"Fuck . . . I wish you'd drop the mother act," I said, carrying my half-empty paper plate of fries and trotting after her.

We were the last to board, which suited us for there would be fewer surprises that way. After living in the same set of clothes for three days, I was sure we looked like travelling vagabonds. Vie's stockings, looser than ever, covered more of her ankles than the rest of her leg. My jeans were layered in rubbed-in cigarette ash. I could taste the ketchup from the fries in the corners of my mouth. The bus was half-full, the seats randomly taken. We shimmied down the aisle, appraising all the passengers sniffing the air, rodent-like, as we passed. I had become feral—no longer obligated by the rules of social behaviour. The other passengers seemed to shrink back, muttering, "These seats are saved. These seats are taken." But they had nothing to fear. We were headed to the back for the best view of the interior and its inhabitants. We settled into two seats by the bathroom, the bus doors closed, and the motor sprang to life.

I remember little of the ride back, except I was very high. I floated endlessly, baptizing myself over and over in oblivion. I was aware only of the times that Vie jabbed the needle into the muscle of my waiting arm. No one noticed or seemed to care about our behaviour. Only our frequent trips to the washroom distinguished us from our fellow passengers.

Vie sat erect: her wispy hair parted in the middle and stuck to her head, making her features sharper. Her paleness displayed the brown age spots that dotted her sunken cheeks. I peeked in my compact mirror for reassurance: my face was round and smooth and dreamy. My hair hung down in a mess. My unkempt appearance garnered looks of pity from those who made the trip down the aisle to the washroom. I rested my head on Vie's shoulder, aware that my youth saved me from the more contemptuous looks Vie received.

Cocooned in the dim rocking interior, my needs met, a friend along-side, it was the closest I had ever come to a junkie's heaven.

We pulled into the Banff station twelve hours later. My joints were stiff as Vie elbowed me awake. As I stepped off the bus, the first blast of frigid air hit my face. It revived my senses briefly.

It seemed surreal walking down main street, weaving our way through the tourists and the skiers. I thought of my high school boyfriend, Bill, who'd been on the ski patrol at Sunshine. He'd looked so good in his uni-form. With him coaching me that year, I'd finally learned to ski. The mem-ories of swishing down the packed runs brought me no pleasure today. I pushed my hands deep into my jacket pockets, my ears burned from the cold, and I began to fall behind. As each fleeing car passed, ignoring our out-held thumbs, I longed for the lost womb-like warmth of the bus.

My head lowered like a battering ram as the snow-swept road beckoned. As we trudged past the last hotel, the forest reared up on either side of the highway and enveloped us.

We walked on, intent on placing one foot in front of the other and catching a ride with someone, anyone. We did notice when the snowfall began moving from the odd light flake to a freefall, but we continued to plod down the highway in silence. The wind swept over us, impairing our vision. Through the half-open slits of my eyes I commanded my unwilling muscles to forge on while damning the struggling figure in front. I won-dered why Vie did not signal to return to the town and stoically kept up the pace. The silence was broken only by the shrieks of the wind and the sound of our feet crunching the snow.

We had no hats, gloves, or even a scarf. For this I blamed Vie—the stu-pid bitch and her dumb ideas. "Travel light," she'd said. But who in their right mind travelled light in the middle of a Canadian winter? How could I survive if I didn't start thinking of something more than when I'd get my next fix? With the wind lashing and pelting us with snow, each step forward became more of a struggle. The wind's rising fury and frigid air reduced my breathing to quick whiffs.

Ahead, Vie faltered and fell. I raced forward, grabbed her, and pulled her back up to her feet.

"Jesus . . . Beth . . . I'm so cold."

This was the first time I'd seen Vie's hard shell crack. I stepped back, frightened by her fear. I reached out and fingered the unlined jacket hanging around her shoulders; the broken zipper left only the worn sweater underneath to offer any protection from the cold. Her Hush Puppies were soaked through, and her wet pantyhose drooped even more. The wind twisted her A-line skirt, driving it between her legs like a diaper. Her hair was white with the snow, and, worst of all, she was shaking uncontrollably.

"Shit . . . shit." I hugged her close. My ski jacket at least was a winter garment, with a waterproof outer shell. With my collar turned up my head was only partly exposed. At least I'd been thinking the day I boosted it. Was there enough room in the jacket to somehow squeeze Vie in?

"What'll we do?" she wailed.

"Someone will stop," I said, aware that not a single vehicle had passed us in at least half an hour.

"There ain't going to be no cars . . . have to be a fool to drive in this."

I stamped my feet for warmth. Vie had just surrendered leadership. "We gotta walk back."

"We're too far out, we've been walking for at least an hour . . . I can't make it . . . I'll freeze . . . .Christ . . . it's so fucking cold."

I looked up and down the highway trying to hide my own desperation. My feet were numb in my leather lace-up boots, my hands were bare and my ears were freezing. My bell-bottom jeans allowed the frigid air to creep in like a lover's cold hands.

"Moving . . . must keep moving. C'mon . . . .we'll walk back on this side and if a car comes, good . . . if not?" I clasped Vie around the waist, and began dragging her along. She offered no resistance, and the wind pushing at our backs eased our progress.

We walked at a sideways tilt so I could spot a car coming in either direction.

The screech of the wind was rising, and from the numbing sensations along my legs I knew the storm had not peaked yet. "We're the only bitches crazy enough to walk out in the middle of a blizzard." I had to shout now to be heard above the persistent howling.

"What?" Vie shouted into my ear.

I screamed back, "Nothing."

I shook my head. Vie was a pain in the ass. My pace was slowing as I fought against the fatigue overtaking me. It was a struggle to keep lugging her along, and Vie was not co-operating any more. With the snow whirling in all directions I knew I would not be able to see a car until it was on top of us.

"I want to sit down."

"No, must keep moving"—I tightened my grip.

Vie jerked free and collapsed in the snow. "I can't . . . I can't," she whimpered.

I squinted up and down the highway. Nothing but the white screen of snow greeted me. "Get up!" I strained to pull Vie upwards, but she remained slumped, shrinking into the snow. I clasped Vie under her arms, lifted, and yanked, but she was not moving. In desperation I slapped her, but she remained prone. I fought an urge to kick the shit out of the crumpled woman, but my thoughts were bouncing around as I hopped from one foot to the other.

I must have a plan. How could I just leave her here? How could I leave all that dope? I wasn't sure I could. But did I want to freeze to death? Perhaps if we lay together the warmth of our bodies would keep us alive. I squatted down to plead with her as a last resort. Then I'd have to leave and walk back; there seemed no other way to assure my survival.

I began pointing down the road, "Look . . . look!" I was sure I saw two dim lights ahead in the distance. I began running towards them. Vie shouted after me, but the wind tossed the words away. I could see better now: it was a half-ton truck inching its way along.

I raced closer, waving my arms. "Please . . . please," I prayed. The truck slowed and stopped next to me. I flung open the door. "Could you give us a lift? . . . Please!"

A man whistled low. "You're nuts, being out here alone on a night like this."

"It's a long story."

"Well . . . I don't want to hear it . . . get in before you freeze to death." The man had a kindly face—one of a man too—much in the sun.

"Will you pick up my girlfriend? She sat down up there and I don't think she can last much longer."

"Good God . . . of course. Sweet Jesus . . . what next?" The truck started off while I huddled close to the heater.

I directed him to Vie, almost invisible next to the road. I jumped out and dragged the pathetic creature into the warmth of the truck.

"I thought you left."

"Fat chance," I said, giving no hint of how close I'd been to doing just that.

"Christ . . . she looks like she might be going into shock," warned the man as Vie began quaking . "Let's have a look." His capable hands felt her legs and face. "Take her shoes off."

I removed Vie's dripping Hush Puppies and again the man's hands probed the woman's cold feet. "I'm not sure . . . but I don't think there's any frostbite . . . a little longer and she might have lost a few toes or fingers." He gestured to the dashboard. "Here, put those up there . . . might dry out . . . and slide into these." He reached into a duffel bag on the floor and found some thick work socks. He removed her wet suede jacket and wrapped Vie in a wool blanket that had lined the back of the seat.

"You should be thankful I have a meeting I can't miss in Calgary."

"Been skiing?" I asked, seeking some way divert his attention away from us.

"Yah . . . took the whole family up for a week at Sunshine. I left them after lunch at the lodge since I heard they were not recommending any highway travelling. I knew I best be going before it got any worse. But what the hell were you doing out there?" He started moving the truck slowly down the vast ribbon of white.

"Sounds dumb," I admitted, trying to think of some plausible story. "We didn't see the storm coming in, and we were in a real rush to get back to Calgary . . . ummm . . . my mother is sick . . . and as you can see we're not dressed for this weather. We kept figuring that someone would stop, but all of a sudden there's no traffic and we're freezing and there's a storm blowing in." I finished and took a better look at the man. He was graying slightly at the temples and had a handsome profile in spite of the deep lines in his face.

"What do you do?"

"Oil man." He strained to keep the truck from being swept to the ditch by the howling wind.

He darted a glance at us. "You're lucky . . . I don't normally pick up strangers . . . not even women in distress. But my God, the way you came out of that storm waving your arms, I almost thought you were a ghost . . . I just had to stop."

"What's so important about that meeting tomorrow?" I wanted to side-step any conversation about ourselves.

"More a matter of who's getting transferred, and where. I may be in Houston in a month."

Vie had curled up beside me and was sleeping with her head resting on my shoulder. How quickly we could change roles, I thought.

"By the way, name's Michael," he glanced over smiling.

"Glad to meet you. Beth and Vie. You know, of course, that you are our knight in shining armour." I attempted to laugh.

"You really have no idea how lucky you two are."

"It's just another way to die," I said, and hugged Vie closer.

◄○►

After two hours of slow driving we made it to Calgary, just ahead of the storm. Michael overheard our plan to stay at the Beacon Hotel, and he offered to drop us off there. He said nothing about my sick mother, but he seemed genuinely concerned for our welfare. As we said our good-byes, he pulled a few twenties from his wallet.

"Thank you," I said, but refused the money he tried to press in my palm. He shrugged. I touched his gloved hand and he waited until we disappeared into the hotel lobby.

"What a nice guy," I said, after we checked in.

"Ya, you should have taken that money . . . the guy was a real mark."

"After what he done for us . . . no way."

"Suit yourself, but you'll learn soon enough that down here on the street you take whatever ya can get." As the unlocked door swung open, we flung ourselves on the double bed, wrapped ourselves up in the blankets, and gig-gled with relief. "I thought I'd never feel warm again," Vie muttered.

"Me neither . . . that was too close for comfort. I couldn't understand how come you kept walking. We should have headed back." I couldn't help my accusing tone.

"Ya know damn well, it's because I kept thinking any minute we'd get a ride."

"But Vie, there weren't no more cars coming and still you walked on—it just didn't make any sense."

"I had my reasons and for now I'll keep them to myself."

Vie wasn't going to give an explanation, so I abandoned the subject. I was tired of her defensiveness. If it weren't for her dope, I'd have been long gone. I felt the first stirrings of the sickness and waited for Vie to warm up enough to give me a fix.

I was soon nodding off while Vie made a phone call to Gloria, at the Calgarian Hotel.

As soon as she hung up, she prodded me. "Get up . . . you gotta do me a favour."

"What?" I pulled the covers tighter around me.

"I need ya to go down to the bar and sell Gloria some caps. Oh . . . and don't tell where we're staying 'cause there's a panic and I don't want to be bugged all night."

Vie had put me through enough already, I thought angrily, pushing away the blankets. "How many does she want?"

"Five . . . I want ya to get going . . . 'cause I got some personal calls to make and I don't want you hanging around." Vie placed five chalky capsules in my outstretched hand.

I sat down again on the bed and wrapped them in foil from my cigarette package.

"Will you hurry up?"

"Okay . . . okay, I can take a hint." I put on my jacket and stomped out.

I waited about ten minutes in the bar—time enough to assure a beefy man that I did not want his company. Gloria, wearing a black pantsuit with a top cut so low that it grazed her nipples, rushed over. The beautiful face was awash in rivers of sweat, and she held a Kleenex to her forehead to stem the flow. "You got?"

"C'mon, I don't want no one to know." I led her to the washroom, annoyed about her asking outright.

Our transaction was completed. Gloria rushed into one of the cubicles while I hid the money in my boot.

"Where ya at?" Gloria called from behind the door.

"Nowhere." I retreated, knowing she'd spread the word about Vie's stuff. I threaded my way through the smoky bar towards the lobby where I sat on one of the leather-covered chairs across from the reception desk and had a leisurely smoke. I was waiting until I felt Vie would have had enough time to make her damn personal calls. I winked at the males passing by and stared down the night clerk. When I thought he was about to call the police, I flounced out.

Satisfied I had no one tailing me, I hailed one of the yellow cabs that lined the block. Back at the Beacon Hotel, I bounded up the stairs to the second floor. A darting look behind and I scurried along the hall, sure I had not been shadowed.

I rapped on the door, then stood dismayed as Vie gestured for me to enter. A stocky man with thick, short blond hair was holding Vie's hand, his tight lips pulled back into an insecure smile.

Vie seemed annoyed. "Did you meet up with Gloria?"

"Ya . . . they don't know where we're at." I felt unwelcome as I handed the money over.

"This here is Terry . . . my old man. I already told Terry all about ya."

"Nice to meet ya," I said, though I was sure that it wasn't going to be nice at all.

"I picked up a few of your things lying around." She handed me a yellow comb and a couple of bars of stolen motel soap. Her voice heightened with pleasure—"Terry's the reason I wanted to get back 'cause I was sure that he'd be out in a few days. Tonight, when I called his Mum, I learned he just got out and was wondering where I was at. So, he was home when I called and came right over."

I propped myself against the radiator, knowing what would come next.

"So, it's been fun but now I got my Terry . . . and I think it's time you moved on."

"The ride's over then." I stared at the grinning man who had replaced me. There would come a time when I would even this score.

"The ride's over," Vie concluded, emphasizing the word *over* for effect.

"Well, can I buy some caps then?" I counted my money. "All I got is fifty-five dollars . . . how about three caps . . . and I can owe you the rest?"

"Nah . . . I already done ya enough favours." Vie yawned and added, "Two for fifty dollars."

"Better than nothing."

"That's all there is on the street . . . so remember I'm doing you a favour by selling dope that I should hang onto for myself."

"And for me," Terry said. Vie patted him on the shoulder.

I tried to ignore Terry as I handed over the money and received two caps. I picked up my purse and, gripping the brass doorknob, asked, "Can I drop by tomorrow and score again?"

"If ya got money." Vie and Terry both nodded.

"Okay then . . . see ya around . . . I guess."

"Just you, though, Beth . . . don't tell no one wheres I'm at and don't bring no one with ya."

"Yah . . . don't worry, and thanks, Vie."

As I opened the door and slipped into the hall, Vie called after me. "And here I was thinking you might forget to thank me."

Just like Vie to have to have the last word, I thought angrily, and as the storm coated the city with its rage I headed back into the night.

Chapter Fourteen

I PACED UP AND DOWN the strip. Beneath the skin-tight blue jeans my hips swayed with each step. The effects of my last fix muted my discomfort as winter winds reddened my cheeks and cracked skin. I could feel my lips peeling under a heavy application of lipstick.

As we passed each other on the stroll, Big Marie turned and butted her cigarette on my chin. "Think you can rip me off, ya little shit!"

"What the fuck are you yammering about!" I'd said, trying not to show my fear and pain. I knew her cruelty was unpredictable.

"Ya ripped off my man, Old Jimmy." Big M pushed me for emphasis, and I fell to one knee.

"But he's in jail." I resisted the impulse to push the larger woman back. I rose, planted my feet apart, and braced for another assault.

"Ya pay me and I expect it tonight." Big M gave me a slap across the ear. Her spiked boots clacked ominously back down the strip.

I knew that the violence between Big Marie and me would continue unless I could take on this six-foot tank of meanness. I fled into the Regis Hotel and spotted Vie sitting alone at one of the tables.

As I crouched to consult her about Big M, I noticed she was wearing her Hush Puppies from our Vancouver trip.

Engaged in finishing her smoke, Vie yawned as if the matter was of minor importance. Lifting her eyes to me, she warned, "If she thinks she's owed, then pay up or else it will get worse than just a little burn on your chin."

"But if I pay then she'll always be after me. She'll think I'm weak."

"Ya are weak . . . .ya got no protection . . . pay her. She'll turn her attention somewhere else before long and, in the meantime, you'll keep your pretty face from being an ashtray." Terry beckoned from the exit and Vie left.

I stayed in the bar and pondered Vie's advice. After considering the alternatives, I searched my bag to find the money I'd give Big Marie on our next pass. The shit-kicking I'd laid on Debbie on Christmas Eve was a start towards a place in the pecking order, but I had a long way to go. I'd better start thinking about protection.

I walked along reliving the run-in with Big Marie and Vie's apathetic response. Non-threatening Jacob was the one person whose friendship I'd encouraged. But Lanny was crashing with him and he made me uncomfortable with his friendly manner and his frosty blue-flecked eyes. He'd been down to the strip the last couple of nights watching me. I wondered if I should escape to Vancouver again. It was difficult to avoid him: no matter where I was, he was there too.

I'd tried to duck and ignore him, but all my slights further enticed him. There was something troubling about him. I crossed the street and gave the clerk—with his brass name-tag that said Duncan—a smile.

Last night he'd changed rooms for me. His vigilance kept unwanted visitors away. Otherwise I figured Lanny would be camped outside my door.

To insure his continued good will, I placed twenty dollars on the desk. A knobby hand slid it away and he offered, "Time for a cup of tea?"

I enjoyed the lilting sound of his voice with his thick Irish accent. "Thanks. Not tonight . . . things I gotta do." I grinned, and blew him a kiss. My legs were aching from the hours of street walking as I climbed the stairs.

On the top floor, I opened the first door on the right of the stairwell and let myself into a clean but cluttered room. I took off my high-heeled boots, flopped on the double bed, and removed a wad of bills from inside my bra. My fingers flipped through the money before picking up the bedside phone.

After a few rings a female voice mumbled, "Hello."

"Hi . . . it's Beth, and I was wondering if you could use some company tonight. . . . I hope it's not too late?"

"Yah . . . you still want to borrow those records?"

I stifled a yawn, "Un-huh . . . I do."

"How many?"

"Seven."

"See ya, say . . . in a half-hour."

I clicked down the button and called the front desk. "Duncan, would you call a cab and ring me when it gets here."

"I thought you were through working for the night."

"Me too." I yawned, too tired to muffle the sound.

"It ain't right, you working till one or two in the morning every night . . . you gotta know when to quit."

"No lectures . . . okay?"

"Right . . . just be down when I call."

"Thanks." I hung up. My hand slipped to the underside of the mattress and I pulled out a cap from a small hole burned there. I held it high and rolled it between my fingers. It was my reward for the hours spent along Seventh Avenue, my consolation for the men who found their release in me. My feet slid across the floor of the bathroom in the hurry to savour its numbing effects. Only it could wash away the stink and free me from the clammy feel of the men who had claimed me.

The needle was positioned into the lesion on my right vein when a knock on the door made me jump. Swearing softly I tried again to find the elusive opening. The knocking resumed, this time louder. I called out, "Just a minute." My focus remained on pushing the cloudy liquid into my arm. This time I made it. Wrenching the point from my flesh, I tried to flush the bloodied fit with some hot water from the tap. The rush tingled up and down my spine. But I'd no time to relish it as I concealed the fit in the medicine cabinet. A yank on the toilet chain and I was running to answer the persistent pounding.

I opened the door, saw the blue uniform, and jumped back in fright. Then I recognized who it was.

Bruce strode in and closed the door. "What took you so long?" His voice was gruff.

"I was in the washroom." I backed against the pine dresser and watched him warily.

"I think you just fixed," he said.

"And if you wanted to . . . you could bust me any time you felt like it . . . so don't come down on me now." I glanced at him, unsure of how far I could push him.

My answer seemed to relax him, and he settled himself on a chair, stretched out his long legs and lit a cigarette. As he puffed, he looked me over. I knew he guessed that I'd dropped to under one hundred pounds on my five foot eight inch frame. "How are you, kid?"

"You didn't come up here to ask how I am . . . which is fine, thank you."

"True . . . true, but you do look tired." He offered one of his cigarettes.

"I am," I admitted, as he flicked a Bic and lit it for me.

As the cop's eyes wandered over the place, I tapped my foot, trying to hide the wave of anxiety that washed over me. "You take pretty good care of this . . . not like the room you and Sue lived in."

I brightened at this praise. "Sue and I together are just naturally pigs."

Noting the tapping foot, he remarked, "You don't seem all that happy to see me."

"I am . . . it's just . . . I got a cab coming."

"Where would you be going at this hour?"

I frowned.

"I'll be brief then. I have permission to take you to see this Peter of yours . . . on one condition."

Not quite able to believe what I just heard, every muscle stiffened. "Wha . . . what?" I stammered, bouncing up and down with excitement.

The cop threw back his head and laughed. "Not so fast . . . you haven't heard what it is." I held my breath. Glowing cinders scattered across the ashtray as he butted his cigarette. "You must question him about several ARs we believe that he might have been involved in."

With a sinking feeling I shook my head. "He'll think I'm a rat . . . he hates rats."

The cop shrugged. "Either you want to see him or you don't, up to you kid." Sneaking a peek at him, I saw his brown eyes twinkle.

I clued in. No one needed to know any more than what I chose to tell them. With this sudden flash of insight, I smirked. "No, I'll do it."

He grinned, satisfied. "I was hoping you'd feel like that. Now, I'm working on the problem of when, so don't leave town or move again. I should have everything organized in a week or so."

I grabbed the big man around his waist and hugged him. He smiled and I stepped away embarrassed. The cop picked up his hat, and turned to go. "Okay, I'll be in touch. And Beth, be careful—there's a bust in the works." The door slammed and I was alone again.

His warning went unheeded, as I jumped on the bed with new-found energy. The ringing of the phone snapped me out of my euphoria. I lifted up the receiver. "What?"

"You coming down or what . . . your cab's been here for ten minutes and the meter's been running the whole time," the Irish-accented voice cracked back.

"Oh, my God, I forgot. I'm so sorry Duncan, I'll be right there." I smashed down the phone and sped around the room searching for my money and misplaced keys, then went flying down the stairs to the cab.

Once there, I hastened inside the building and pushed the intercom button. A buzz and the locked door swung open. I stepped through, puzzled that Sandi had not asked who it was. During the elevator ride I found myself vaguely uneasy. The elevator stopped and the steel door slid back. I stepped off, unsure of myself, and made my way down the hallway to the apartment. Here I knocked ever so lightly. The door burst open and a pair of masculine hands fastened around my neck and I was wrenched inside and slammed up against the wall.

"Oh, shit," I said, just before the mammoth hands began applying a tightening pressure around my windpipe.

"Surprise," shouted another man, as he ripped my purse from my shoulder and dumped the contents on the upside down coffee table.

The suffocating hold on my throat was released and I was flung to the sofa, where I landed beside another hype called Marko. As I tried to straighten myself I spotted Sandi sitting in the kitchen, her compact hands on her knees and a pair of hand-knitted blue slippers on her small feet. In the bedroom I heard the sounds of a scuffle and knew instinctively that Blade was being roughed up.

"What are you doing here?" demanded one of the men.

I relaxed ever so slightly realizing these were city bulls, not the dreaded horsemen. "Just visiting."

"You can do better than that, Beth . . . it's almost one thirty in the morning."

"I couldn't sleep."

"You'll all sleep just fine in the city cells . . . just as soon as we find the stuff," the bull, who first nabbed me, warned.

I settled into the folds of the sofa and watched impassively as two of the bulls tore the curtains down, twisting out the rod as well, then began cutting and rolling up the carpet. I glanced and saw that they'd already been through the kitchen. All the cupboards hung open, their cereal and dishes spilled and mixed on the floor. Understanding that they hadn't found the dope made me edgy; I knew it must be in here somewhere.

Their frustrations mounting, the bulls' search escalated into a frantic rampage. They tore down light fixtures and inspected them, ripped out and discarded the wall plugs. They shredded the bathroom linoleum.

"Where the fuck is it?" One bull turned to Sandi, who looked up blankly.

"I haven't any idea what you're talking about."

"We'll find it . . . we will," he promised, as he and another bull dragged Marco off the sofa into the bedroom, leaving me alone in the living room.

I peeked into the kitchen at Sandi, who, seeing the questioning expression on my face, winked and pointed to the phone, the only object in the kitchen that had been left alone. The light beige phone blended in perfectly with the table and was almost buried underneath a pile of food debris. I raised my eyebrows in understanding just as one of the agitated bulls came charging out. "Where in the fuck is it . . . where?"

He yanked me off the sofa and, pulling a knife out of his pocket, rolled the sofa over and slit it open; his hand rifled through the piles of stuffing he dragged out. I stood a few feet away, my eyes downcast, afraid that they might stray to the kitchen and give the game away.

Four enraged bulls emerged, herding Marco and Blade ahead of them. One of them screamed, "I know it's here!" As if he had given the others a command, they sprang into action while I and my fellow hypes were lined up against the wall to witness, again, the destruction and the fruitless scrabble over the ruined apartment.

I was terrified that any minute the phone would become the next target. Finally, in defeat, the bulls marched to the door. The last one out turned and snarled, "We'll be back."

As the busty girl emerged from the kitchen with a grin, I remarked, "I hate to say this Sandi . . . but I don't think you're going to get your damage deposit back."

We snickered, and Sandi opened her fist, revealing the two balloons that had eluded the bulls. Marco took a position by the door, watching through the peephole for any return of the raiders. Soon we were all fixed and nodding happily, surrounded by the disorder created by the enforcers of law and order.

Chapter Fifteen

I SETTLED INTO THE REAR seat of the police cruiser, ignoring the rumblings of my stomach. I tried closing my eyes and shuffling through my emotions, but a scene kept playing in my mind like some old black-and-white newsreel.

I had been working my chunk of pavement between the Calgarian and the Beverage Block. A short woman with cropped hair had sidled up to me. "You Beth?"

"Who's asking?"

"I got a message from Peter."

My face relaxed. "Well . . . what is it?" I'd asked, relieved at the acknowledgment that I was still alive.

The woman cracked her gum. "He wants you to pack some stuff in with you."

I took a step backwards and spit, "You tell him to go fuck himself." I puffed out my chest, moved forward, and towered over the smaller woman.

The woman smirked. "All I'm doing is passing on the message he done give to my old man . . . so don't come down on me for it . . . okay?" She cracked her gum one more time and waddled away.

His gall to ask such a thing: Packing dope and going into the joint with two bulls. He must have lost his mind.

"Awfully quiet back there"—Bruce's voice jarred my thoughts.

I opened my eyes and saw him studying my image in the car's rear view mirror.

"Just thinking."

"Heard you were in on that raid at Sandi and Blade's. Man, were they pissed that they couldn't find anything."

I smiled. "Yah, they missed it."

Bruce rose to the bait. "Where? They told me they went through that place with a fine-toothed comb."

I stretched and yawned. I was more interested in my own thoughts than the cop's question.

Thank God, Duncan had remembered to leave word with the day clerk to give me a wake up call for eight. I'd wanted plenty of time to get ready. I had washed my hair and parted it in the middle so it fell on either side in a wavy mass. I'd taken pains to paint my nails with rose polish to hide the peeling layers. A tube top showed off my bust with just a hint of cleavage showing. A pair of wide-leg cords fit around my waist with a wide belt buckled in the front. I'd bought a pair of leather boots with high heels, although I was concerned they might make my size-eight feet look large. I was not worried about the boots making me tall, for Peter found that look attractive. Everything I wore today accentuated all my assets.

Bruce had said to be ready by nine, and I was pleased that I'd managed to pull it all together.

"Cat got your tongue? I asked you a question, remember?" Bruce reminded me.

I tried to hide my amusement at keeping him waiting. "No . . . just tired . . . ain't used to being such an early bird . . . oh yah . . . the dope was in the phone the whole time." I couldn't help my giggle of satisfaction.

"No shit? Will the boys ever be pissed off when I tell them."

I stretched across the seat. "I'm going to catch a little shut eye."

I rested my head against the door and tried to drift off, but kept thinking of how I'd feel in a couple of hours. My last fix had been at eight thirty and by the time we got back to Calgary I'd be in bad shape. I felt uptight and my stomach churned again. I hadn't eaten but I doubted I could hold anything down.

New fears mingled with old ones. Would Peter be happy to see me? Why hadn't I been allowed to see him? Was he done with me? Why would he risk asking me to pack dope in?

It had taken two weeks to make all the arrangements and I had worried each day that the whole thing would be called off. But Bruce came through and I trusted him, in spite of the danger of my association with him. I was also aware he cared what happened to me—a rarity in my life these days.

I'd recently made the mistake of phoning my parents. My father had screamed his rage at me for having a cop visit him at work. The humiliation of being questioned about why I was not allowed back home was the final straw. I'd tried to explain I'd not put any one up to an office visit, but my father shouted me down. He never wanted to be that embarrassed again. I damn well knew why I was not welcome at home and it would be better if the family did not hear from me at all. My father usually dealt with my situation by avoidance and silent dismissal. I had become his ghost daughter. Perhaps he was right: severing our tie would be better since I was the only one still clinging to it. It was too painful to think of them. Seeking to understand their motives was useless, but I could not let it go because I had once been a real daddy's girl.

My father's anger triggered my feelings of betrayal. It was frustrating that he could not see that no one was more distressed by my lifestyle than I was. I had no empathy for his position when all he had to live with was humiliation and I had to live waist-deep in shame. In an effort to stop his verbal assault, I'd asked to speak to my mother. But he'd refused, shouting he didn't want my mother upset and talking to me always upset her. The family did not want to hear from me again, he bellowed, until I had taken positive steps to straighten out my life. He'd also said he hoped I'd live to see another New Year.

It was a joke to say "straighten out" when I'd no one to turn to, no place to go, and no money or assets other than my body. I'd walked through a door that society locked behind me, and my family seemed intent on keeping it that way. The one person I'd confided in about my father's position was Bruce, so he was the cop who'd angered him. As head pathologist at The Calgary General Hospital, Dad was well known in the medical community and friendly with homicide detectives. Had Dad's status made any difference to my situation, I would have used it to my advantage. But my family had left me with one gift, and that was the ability to speak well. I could communicate with lawyers, judges, and social workers, using educated language to argue that I that I did not belong in the world I was in. In me, they could hear the voices of their own children.

The other cop with Bruce was his rookie partner, Alex, the same one who'd taken Sue for coffee the night I was introduced to them. He was speaking with Bruce quietly. The hushed male voices began to have a lulling effect, my emotions quieted, and I managed to doze.

When I awoke, I sat up and peered through the cruiser's windows. The badlands near Drumheller stretched along the horizon like a curled brown hand. A straw hue blanketed the land with only a smattering of snow to offer any contrast to the desolation of the place. Scattered throughout the bleak scene were unusual clusters of irregular-shaped mounds of rock. This land was nothing like I had ever seen.

"What time is it?" I asked, keeping my face pressed to the window.

"Coming on ten thirty," the rookie said.

I figured the sickness would not start for at least another half-hour and so resumed my study of this strange locale.

"Almost there," Bruce said.

I searched the bottom of my bag for my compact. I tried to touch up my cheeks with an application of rouge and smeared some gloss over my lips. I patted my hair into place and hoped I was presentable.

The town of Drumheller came into view, nestled between the sliced tops of the surrounding hills. It reminded me of pictures I had seen of old cowboy towns in the arid American South West.

The police cruiser wound along some tame twists and turns, towards a stark, stone building. The fortress rose above the contours of the Badlands, surrounded by a tall wire fence. The gatekeeper, a uniformed guard, sat in a glass booth where a pair of electronic gates hung open. He waved us through to the parking lot.

With a uniformed man on either side, I was escorted to the entrance of the building. We walked down a hall to a station. Inside, a couple of guards sat watching TV screens showing pictures of different cell blocks. Bruce stepped up to the booth and one of the men directed us down the hall to the left. We marched along, with Bruce in the lead, until the way was barred by a steel door.

Bruce touched me on my shoulder. "I'm not going in with you, kid. Good luck."

An unseen finger pushed a button, a buzzing sound pierced the air, and the barrier swung open. I stepped inside and the door banged shut behind me. I assumed I was in the main visitors' room, for it was like a community hall with lacquered tables surrounded by plastic chairs. Benches lined one side. Bars cut across floor-to-ceiling windows. The linoleum floor was checked in black and white squares. I took another few steps inside. I saw the guard behind a glass partition in the front of the room, glancing up and taking silent note of my presence.

I spotted a male figure near the back, leaning against a door marked PRISONERS' ENTRANCE. His arms hung loosely at his side as he blended into the wall in his prison khaki pants and matching short-sleeved shirt. His head was bent, his hair pulled into a severe ponytail, and his chest and arms were fuller. Finally, he nodded.

Our eyes met but neither of us moved. It was a stalemate. I could feel my anxiety and nausea building.

Peter stepped out under one of the overhanging fluorescent lights, "Got a smoke?"

I did not speak for fear my voice would give away my mixed emotions. He moved reluctantly forward, and I began burrowing for the pack of Players in my bag.

He grasped my arm and led me to one of the benches a few feet away from the guard behind the reinforced glass.

I sat down and held out the cigarettes. He took one with an air of disinterest. When I offered the lighter, my hand began to tremble. He placed his large hand over mine to steady it. He let go. I felt an immense strain, as if he was an old acquaintance with whom—after the obligatory "Hello. How are you?"—I'd found little else in common.

Peter inhaled deeply. "Hell of a lot better than the shit-ends we get to smoke in here."

I could feel my insides twisting as I waited for something more. I studied the familiar profile. The straight line of his nose and the scar that cut across his cheek had once been reassuring, but for the first time I saw the hard lines around his mouth and eyes. His cold manner, so different from the playful man I thought I knew, left me at a loss.

"I sure didn't come here to discuss the finer points of tailor-mades. . . . Ain't you just a little glad to see me, or is this how you treat all your visitors?"

He shifted on the bench and all the warm images I held of our relationship went blank.

"Surprised would be more like it." His words were ice chips. He dropped the ash from the cigarette on his pants and rubbed it in a circular motion.

"Do you know the trouble I had to get in here?"

"I wonder what trouble . . . when you get two pigs to come with you."

"Is that it? . . . you're pissed off cause of that? I . . ."

"First, tell me what they want."

"I told them I'd find out about your other ARs." I could feel him stiffen.

Afraid he was going to leap off the bench, I placed my hand on his thigh pressing my fingers into the rough cotton of his pants. My words tumbled into a rushed plea, "Don't you know I'd . . . say anything . . . do anything to see you? You gotta understand I wasn't going to ask you anything. This was the only way I'd get to see you again. I'd never rat." I released my grip and clasped my hands.

He settled back onto the bench, his jaw set in distrust.

"Why won't you see me? I just don't understand why I can't see you! It's so unfair!" My lips started to quiver. He made no effort to look at me. Instead, he seemed engrossed by the smoke rings that he was blowing towards the guard behind the glass.

I rubbed my wrist across my eyes, then I kicked his foot, "Well . . . ain't you going to answer me?"

He crushed the smoldering butt under his black leather boots. "I never said I didn't want to see ya."

"Then why aren't I on your visitor's list?" I thrust my hands into my pockets.

For the first time he turned to me. "Because you're a bad influence."

Seeing me blanch, he explained—"You don't understand . . . you think they're going to let a known junkie in off the streets to see me? No way, and let's be honest here, you are a known junkie." He stretched my arm out, as if he could see the tracks beneath my sleeve.

I jerked away, "Other junkies get to visit their old men inside . . . why not me? Am I so different? I just don't buy it. It's a load of crap."

The muscle on his cheek twitched. "It's not a load of crap . . . we were known accomplices—you know they know that . . . or have you forgotten?" He stared down at my leather boots, and I thought I detected a slight overtone of regret. "You think I haven't tried to get you on my list . . . but I have."

I rubbed my cheek before lashing out, "You couldn't have tried very fucking hard . . . I ain't even got so much as a letter from you in all these months. You can't tell me that they refuse to let you write."

He grabbed me by the shoulder and shook it. "Don't use that kind of language." His voice surged, then faded; "I don't like hearing that from you."

"What?" I searched his face, then brushed away his hand. "The word *fuck* is the least of my new bad habits."

In a uneven move to leave, I stood up.

He clapped his hands together in recognition of my performance. "Yah . . . I heard you've been out selling your wares every night for any jerk who's got two-bits." He rose as if giving a standing ovation.

I slapped at his arms. "You think you did me some high and mighty favour . . . by being in here? All you did was leave me with no place to go and a fucking habit to support. Christ, if I wanted a lecture, all I had to do was phone my parents, not get up at eight in the morning to go visit some loser in the joint!"

The guard tapped on the window. "Watch the tone!"

Peter sat down and crossed his arms.

I was the locksmith, probing with a rusty key. "Who told you about 'selling my wares'?"

"Who cares . . . that's not the point." He turned, reached up, and gave me another shake. "What the fuck did I fall for . . . so you could lay down for any john with a few bucks in his back pocket? What a fucking waste."

"Well . . . at least you're in here getting three squares a day and free room and board. A hell of a better deal than I got at the moment."

The rising colour in his cheeks matched my own as he spat out, "Why didn't you go home like I told you . . . look at you . . . you look like shit . . . a fucking skeleton." He dragged his finger across the first few beads of sweat that had begun to cluster on my forehead. "Even getting sick . . . a fucking mess. What happened to you? I thought seriously about not seeing you, and now I'm sorry I changed my mind!"

I looked down at the top of his head, and struggled to hold my voice steady: "You know bloody well what's happened . . . I'm wired. I got no way to support a habit, except by 'selling my wares.' I got a family who wants nothing to do with me . . . I'm alone . . . you just don't get it . . . DO YOU? Even you, the one person I thought I could count on, treats me like a piece of shit. You're sorry . . . well, I'm sorry I made this trip. I am a whore, but at least my time is worth a lot of money and I'm not going to waste any more of it."

The guard rapped on the glass again.

My face whitened and I felt sick. Peter's hands grasped my hips and he pulled me down to his lap. As if his resolve had cracked, he said gruffly, "Things change baby . . . I ain't the same . . . neither are you . . . and I warned you that some day that would happen. You don't know how it eats me to hear those stories of you. Why am I here if you're going to burn yourself out? If I do ever get out, there won't be anything left of you." He tried to pinch my waist as if to make a point. It was the first glimmer I had seen of his easy manner and I took it as a hopeful sign.

"Why would I want you anyway then? I'll probably have some other old man," I reproached him, but did not resist his embrace.

"When I'm sprung I'll give any old man you got the boot." His laugh dispelled my anger.

He stroked my hair and I pressed my face against his chest. "I'm so lonely."

"I know baby . . . I know." He rocked me like a child, while my tears stained his shirt. He bent over and instructed me, "You gotta get an old man. You're nothing but a sitting duck out there without some old man . . . any old man . . . it's all I can do to survive in this mother-fucking weird place. I can't be worried about you alone on the street. Understand . . . I done all I could for ya . . . and now you gotta get it together . . . look out for yourself . . . you owe me at least that much." I tightened my grip on his arm.

I stretched my hand to untie his hair, letting it fall across his face and raised my mouth. The guard shouted through the grates of the glass, "No close contact."

The mood was broken. Peter dropped his arms and I slid back to the bench. I watched him fold again into the unfeeling stranger I'd just managed to reach.

"Fucking screws," he muttered. "We weren't even allowed to sit at the back—no, we have to sit right under their noses. . . . Got another smoke?"

I offered the pack. "Keep them."

"Ain't allowed . . . another fucking rule."

As he lit up, I ventured a question. "Why'd you want me to pack in dope?"

"Because you could get it," he said, avoiding looking at me. "I got one word of advice, then I'm gonna split . . . 'cause we ain't got nothing more to say to each other . . . and I ain't putting on another show for that old screw. If you can't go home, and Beth you really need to . . . then like I keep trying to tell ya, get another old man . . . one who'll look out for you."

He stood up. "And if you write"—seeing my puzzled look, he growled— "Yah . . . you can do that . . . whatever they told ya . . . well . . . don't expect me to answer . . . 'cause I ain't very good at letter writing." He strode back to the PRISONERS' ENTRANCE and kicked the door with his foot.

The guard pushed a button, and he was gone. I stayed on the bench as the sound of his heavy boots boomed across the empty room.

"Visit's over miss . . . in case you haven't noticed," said the guard.

◄o►

Stuck in the back seat of the police cruiser, I felt my sickness grow, flooding me with new miseries. Bruce, glancing in the rear view mirror, observed the withdrawal—the sweat on my forehead, my frame shivering from attacks of the chills, the black eyes, and my running nose. He saw that I, too, was watching him, and looked back to the road. He snapped on the radio. "I'm sorry it didn't go the way you'd hoped."

"Yah," I mumbled, as the wailing of country music furthered my dreary mood. I began to sway back and forth, while Tony Orlando sang, "Tie a yellow ribbon 'round the old oak tree. . . ." I gripped my chest as my heart raced faster. A current of emotions swept me along until I embraced my suffering. The cruiser sped along the ribbon of highway that cut through the flat fields.

My thoughts cycled back to grade eight and my first day at Mount Royal Junior High School. My mother had insisted that I wear a cut down, A-line two piece suit that had once been hers. She informed me, in that cool detached way of hers, that it would be a shame not to get some more use out of what once had been an expensive outfit. But it accentuated how undeveloped I was. Too tall for my age, my legs looked like sticks and my bony knees like doorknobs beneath the tartan colours of the tight skirt. I could still feel the Stanfield T-shirt soaked with the nervous sweat that clung to my flat chest as I stood in front of the classroom. As the teacher introduced me, my classmates marked me then and there: rejection, isolation. One moment can define you as either a geek or a prom queen. Alone in front of a bunch of peer-conscious thirteen-year-olds, I would never forget those judgmental eyes. It was the same look I'd seen in Peter's eyes from the back of the visitor's room.

As the car slowed, I sanded away such thoughts. We'd just entered the city limits. The sight of the Calgary Tower jutting in the distance made my spirits rise; even from here I could feel the pull of the east end.

The cops, perhaps obliged by my unspoken urgency, drove to the corner of Centre Street and Seventh Avenue. Before we'd come to a complete stop, I made my escape. Over my shoulder I called to them, "Bye . . . thanks."

Bruce rolled down the window and shouted, "I'll see ya sometime and we'll talk . . . okay?"

I did not turn around as my feet pounded towards home, the Empress Hotel. I raced across the hotel's lobby and bounded up the carpeted stairs, oblivious to everything except what lay waiting in my room.

I had three caps and this time I'd use them all. I would overdose myself. It would be a painless way to go. I squatted on the edge of the toilet and forced the liquid into my arm. My body plunged forward, my head slammed into the upright porcelain sink. The room was still. I lay crumpled on the yellowing linoleum. I could feel the sweat, still wet on my face, mingling with the blood that seeped from the gash on the top of my head. I saw everything, as if it were a part of me but lost in a dreamy fog. I wondered why the body did not move as the floor and the person I assumed was me melted into one. I felt pulled towards a dark tunnel where I went spinning downwards faster and faster.

Something hit my cheeks again and again, pain like an electrical surge shocking my deadened senses. I tried but could frame no words, and my eyes refused to open. Heavy slaps continued, accompanied by a male voice, "Beth . . . wake up . . . damn you, wake up!" Slam. Slam. The blows continued raining on my face.

A faint "Fuck off" worked its way from my lips.

"That-a-girl," the voice encouraged. My eyes still refused to open as I was lifted up off the floor.

The voice commanded, "Walk . . . walk . . . walk!" My limp body was dragged around the room. The tone continued, loud and persistent in my ear, "Walk . . . damn you . . . walk . . . I said walk."

I managed to mutter, "No . . . no walk."

"I don't give a shit . . . you walk."

I pried open one eye a crack, and stared at the man who kept forcing me around the room. Lanny. He was stronger than I would have thought, and he lugged my rag-like body back and forth.

"Go 'way."

"No fucking way . . . walk . . . hear me? . . . WALK!"

"NO . . . no more."

"YES . . . you will walk!"

I did not know how long it was before I began trying to place each foot alternately down. "Good girl . . . C'mon . . . that-a-girl."

"Cigarette?"

"In a minute . . . just keep walking a little longer."

"Cigarette." I stiffened.

Lanny knew if I had the strength to start resisting him, then his efforts to keep me moving would require more energy than he had. He lowered me onto the bed. I lay there unmoving.

"No . . . no . . . sit up!" My cheeks stung, as an open hand crashed across them.

My eyes flew open and I thought I saw a look of delight. I held my arms over my face, suspecting he was enjoying himself. "Stop!"

He picked me up. My head tumbled against his sweatshirt and smeared it with blood. "If you nod out . . . you could go under again."

"What are you doing here?" I made no move to escape the arms that held me.

"Been hanging around outside since about two thirty . . . got some news for ya . . . then you come barrel-assing in. . . . Shit, I didn't even know you was out . . . you see me?"

I shook my head slightly.

"You was in such an-all fire hurry. I had to see what was going down.

Had a hell of a time slipping past that desk clerk. He's even worse than the one at the Cecil. You left your door open, so I just came in and there you was in the can, lying in a pool of blood. Fuck, the fit was still in your arm . . . hardly no heart beat t'all. You're real lucky I came . . . yah, real lucky."

"Yah . . . real lucky."

Lanny propped me up amidst the pillows—"You sit up. I'll get something to wash off that blood and we can see how bad that cut is."

"Cigarette?" I rubbed my nose.

He took the pack of Export As, slipped one in my mouth, and lit it.

I inhaled. He wiped off the dried blood and swabbed the oozing wound. "Ain't that bad, just a cut and your hair will cover it. Don't think it needs stitches . . . and even if it does, ain't no one going to see it anyhow."

He gave me a poke in the ribs. "How come, Beth?"

I took another drag. "Peter . . . don't want me no more." The words formed and broke, yet did not hurt as I thought they would have.

"He tell you that?"

"Not exactly. Told me to get another old man . . . one who can look out for me." My head rolled forward. "He took a fall, and I fall for any guy with a few bucks in his pocket."

"Ah, Beth," Lanny said, stroking my matted hair. "He ain't worth it . . . c'mon . . . besides, what's wrong with the guy . . . you're one of the top girls on the strip . . . ain't no shame in that. I'll look out for ya, any guy can see what a prize you really are."

"I don't want any one else . . . I only wanted him."

"But he don't want ya . . . and ya can't be alone out here . . . whether ya like it or not I'm gonna look out for ya." With that he lay down beside me and I angled closer, enjoying this bit of unexpected comfort.

◄○►

Although I was on the street by seven, my mind was unfocused and my head wobbled. Large hoops hung from my ears and weighed my head down further. Despite my high heeled boots, I shuffled along the sidewalk like an oldster. I thought the beige concealer that covered my bruised face and combined with red blush gave me an Andy Warhol look.

Lanny had held compresses over my forehead in hopes of getting the swelling down, but to no avail. He'd also helped wash my matted and stained hair. It was now parted on the left side so that it covered the cut.

I'd stared at the half-inch gash in the bathroom mirror. It would heal, leaving a constant reminder of this day. The cut was near the hairline, so the scar could be hidden and pose no threat to my earning potential.

The Chinook wind that had blown all that day died, replaced by gusts from the north. The cold was numbing but did little to clear my grogginess. I attempted to hold my hair in place. I must have a concussion. My legs moved like stones: all I wanted to do was sink to the pavement and sleep.

From inside the All Night Arcade, Lanny watched me hide behind the other women clustered in front of the Regis Hotel. He darted out, to jerk me in front of the other women. Still feeling sluggish, I tried to straighten my spine as his colourless eyes remained expressionless.

"Now how are we going to get to Van . . . if you don't hustle?"

I rubbed my lip, trying to think up a retort and save face in front of my peers. He withdrew back into the warmth of the arcade, leaving me front and centre on the busy street. I shrugged at the stares of my mates and tried to oblige Lanny's request by appearing more interested in the male passersby.

I bombed badly many times before my line—"Want a date?"—was accepted.

For the rest of the night, Lanny followed the johns up to my trick room in the Carlton Hotel. His hovering bugged me: he was more like a fly over a bowl of fruit than a bodyguard. But as the hours passed and my senses cleared, I began to appreciate his surveillance. It gave a feeling of safety that I hadn't known since Sue and I worked together.

As I milled among the working girls along the strip, I noticed Gloria and Big Marie on the outer edges of the group sharing a laugh and staring. I turned my back to them as Gloria called out, "Got an old man do ya . . . things'll be real good now." The two of them doubled over in loud guffaws. I flounced away, giving them the finger as I passed; instead of incensing them, it added to their merriment. I stomped towards the York with Lanny trailing after me.

It was past 2 AM when I finished with my last trick. Lanny had waited outside the door while I wrestled with a fat, drunken slob who took forever to come.

We entered the familiar lobby of the Alexandria Hotel where a frowning face promptly informed me, "You pay double rates . . . if that thing is staying." Too weary to argue, I approached the desk and dropped two twent dollars bills on the registration book. Lanny, reclining in a lobby chair, glared at the old man. I hurried away from the Irishman, who in the past had been kind.

"A few more days and you won't have to put up with any BS from that old shit."

"The cops knew where I was this morning. I needed another room and I like that old shit and his BS." I gave him a push. He said nothing.

As I locked the door, I was aware of aching all over. As I lowered myself to the bed, my head was pounding and my stomach hurt.

I'd started to stretch onto the bedspread when Lanny demanded, "Gimme the night's take . . . and I'll score."

I crossed my arms. "I make it and I don't give it to no one . . . understand?"

"Ah . . . Beth. I just wanted you to get some rest . . . and I thought I was doing ya a favour." He moved closer and caressed my knee.

I thought over what he'd said, then removed my boot and threw him a wad of bills. The hand left my knee and snatched the money. "Better not disappoint me."

He flashed a grin, "Never," and was gone.

I eased back down on the bed, bothered by the dull pains in my stomach. I rubbed the tight skin and realized that when I was not high, the pains began. "Could it be the flu?" I wondered aloud. I closed my eyes and blocked out this discomfort.

I moved to the desk in the corner and found what I was searching for—a piece of hotel stationery and a dull pencil. I positioned myself on the chair and began forcing the lead onto the page.

> *Dear Peter,*
>
> *You really are an asshole. How stupid do you think I am? Known accomplices . . . bullshit . . . on the street maybe, not the joint. I know I haven't changed, and who are you to judge me any-*

way? I'll think of you sometimes, because of the good times we once
had, but mostly I'll think what a bastard you turned out to be.
Beth

P.S. I'd say see ya around some time, but we both know that
isn't very likely.

I slipped the letter into my purse as the door swung wide and Lanny
returned. I caught the balloon in my right hand. Minutes later, satisfied, I
crawled between the sheets with all my pains and doubts banished by the
heroin's blanket of forgetfulness. I snuggled into the pillow, ignoring
Lanny as he crept in beside me. He brushed my cheek with his lips.
"Night, Beth."

"Night," I said, then dropped like an anchor into a dreamless sleep.

Chapter Sixteen

Supporting both our habits was an exhausting grind. The long hours began with working the four o' clock supper crowds and ended at two or three in the morning. The tricks at that time of night were the worst, usually drunk; but thoughts of the warm West Coast made them bearable. It would be a fresh start in a new city, with no past history to drag me under. And the dope there was plentiful.

I'd worked until there was an hour to spare to catch the last flight to Vancouver. Lanny hailed a cab and we were on our way to the airport. Inside the warmth of the car, I leaned my face against Lanny's jean jacket and dozed off. But it was not long before he was shaking me. "Money." The cab idled as I handed it over and watched the thin man pay the fare.

Inside the airport, Lanny arranged for the tickets, then hustled us along to Gate B.

In a short time he'd become a most helpful companion. He organized everything, including the scoring. He was always close by, so I'd no worries of a bad trick. The one detail he left to me was making the money, and I was good at that. He drove me hard, coaxing me out of bed by three-thirty and prodding me to keep going until I was the last one working the strip. I accepted his explanation that we must get a stake together before leaving. However, the periodic fixes I received for my labours did not blunt the long hours. I'd made up my mind that once in Vancouver I would slow the pace.

Weariness trailed my every move. Secured by the seat belt, I fell asleep. When we were airborne, Lanny shook me awake to take the fix he'd readied before we'd left. I remembered stumbling into the washroom and jabbing myself. Then the lull of the engine filled my head as sleep overwhelmed me again. After that it seemed a matter of minutes and I was in another cab on my way to the east end of Vancouver.

I was surprised when it stopped in front of a seedy run-down cafe on Hastings Street. A sign hung precariously in front of the dilapidated building advertising MAH'S CAFE. The faded lettering was more noticeable in the darkness, as several of the light bulbs inside were burned out. I held Lanny's hand as we entered the place.

Crowded together in booths were hypes—old ones, young ones, high ones, and the desperate eyes of the sick ones. An odour of grilled food hung in the air and mingled with the cigarette smoke that blanketed everything. He guided me to a table at the back, near the washroom. As I slid into the booth my boot stuck to a sticky substance on the floor. As I worked to free myself, a steady stream of bodies came and went into the washroom. Lanny surveyed the faces, searching for a familiar one. A middle-aged Chinese woman in a dirty smock approached. "Ya . . . what ya want?"

"Two coffees," Lanny ordered.

A woman, her dyed blue-black hair shimmering under the paneled lights, skidded in across from us.

"How ya doing, Lanny?"

"Oh, Laura . . . I didn't see ya." He did not seem surprised.

"Figured that."

"Beth . . . this is Laura. Used to be a Calgary hype . . . then she got smart."

Black eyes surveyed me, then Laura dropped her eyes and resumed a conversation with Lanny. "Well, if you're going to be wired, this is the place . . . that's for sure." A slight hesitation followed. "Bringing a new one . . . eh?"

"Watch your mouth," he warned.

"Ya want or not?" Laura bit back.

"Yes . . . we want," I interjected, uneasy with the tensions that surrounded these two.

"Well, there you go," the woman smiled.

Lanny flashed her a dirty look. "Ya better come through," he growled, as he passed the money to Laura under the table.

"Or else?" Laura replied, leaving.

"How long will she be?"

"Only a few minutes . . . this place is crawling with pushers . . . you just got to know which ones they are . . . 'cause the others would love a chance to sell ya icing sugar, thinking you're a stupid hick from the prairies." He snorted, as if he sympathized with that point of view. He lit up an Export

A and stared off into space with a calculating expression.

He belonged in this setting more naturally than any place in Calgary. I glanced around, aware now that all these hypes were worn and ugly. The couple in the next booth had hair so filthy that it was impossible to tell which sex was which. Through the separated tendrils covering their faces I could see junk sores, and I caught a whiff of body odour. I could sense, feel and smell Rounder here.

"Where do the hippie types hang out?"

"Granville Street—won't find no snobs here" he said, tapping his cowboy boots.

As I puzzled over what he meant, Laura coasted back and transferred the dope to Lanny with a handshake. He left for the bathroom to taste it.

Laura pulled her lips tight to hide her protruding front teeth, then she held a hand over her mouth and asked, "Known him long?"

"Not really."

"Oh." She patted me on my shoulder.

At this patronizing gesture, I jerked away.

A shriek at the front made me jump around in time to see five or six men lunge towards a man in one of the booths. This was followed by choking sounds, and I froze in fear. The place went silent as the scene was played out. We all were accustomed to danger: it came from within, sometimes it came from without. A few ducked out the back door, several others bolted out the front, but the rest, like Laura and I, stayed, afraid to draw any attention to ourselves. We watched as the helpless man was carried struggling from the booth and disappeared with the men.

In a matter of minutes it was over. The remaining patrons relaxed and things returned to what they had been before the entry of the horsemen into our territory.

I leaped up as Lanny returned. "You saw?"

He nodded and led me outside. "It happens in here at least twice a night . . . one thing about Van, it's crawling with narcs."

My heart was still beating hard as we walked into the night. Brightly dressed pimps and colourful women in suggestive outfits paraded along, while groups of young and old stood in shadows whispering the language of the street. We hiked along to a clapboard building with a Victorian facade of neatness, standing between two tenement buildings.

We registered as Mr. and Mrs. Boyd. In our room we fixed again. Then, Lanny turned mean. "Enough goofing around . . . ya can go to work now."

I draped myself over the bed and ignored his remark.

"Didn't ya hear me? . . . I said I want ya to go to work."

"I don't want to."

My attitude infuriated him. He rushed closer, grabbed hold of my sweater and jerked me upright. "I don't care what ya want . . . I want ya to work . . . now."

I brushed his hands away. "It's late. I'm tired. I worked like a dog to get us here and I won't work a strange city, especially at this time of night. Get real for Christ's sake." I made to move away from him. But he caught my hair and pulled my face close to his. "You're pissing me off. "

"No . . . you're pissing me off. "

His answer was a cuff the across the side of my head with his open hand.

"You bastard." I threw my arms up to ward off another blow and ran across the room, easily ducking away from him.

His face whitened and his fists clenched as he came after me. I was backed into a corner. "You gonna go to work?" he demanded, pushing me into the wall.

"Fuck off. Jesus Christ . . . what's the matter with you," I screamed as a fist slammed into my head. I swiped at the trickle of blood that ran down my nose and shoved him away. He rammed his body into mine and I landed on the carpeted floor.

"I'll tell you what's wrong with me . . . YOU . . . a spoiled bitch who always gets her own way. . . . Peter was pussy whipped . . . if that idiot had any sense he'd have turned you out and the two of you could have still been playing lovey-fucking-dovey on the street. . . . Now I'm going to teach you who's boss around here."

"Get off me!" I yelped, twisting violently.

He pushed my left arm up my back until I thought it would snap. I whimpered in pain. The pressure never wavered as he dragged me to my feet, forced me to the door, then threw me out. "I've been patient long enough . . . now get to work."

The door slammed and I began banging on it. "I paid for this fucking room . . . let me in . . . let me in . . . let me in . . . let me in." No one seemed to notice or hear as my fists pounded on the door.

Someone in one of the neighbouring rooms shouted, "Shut up!"

I persisted in rapping my fists on the closed door, which opened as Lanny yanked me back inside. "You bitch . . . ya need some smartening up," he said, belting me across the side of the head again.

"You prick . . . you don't give a shit about me."

"Ya ain't so dumb after all." He waved a finger under my nose—"Too bad there's nothing you can do about it."

I pushed past him into the washroom, where I held a wet face-cloth over my head and sat on the toilet thinking. I would not stay with him. I must dump him . . . but how? After stemming the blood, I slunk back out to him. "Lanny, I'm sorry, but I'm so tired and this being a new city and all . . . I thought you'd give me at least the night to rest. Then tomorrow I'll find my way around . . . and I promise that I'll work doubly hard to make up for it."

He lowered his fists. "Okay . . . just tonight . . . but tomorrow you better work your lazy ass off."

"I promise I will, just don't be mad. Why don't you have an extra fix?" I smiled and climbed into the bed. I closed my eyes, waiting for him to come and lay beside me.

I began to think that he would stay chain smoking by the window all night, but finally he nestled in next to me. I could feel his muscles flexing as if he knew I would try to flee. I lay still, measuring my breathing. Inside I was churning as I listened for his answering rhythmic breath. The wait stretched into hours before I was sure he slept. Then I glided from the bed and made my way to the washroom where I found the hidden balloon. Thank God, he always stored the dope in the same spot behind the toilet.

Then I returned to the bedroom and rifled through the pockets of his discarded jeans until I found my money. He rolled to his side, and I froze. At last, reassured he still slept, I gathered my clothes and darted to my carrying case by the dresser. I tiptoed to the door, which I opened and closed soundlessly behind me. Outside in the hallway I dressed and then ran along the hallway, to the safety of the street.

◄○►

I sprang upright, then doubled over, moaning. I struggled to stand and hobbled across the cold floor. My hands fumbled under the dresser until I retrieved a bulging balloon. The top drawer revealed a fit and blackened spoon. The fix brought relief.

I closed my eyes and rubbed my stomach as the pain diminished. Sitting up, I surveyed the tiny room and wrapped the blanket tighter around myself in an effort to keep off the chill. I'd a lot more money and a much larger habit since I no longer supported Lanny's. Above, a mobile circled and drew my pinned eyes to the painted clown faces. I followed their hypnotic movements and retreated into another world.

I could hear the wind purring as it rustled through the budding branches of the poplar and maple trees. Below, crested waves crashed onto salt-stained rocks, licking at the exposed embankment. Above the sea, perched on a high grassy bank, stood a white-washed cottage. Velvet moss trimmed the shingles and ivy obscured the slumping verandah that hugged the single story building. Along the hardwood floors I glided, relishing the smell of the ocean breezes waffling through the open screens.

Crackling with life, a stone fireplace filled the living room with warmth. A bag of marshmallows forgotten by the hearth was growing together into a gooey mass. Rain pelted against the window and I pressed my face close, fascinated by the mini rivers cutting the glass with their shifting patterns. A finger tracing the fleeting designs, a feeling . . . a feeling of. . . . "Fuck!"

I shrieked, coming out of the nod. I lurched to grasp the cigarette that I'd dropped in my stupor. The first bubble of a blister was forming and I squashed the offending butt in the ashtray. I studied the burn, a red circle of skin on the inside of my thigh. I rose and lifted a pair of bell bottomed cords off a metal chair. As I dressed, I observed the clouds that blocked the morning light. I brushed the knots out of my sleep-tousled hair and reached for the bomber jacket hanging on the bedpost.

The last of the morning rush hour traffic still clogged the streets and thickened the air. The sky spit rain as I hurried towards the Royal Hotel and breakfast.

I slid into the coffee shop by the side door, choosing an empty booth by the window. Here I watched the well dressed men and women, briefcases swinging by their sides, umbrellas held aloft advertising their respectability.

"Suit parade." I waved to the waitress to attend to my order. My mouth was watering at the thought of the sweet toasted butterhorn. The chocolate milk was thick and creamy, soothing my chapped lips and raw throat. I was waiting for the clock above the busy cash register to signal 10 AM, the opening of the post office.

I'd heard nothing from Peter since my visit. Every day for weeks I'd expected a letter. If my mother had been sitting beside me she would have asked, "What planet are you on?" I shook my head, relieved that she was only an unwelcome pop-up in my brain. I lit another cigarette and then, with some satisfaction, saw that it was almost time.

The postal clerk pushed a small white envelope at me. I swiped it eagerly, inspecting the postmark—it was right . . . Drumheller. Oblivious to the clouds that belched with rain, I returned to my room to savour the letter. I hastily ripped the envelope.

> *Dear Beth,*
>
> *I didn't mean to hurt you, it's just like I was trying to explain, three years is a long time, and you won't be the same by then and neither will I. I probably dug you more than any chick, when we were together, but that was then and this is now.*
>
> *I wanted you to get another old man so there would be someone there for you, 'cause between you and me, you know that you need some looking after.*
>
> *I heard about your troubles with Lanny. You got to get your shit together.*
>
> *Can't you tell the difference between someone who cares and someone who'll take you for what they can get? I thought you were a good enough con artist not to get conned yourself. I don't mean to lecture or nothing, but I can't give you nothing and it's hard enough to survive inside without thinking you're fucking up so bad. Write me anytime and let me know how you're doing.*
>
> *Luv Y's*
>
> *Peter*

I crumpled the page and threw it to the floor. It was nothing . . . nothing . . . he could have written that to his sister. A tear threatened as I slammed my fist on the pillow. Why did he have to write that?

"You and me, Baby, nothing going to stand in our way, you watch my back and I'll watch yours. Can't take us down . . . we're a team." I'd believed him. Why couldn't he write something like that? I needed something to cling to.

"Luv Y's, my ass." I ground my wet boot over the letter. Then I flew down one flight into another darkened hall. I moved past a couple of narrowly spaced doors that all looked the same except for the fading numbers hand-painted on them. I knocked lightly on one. "It's Beth."

"Door's open."

I entered a room twice the size of mine. On the wall above the double bed was a pinned collage of hearts and cupids. A matching pink comforter and ruffled pillowcases covered the bed. At a table under the window sat a round-faced girl, her long hair done up in two large side ponytails. She was labouring over a sheet of construction paper, using a small paintbrush to dot each square of the outlined cubes with 7-Up.

"Another acid rip-off ?" I asked, and sat down.

"You bet—a big one—five thousand dollars. I got to be finished before Blade gets home. He's already working on some other deal."

"Ain't ya scared he's going to get hisself killed some day?" I fingered a cigarette and tapped it on the table.

Sandi shrugged, "If it happens . . . it happens, but ya know he'd take a couple with him." She put down her brush. "Did I tell you what happened the other day? We was coming up from the Gastown Hotel, and these four young punks came up behind us and grabbed Blade. They was screaming that he done ripped them off for a pound of hash, and Blade turns quick-like and knocks one flat, then the other three come at him and he pulls a knife and tells them that the first one to lay a hand on him will die. I start saying things like, 'Ya want to mess with junkies, come on . . . we'll tear you apart. We eat chippies like you for breakfast. C'mon on then, let's get it on.' It was real great sport." Sandi licked her lips, a gleam in her blue eyes.

I laughed, "You mean . . . they went for the shit about junkies?"

"Of course they did . . . don't everyone know that junkies are bad people?" She made an ugly face and both of us smiled.

"Can I have some of this pop?" I asked, helping myself to the large bottle of 7-Up on the table. Sandi nodded absently while I sipped it for a few moments.

"You know Sandi, that pain in my gut is getting worse. Last night I must have woke up four times with it. Even the junk only seems to hold it for a couple of hours . . . my habit is going through the roof because of the big fixes I have to take . . . I mean, almost every two hours or the pain is so bad I can't stand it."

Sandi's head, bent low over the construction paper, nodded. "Ya gotta see a doctor . . . I just don't see what else you can do."

"I can't . . . me in the hospital . . . I'd be so sick. I think I'd rather die."

"Don't ya know this is Vancouver? . . . Shit, they'll give ya Methadone . . . no sickness."

"I don't know . . . maybe." I studied Sandi for a few minutes. As usual, Sandi's mode of dress was sloppy. Today she wore one of Blade's old sweaters, a loose one with several burn holes in the front that came down to her knees. A faded pair of blue jeans covered her short legs and her feet were bare. Her raspy voice was offset by a face that held softness in its rounded features.

I pointed to the arrangement of hearts and cupids on the wall, "You do that?"

"Why, don't you think it's Blade's style?" Sandi laughed. "It's almost Valentine's Day and it cheers this dump up."

"Yah, we could all use some cheering up. Speaking of the cupid thing, I don't know if I should send Peter a card as he's not the mushy type . . . and I don't know where I stand with him anyway. I'm alone on an empty life boat."

"Ya heard from him lately?"

"This morning."

"Yah . . . what's he got to say for hisself ? . . . and don't give me no more shit about boats and such . . . Jesus, sometimes I just can't understand what you're going on about!"

I cleared my throat and took another sip of the pop. "You just don't have the heart of a poet, Sandi . . . that's your problem."

"I don't see that as a problem and yours is that you take too long to get to the point . . . just tell me what he said."

"He just told me the same old stuff . . . take better care of myself . . . shit . . . as if I want to hear that BS. The only thing that I can hope for is that Lanny does time with him." I traced my finger around the rim of the cup. "I know Peter will gut that fucker. Just on the principle of what was."

"Shit . . . let's fix and sort all this emotional shit out. Did I ever tell ya the story of how Peter and Blade ripped each other off? Well, it was when both were still into smoke, and Peter went to buy a pound of hash off Blade, and when they made the transaction, Blade, in the dark, didn't check the money too good—just saw a ten on top of the pile and handed over the pound. But here's the good part—the pound was a pound of mud, and both of them had a bitching fight the next time they ran into each other, each claiming the other had ripped them off." Sandi giggled.

I pumped my arm. Sandi made ready for the hit and I winced as the needle drove through the hardened gristle of my infected track. Sandi pulled the point free and shook her head. "Ya gotta see a doc."

I was not to be distracted from any story of Peter, "Who won?"

"They both gave each other a pretty good shit kicking as I remember. One of the only times that Blade ever been ripped off. Your old man's pretty smart hisself—I done heard that he turned around and sold that bogus pound to someone else. In fact, he's one of the few that ever won Blade's respect."

"Peter always was pretty wily. What kind of dope is this? . . . Man, is it good!"

"I've been saving it for ya." Sandi began to prepare her own arm.

I moved to stand, but instead thumbed my nose. "You should lock the door."

"Don't make no difference . . . relax."

"Where did you get this stuff? I haven't had a buzz like this in a long time."

"Blade brought it home the other night. It hasn't been cut too bad and he told me to save ya one, for all the dope that you done laid on us."

I raised my voice raised in protest. "That was nothing, after all you guys did taking me in the night I ran from Lanny. Fuck, I don't know what I would have done if I hadn't bumped into you . . . and shit . . . I had more dope than I could shoot myself." I paused as I swayed in the chair. "But it's not so lonely since Sue's been staying with me. She didn't come home again last night. I hope she's okay."

Sandi finished fixing and her head dropped to the table. "Sue can take care of herself. Been doing it for a long time. I just want you to know that I think of ya as a good friend and I feel pretty close to ya. So listen to me when I say, Snakey Sue looks out for Snakey Sue. Don't ever think otherwise. Probably has a mark somewhere."

I touched Sandi's arm. "I pretty much know that, but heh, I don't have many friends and I think I'll try to keep the few I've got."

"Junkies and friendship usually ain't a good mix," Sandi reminded me, as we slid into the velvet hands of the nod. Our breathing became shallow and our hearts beat slower, pumping streams instead of rivers.

The door banged and both of us jumped. Blade stood there, his face flushed red. He was of average height, but with a powerful build. In his worn leather jacket and scuffed motorcycle boots he looked tough. Many girls around commented on how good looking he was with his brown eyes and blond hair. But he was too serious for my liking. At times he reminded me vaguely of Peter, with his daring schemes and rip-offs, but there was a coldness in Blade that made me apprehensive.

He strode across the room and hollered, "You fucking bitch . . . I tole ya I needed those acid tablets done by the time I got back."

"I was working on them," Sandi snarled as he leaned over her.

Then his fingers tapped across the construction paper. "Ya haven't even started cutting them out yet!" His hand closed into a fist as if to hit her. Sandi reached for the glass pop bottle on the table and raised it up by the neck. The fizzling remains splattered to the floor as she swung it in a wide arc narrowly missing his head. "How dare ya come in here, acting like that. Couldn't ya see I was busy?"

"Ya . . . fixing my dope." He moved sideways, ducking her wild swings. "If ya hit me . . . ya ain't going to have no teeth left." He made a grab for the bottle as Sandi brought it down and grazed him across the top of his head.

I watched Sandi slowly back Blade up against the wall. My ears rang with their rising curses as they struck wildly at the other. As one of the cupids fell and fluttered to the bed, I made for the door.

I'd just started up the stairs, when I heard the door slam. Sandi started kicking it, screaming, "YOU BASTARD . . . YOU BASTARD . . . I'LL KILL YA . . . YOU BASTARD . . . YOU'RE DEAD . . . YA HEAR ME . . . DEAD!"

I bolted to my room. Noting the discarded letter on the floor I muttered, "Cupids and pop bottles," and kicked it under the dresser. I sank into the mattress and let the drug lift me to the place of emptiness.

I pried open a eye as Sandi entered and sat down on the bed. "You going to be okay?"

"Shit ya . . . he'll come looking for me and beg me to forgive him, it always ends that way." Sandi shrugged.

"Why go back?"

"Because I love that bastard. We've been together since I was fourteen. A fight don't mean nothing. I didn't think I could ever forgive him after I had that abortion and saw my baby being flushed down the toilet. Fuck, the coat hanger! Man that hurt. He forced me to have it, but we're still together. He's broke my arm and I've cut him. We always work it out. Besides, you ain't gonna tell me that you and Peter never went at it . . . shit, it's part of the life."

"Can't recall going after him with a pop bottle."

"Whatever . . . someday you'll come clean on the shit and not the glory."

"You forget what a constipated bunch junkies are," I retorted, on my knees finding the trampled letter in the dust under the dresser. Then I offered Sandi a smoke and we stepped from one world into another, sinking into the arms of our one true love.

◄o►

My eyes flashed open. Peter was not here, although a minute ago in my dream I could have smelled him and tasted the blood that covered him. The pain was back and I rubbed my stomach as if to exorcise it. The neon sign from the bar across the street flashed through the threadbare curtains. Sue had not come home tonight. I stumbled out of bed and made my way to the drawers. Using a beer bottle full of water, I fixed myself. The pain was waking me every few hours; it felt as if beavers chewing on tree bark were trapped inside my stomach.

I sat back up, lit a smoke, and turned on the light hanging from the ceiling. I longed to tell of my loneliness, the sickness in my gut, and how hopeless I felt. But no words could build the bridges I desired. I began in a stilted style.

> *Dear Peter,*
>
> *I ditched Lanny because he beat me. I'm sorry you heard about it before I could tell you. Being on my own hasn't been too bad and is better than being with some asshole who used me. Its been five weeks now and certainly the weather here is much better than in Calgary, so I can't complain too much.*
>
> *I've bumped into some of the old crowd. Sandi and Blade live here in the same building so I see them often and Sue's rooming with me. Also heard that Vie and Terry are here but haven't met up with them yet. The reason I'm writing is that I didn't mean all those things that I wrote you last time. I guess you didn't mention anything about that in your last letter 'cause you knew that you'd hurt me and I just wanted to hurt you back. Least ways that's my take on it. You told me that the seasons change, but I never thought that could happen to us.*
>
> *I dreamed tonight of the night the bikers caught up with us. Do you remember eventually going to the hospital and telling them that a dog bit you? Of course they didn't believe you, but you always had a way of making the unbelievable sound believable. It certainly wasn't one of our best times, but, like you said, we watched each other's back and were always there for each other.*
>
> *No hard feelings, only sad ones. All I can say is that I don't want to burden you with my shit but I still care even if you don't. I know you hate letter writing and thanks for the effort. You must have got the message I sent with Dela when she went to visit Chess last month, on being able to reach me here at C/O General Delivery, Vancouver Main Post Office.*
>
> *Love, Beth*

I folded the piece of paper and forced it into a pocket of my purse. I fixed again and this time I slept with no haunting remembrances.

Chapter Seventeen

GRANVILLE STREET WAS FILLED WITH headlights like streamers. Both on and off the road, people clustered around this stretch of pavement, while signs bursting with coloured lights added to the festive atmosphere. Drivers slowed to leer at the girls along the sidewalk. I stood a little to the left on the corner of Granville and Davie Street. Bored, I patrolled my square of sidewalk. A cigarette dangled from my lips and I rolled it from one side to the other with my tongue. I was thinking about the latest move Sue and I had made. Driven by our obsessive fears that the narcs would find us, we routinely pulled up stakes every few days. The more paranoid we became the faster we fled, as if the constant change would buy us safety. I could hardly remember all the places we'd stayed in the last few months.

My new boots pinched my feet so I leaned sideways into a lamppost to ease the pressure. I'd been standing in the same spot for hours with no action. My feet were killing me and I was unable to shake my bitchy mood. A blue Camero whizzed past, crammed with whooping teenage boys. One of them hollered, "Fucking whore," and flung a handful of marbles at my face. They landed short and scattered down the curb. I lifted a middle finger at the retreating vehicle.

A young girl approached, the small features not quite formed. She stretched a tiny hand towards me, "Spare a couple of bucks?"

"Use your butt, like the rest of us," I snapped. The youngster melted into the crowd. I took a deep drag on my cigarette. The faster the kid realized what life was down here on the streets, the sooner she'd go home.

A black Mustang roared up and the driver waved me over.

A man, middle to late twenties, looked me over. "How much?"

"The usual."

"Twenty-five then." I hopped into the shining car. As I slammed the door, my sixth sense banged into my consciousness, but I suppressed it and flashed him a grin.

"Where to?" the man asked, as he shifted the gears and gunned the motor.

I observed him carefully, noting his piercing eyes, dark hair, wiry build, the tight jacket that covered a white T-shirt, and the poor quality dress slacks. He seemed average enough, but there remained an elusive something that made me uncomfortable. "Take a left here," I instructed, directing him to Chinatown and the rundown hotel where I brought my tricks. Hoping I could gauge the man better by his responses, I tried to draw him into a conversation. In this trade, the ability to measure up a john was crucial.

"What's your name?"

"Jim."

"You from around here?"

"Yah."

"Got any kids, Jim?"

"I want a piece of tail not a bunch of yap."

"Take it easy, no harm intended. A little conversation usually helps to relax things, but if you prefer none . . . ."

Not taking his eyes off the road, he grunted.

A bit rough, but I'd had gruff ones before and tonight was so slow. He'll be okay, I reassured myself. "Park here," I said, keeping my voice level. He parked the car in front of a dilapidated building. Two small businesses were on either side of a grubby glass door. A weather-beaten sign read WONG'S ROOMS. It jutted over the sidewalk, casting a shadow. Metal hinges groaned in the wind.

I led the way through the door that advertised, in faded gold letters, REASONABLE RATES. The entrance was small and dimly lit. Several yellow arrows on the wall pointed up a long flight of wooden stairs. At the top, an oriental man peered over and then pushed a button and a steel door swung open. I wrinkled my nose at the musty odour of the hall and proceeded up the creaking stairs. I paused to nod at the little man, who sat back down and continued reading his newspaper.

I halted halfway down the corridor and pulled a key from my purse. The door opened to reveal a tiny, grime-coated room. As we stepped in, I noticed with relief that the trick was about the same size I was, about five eight. I smiled and held my hand out, "The twenty five first."

"I ain't paying for the likes of you . . . get your clothes off, bitch!" he snarled, slamming the door shut.

"I don't play rough . . . and I don't do it for free."

"And I said peel those clothes off, cunt!"

"Get someone else, I've changed my mind." I made a move towards the door.

"Well, I haven't." The man grabbed at my halter top and tore it from my body.

I covered my breasts with my arms. "Get out! I told you. I don't play rough!"

His answer was a fist into the side of my head. The power of the blow knocked me backwards and I toppled to the bed. He lunged after me with his fists swinging. I kicked frantically and succeeded in fending him off.

The standoff continued, with the man punching wildly as I kicked back desperately. Again and again I screeched out my fear, sure the watchful owner would come. My cries did not stop the assault; the man continued to flail away with more hits than misses.

Suddenly he came crashing down, crushing me beneath him and the attack escalated, as he bit down on a exposed breast. I clawed at his eyes, howling in terror. But his hand clamped over my mouth and silenced my screams. I continued to struggle, while his other hand found my throat. Under the growing pressure on my windpipe, I froze, afraid to further enrage him. I focused on his tight white mouth and impenetrable eyes. He responded by relaxing his hold on my throat, and I gulped at the unexpected return of air. He shifted his weight to better pin my arms and hands. Briefly free, I pulled on his short thick hair. His head jerked back in surprise, and I rolled out from under him.

He swiped, but I was too fast, reaching for the doorknob. He leaped across the bed and landed there in front of me. Shaking his index finger he advanced, backing me up step by step to the wall, where I waited for his next move.

"Look at the light," he commanded.

I knew he wanted to land an upper cut and knock me senseless. I shook my head. He aimed another blow to the side of my head and my ear echoed with the ringing accuracy of the punch.

I was going to die here, alone and afraid, in this dirty room and no one would know or care. The man's fist whistled again through the air; this time expecting it, I ducked. He broke off the attack and hung his fists by his side.

"Get dressed!" He threw my top at me. I did as I was told and wriggled into the useless halter-top. As I fastened my jacket, he grasped me by the arm and forced me from the room. "You're coming with me," his cold clipped words increased my terror.

As we snaked our way back down the hall, I gathered my wild thoughts together. If he gets me into his car, I'll end up a nameless floater in the harbour. That image spurred me into action and I wrenched free. I ran headlong towards the office, with my attacker in pursuit. "He's crazy! He's crazy!" I bellowed.

The tiny man stood up just in time for me to whirl him around. He became the buffer between me and the furious man.

"You go," the little man ordered. "I call police."

My attacker ignored the warning. He continued cursing and lunging around after me, while the owner, now in the middle, twirled around with me as I attempted to stay out of the man's reach.

"You go!" the owner shouted, becoming angry. The john made a final grab for me and then backed off. "I'll find you later," he threatened, and then walked down the stairs.

I tried to catch my breath.

"I call you cab," the Chinese man said. "You sit here." He pushed his chair at me as he dialed from the phone on the wall.

When he was finished, I asked, "Why didn't you come . . . I was freaking out. Didn't you hear me scream?"

"No speak English so good."

"Like fuck you don't." I held onto my pounding head.

"You get cab, you go home." He patted my arm.

"I can't, I have to go back to work." My hands covered my face as I bent low, trying to swallow my sobs.

◄○►

I confided the horror of this experience to Sue later in the cramped Gastown apartment we currently called home. Sue smiled from her twin bed, bounced up, and inspected the outline of a purple bruise on the left side of my face.

"Got ya good . . . I think it's getting worse out there. Only last week a guy I was giving a blow-job to pissed in my mouth. Can you imagine? Unbelievable! It's bad enough society comes down on us . . . but my God, when your own customers turn on ya. Bad tricks . . . we all get them. You're lucky that guy didn't kill ya . . . you remember the hooker down on Broadway they found last month with her throat slashed?"

"I don't want to hear that." I stood up to again study my face in the vanity mirror.

Sue returned to her own bed, complaining, "But what choice have we got . . . except to take it?"

I began pacing up and down between the beds, fuming. "I don't have to take shit like that . . . God . . . I remember when I helped Big Marie after a trick beat up on her. I was upset then, but now I'm scared . . . it's like working without a safety net. How can you tell if the guy's not right in the head? You only got a couple of minutes to make up your mind, and if it's a slow night like tonight . . . ya think . . . oh, what the hell. And that, my friend, is a sure way to end up dead."

I paused, thoughtful. "I mean it's a job. Salesclerks, waitresses, receptionists, don't have to worry about having the crap knocked out of them . . . and we provide a service too."

Sue laughed. "They don't make as much money as we do and they're not wired . . . they could quit if that happened."

"I could quit too, if I could get off the H." For the first time I mulled over the possibility, but before I figured how I might do this, Sue interjected.

"Ya could do just Chinese. I ain't never had any trouble with one of them. They are all quiet and polite and they don't take forever either."

"Come to think of it . . . I ain't either . . . had a problem with them," I confessed, sitting back down on her bed.

Sue lit a cigarette. "By the way, did ya make any money tonight?"

"I did okay, only got going late and went till almost two o'clock."

"Me too, and I thought that Granville further down would be better, but it wasn't. So I'll come back up and work with you tomorrow. Just a bad night all 'round."

"Yah . . . just a bad night." I said, trying to drift into the nod and escape those fierce eyes glaring from behind the swinging fists.

Chapter Eighteen

VIE LAY IN THE MIDDLE of the single bed with me on one side and Terry on the other. The light-bulb dangling above us had been switched off. The blind had been pulled down as far as it would go, half way, and the neon sign outside bathed the room in a soft glow.

Terry raised his head and uttered a curt, "Good night." With my back to the other two, I responded with a small grunt. As there was no room for a third head on the lone pillow, I'd just placed my arm under my head for support. The door burst open and men stormed into the room bellowing orders. The plain-clothes men swung Terry off the bed and dropped him hard to the floor. The remaining man shouted for Vie and me to lie on our stomachs with our hands clasped behind our heads.

"Terrance William Bradshaw, you are wanted on an outstanding warrant in Calgary." As Terry's rights were read to him I felt relief that it was him they were after. This feeling evaporated as one of the men joked, "Junkies sure do make strange bedfellows. The young one should be in the middle."

I could hear the click of the handcuffs fastening around Terry's wrists and thought of his Stanfields underwear, stained and in need of a wash.

I could see the outline of one of the men as he searched the pockets of our clothes, which were laying in separate but untidy clumps against the wall. I couldn't make out any individual features on the men; without their uniforms, there was no way of knowing if they were horsemen or city bulls. Nor had I seen the badge they'd flashed as the door came crashing down.

"Ladies, we apologize for ruining your three-way, but we have a scumbag due for delivery in Calgary." With his hands bound behind his back, Terry was forced into his blue jeans and hustled away, still in his bare feet.

The raid had taken only minutes; both Vie and I lay on the bed in silence. I waited until I heard the last of the raiders' bootsteps echoing off the stairs. I stood and watched the skin on my arms rise in a blanket of goose bumps.

"Ya know what this means?" Vie asked—her voice was resigned as she rolled onto her back. "I gotta get some money and be on the next flight to Calgary."

I was busy searching my pair of cords and becoming more angry with what I did not find. "Jesus . . . those fuckers stole my money."

Vie held her hair back with her fingers and exposed the silver that inched beneath the topping of mousy-brown colour. "They didn't take you in, so consider it a payoff."

"You're telling me I'm supposed to be grateful." I was on the verge of smashing my fist into the wall, but, spotting a blister on the top of my big toe, I bent down. "I was planning on a big breakfast. I've hardly eaten in days and now look at this." I extended the foot towards the woman on the bed.

"We all got our problems." She coughed, and then, as if the attempt to sit was too much, she lowered herself back to the mattress.

I stomped my injured foot down on the hardwood floor and went to retrieve my pants. "I'm fucking starving. This is just great! What the hell do they want your Terry for? I thought he lived off you?" I heaved my things against the half-open shade.

"Probably bad cheques. Sit down. I don't need to watch a temper tantrum." She offered me half the pillow and patted the bed.

"I want my money back." I huffed, but I edged closer to sit beside her.

"Remember, Terry and I do spend more time together on the street than you and that man of yours. Only fools and desperados pull AR's."

"You ever say that again and I'll kill you." I jumped up and began stuffing my legs into my pants.

Her lips formed a resemblance of a smile before she patted the pillow again.

Still angry, I tossed myself down beside her and placed the brown filter of my Players in the corner of my mouth. My hands stroked the bones of my ribcage. "Ever think of how strange it is—the funny little details one remembers?" I elbowed Vie in the ribs for emphasis—"Peter, for instance, smelled like musty pine needles."

"No one gives a rat's ass how your old man smelled," Vie interrupted.

"Heh . . . I had to sleep beside Terry and he didn't smell so good. That detail I hope I live long enough to forget."

Vie chuckled. "Come on then, let's try to get some sleep. We'll think of something in the morning."

◄◊►

Outside the entrance to Safeway on Hastings Street the two of us huddled under a black umbrella. Vie was whispering orders. "You take the cookie aisle and I'll head to the bakery section. Meet me on the steps of The Broadway Hotel." I nodded in agreement and Vie led the way into the grocery store, where we promptly split up.

After a few twists and turns I was standing in front of a selection of cookies. My mouth watered, as I fingered the chocolate chip, oatmeal, cream-filled Oreo's, and Fig Newtons. I was about to place a bag of chocolate-covered macaroons under my blue rain coat when a tall man with a name tag pinned to a white coat stopped beside me.

"Can I help you?" I noticed that he was only a few years older than I was.

"No . . . I'm just looking," I said, pivoting around to inspect the boxes of Premium crackers lining the other side. But the man matched my movement so precisely that his shoulder touched mine. My frustration increased, for I knew with him all over me I would never be able to steal anything. But the sight of all this plenty and my hunger combined to make me feel desperate.

As the loud speaker announced, "Price check," I saw the man's eyes dart towards the front of the store, and my fingers fastened around the only thing I could reach—a six-cent package of raisins. Before I could transfer it into one of my pockets, he grabbed me by the wrist. "You will take this to the cashier and pay for it." I held the pilfered raisins pinched between my thumb and forefinger as he marched me to the check out.

I threw the tiny package onto the conveyer belt and moved through, mumbling, "Got no change."

I stomped across the street to the Broadway Hotel, questioning what kind of desperado was I when I couldn't lift a tiny box of raisins? My stomach was knotting in hunger, and the humiliation of not having six cents was making me angry. These last few months I was angry most of the time, when I wasn't high. When I was straight, I wanted to kick the living shit out of someone or something.

Vie was waiting under her umbrella and chewing; but seeing me, she smiled and held out a package of donuts.

I ran the last few steps toward the treats. "How'd ya manage?" I asked between bites. "That fucker was all over me."

"You don't blend. You look like a hungry hooker."

"How'd ya mean?" I licked the last of the sugar off my lips with my tongue.

"Hip huggers, halter top, plastic raincoat in a shade only a hooker would wear—whereas no one notices me. They don't expect I'd be a working woman unless they saw me standing on a street corner."

"Ya . . . no one else wears Hush Puppies," I said, grabbing the empty tray and licking off the remains of the powered sugar before tossing it to the side of the road.

The woman tapped her nose and changed the subject—"I'm going to work and then head back to Calgary."

With my stomach full, I was quick to acknowledge this goodbye— "Well, say hello to Sue for me. She left this morning for a few days. I'll see you around sometime, Vie."

As I turned to walk away, Vie slipped a box of Band-Aides into my pocket. "You gotta take care of your feet."

"Yah . . . I only got the one set." I walked into the rain whistling, "It's a long way to Tipperary"—just as my father had taught me to do in another life.

◄○►

I crawled across the floor, my hands clawing through a sea of dust and lint. I inched closer to the bureau.

I groped underneath the wood and found an empty wad of tinfoil. "Shit." I hurled it across the room, remembering I'd fixed the last of it a few hours earlier. I tried to recall if Sue was there then, but my mind emptied, holding only the pain. My hands trembled as I clutched at the dresser for leverage. I struggled into a pair of cords and dragged a T-shirt over my head. Easing my feet into a pair of sandals, I stumbled away from the room that reeked of my sickness and pain.

As I made for Hastings Street, each step activated the agony that rocketed across my sides, exploding into spots of burning pain. The tricks there were not picky. It was a flea-market of desperation, the flesh bargain centre of the West Coast. Here I could find johns even in my bent condition. The rate was less, sometimes much less, but I would take what I could get. It was the last stroll for those too old or sick to work anywhere else.

The cords hung around my hips, my face was stiffened with misery and my unkempt hair was whipped by the wind. A few pedestrians stared with a mixture of curiosity and contempt.

A wrenching jolt of pain made me lurch for a lamppost. My grip tightened around the steel, while a sense of fear swept over me. I knew I would not make it to Hastings Street. Tomorrow was Sunday . . . I couldn't hold out against that too. I must score. I must work. Closing my eyes, I tried to steady myself as I pressed my forehead against the post and prayed for strength.

A wail propelled me into the middle of the road, to flag the approaching cars. A driver rolled down his window, "Crazy bitch!" I felt dizzy as the traffic edged around me, honking with frustration. A young man beckoned. I manoeuvred to the passenger side. "Please . . . a hospital . . . please."

"Right. Anyone can see that you're in bad shape."

I doubled over. The man watched in silence, then pressed his foot on the gas pedal. The five-minute drive seemed an eternity. He braked to a stop in front of letters that proclaimed EMERGENCY ENTRANCE. Then he jumped out by the parking sign, and helped me out. "Good luck."

I nodded my thanks and brushed past him into the bright place. "I need a doctor," I gasped to the admitting desk, then stooped over moaning.

"Name please," a middle-aged woman intoned.

"Elizabeth Hudson." I leaned along the edge of the desk.

"Address?"

"Don't have one." Another round of searing pains jabbed and I crouched low.

Coolly, the clerk looked down. "What seems to be the problem?"

"Pains . . . in my gut . . . I . . ."

"How long have you had them?"

"About three, maybe four months, but now they're so bad I just can't stand it." I tried to correct my curved spine to stare the clerk in the eye, but failed.

"Medical insurance number."

"I don't have it with me." The woman was a robot, and I was dying here on the hospital floor.

"You have to have an insurance number."

"I do . . . I can get it . . . I just don't have it with me." I swiped at the sweat that was starting to drip down my face.

"We need an insurance number." The clerk sat unmoved.

I stifled an urge to reach over and pull the woman from her seat by her hair. Instead, I rapped the desk with my knuckles. "I need a doctor! You'll have a number tomorrow . . . I can't get it right now. You can't refuse me treatment because I don't have the fucking number. My father's a doctor for Christ's sake . . . of course I have a number."

"Take a seat."

I forced myself into a vinyl chair beside a plastic plant. I rolled myself into a ball and rocked back and forth. The blazing lights were burning my eyes and I squinted.

"Elizabeth Hudson . . . Elizabeth Hudson? Is there an Elizabeth Hudson here?" On wobbly feet I rose and followed the nurse into the examining room. I was helped to undress, and was placed onto a small bed with a white hospital gown over me—laid out as if I were already a corpse.

"The doctor will be here shortly."

I used my hands to shield my eyes, as my body contorted into a crescent shape.

"Where is the pain?" a male voice asked.

"My gut."

Experienced hands probed my flesh, causing me to cry out as he pressed the hot scalding spots in my abdomen. "I need to give you a pelvic exam . . . just relax."

I nodded, but screamed at the shock of the steel speculum. "What . . . what's wrong with me?" I continued to whimper, looking to the doctor for some reassurance.

"It is my opinion that you have an STD. It's spread, infecting your tubes. You have Pelvic Inflammatory Disease. However, a specialist will have to examine you to confirm my diagnosis. In the meantime, I'm putting you on penicillin immediately." He noted the bruised and scarlet tracks on my arm. "Are you an addict?"

"Can't you just give me something now so I can go?"

"You are very sick and in need of immediate attention. I'm admitting you. As for your withdrawal—if you can tolerate it tonight—in the morning Dr. Thompson will see you and place you on Methadone."

I curled my hand into a fist and punched the side of the cheap plastic mattress. I forced myself off the cot and to my feet. I must get out . . . to get away . . . to run. Again the pain seared and sent me reeling.

"What do you think you're doing?" the nurse asked.

"I have to get out of here."

"You're not going anywhere except upstairs, young lady."

Later, I remembered crying as a male attendant wheeled me along dimly lit hallways. There was an elevator ride before I was deposited into another, slightly more comfortable bed. I found myself praying for death as the night crept forward. Nothing broke the monotony of my agonies except the odd flashlight that shone briefly into my room. My senses were assaulted as the hell that ticked inside me erupted. First the bed was drenched by sweat, then the mattress was an ice cube.

I remembered something my grandmother used to say: "This too will pass . . . this too will pass." As these words replayed in my head, I succumbed to the rocking motion that had brought me comfort as a small child. "This too will pass . . . this too will pass . . . this too will pass . . . this too will pass."

A white-coated man paused and observed me through his thick lenses. He touched me lightly on the arm. "Elizabeth, my name is Dr. Thompson. May I examine you for a few minutes?" The kindness of his words stopped my rocking.

"You the Methadone doctor?"

"The very same." He busied himself feeling my pulse, then noted the huge pupils, and my running nose. Lastly, he checked my arm. He scratched his observations on a chart. "In a few minutes a nurse will bring you a small glass of liquid. That is Methadone. You drink it all down and it will take the withdrawal pains away."

"Thank you." I began to chew my nails in anticipation of the arrival of the promised drug. Soon, a nurse breezed into the room and handed me a small glass of brownish liquid. I put it to my lips and gulped. My insides rebelled and I gagged. I willed my stomach to settle, then waited expectantly. Within a few minutes, my nose had stopped running. I felt neither hot or cold but rather comfortable, as satisfied as one does after a filling meal. I closed my eyes and slept.

I awoke a few hours later with a woman shaking me. "Miss Hudson . . . Miss Hudson . . . I need to take some blood samples." Although groggy, I was aware that I was hooked up to an IV and my left hand was attached to the thing. I held out my right arm. The technician looked over the offering. "Let me see the other one," she ordered. "Are all your veins like this?"

I nodded, then pointed to an overused vein in my right arm. "You can always get it there."

She poked the needle into the ulcerated flesh. "We also need a urine sample." A cold bedpan was placed under my ass and a paper cup put in my hand.

After the technician had her samples, I rang for the nurse. "Is there a phone I could use? It will be collect. I need to contact my family." In a few minutes a phone was plugged in beside the bed and the nurse waited while I dialed for the operator.

"Will you accept a collect call from Beth?"

My mother's voice answered with a wary "Yes."

"Mum . . . I'm in the hospital."

"Doesn't surprise me."

"I thought you might like to know that I'm here and I want my medical insurance number."

"What . . . you don't even have your number?"

"Listen . . . I don't have time to dick around. The number."

"Well, I haven't kept it up to date. You're over eighteen."

"What . . . you let it lapse? This is just fucking unbelievable."

"You're not using that language on me. If you have nothing else to say than to blame me for the mess you're in, then I'm hanging up."

"Fine." I slammed the phone down hard. I gave the nurse an apologetic shrug and then curled like a foetus on the bed. When I finally awoke there was a hint of gathering murkiness outside the window. It must be about four or five o'clock, I thought. Tomorrow I would ring later in the morning when my mother was at work.

My grandmother would take care of the health care number. For now, it was enough that I felt no pain, and—for the first time in so long—rested. A nurse appeared to give me a sponge bath, which added to my overall feelings of comfort. I nestled into the clean sheets with a deeper appreciation.

This new-found serenity was shattered by the appearance of yet another white-coated male, who clumsily pulled a chair close to my bed.

"Hello, Elizabeth. I'm Dr. Murphy and we're set to do surgery tomorrow morning. You'll have to sign some forms, since we need your permission to remove some cysts on your ovaries that we spotted in your X-rays last night.

"I don't even remember having X-rays," I answered.

"You did, and it'll be fine. In the meantime, you won't be allowed any supper or breakfast—no fluids either. You may, however, wash your mouth out with water. Any questions?"

"No." Just my luck that as soon as I started thinking food, it was fasting time.

Without acknowledging my answer he stood up. "Right, we'll see you in the OR around eleven."

The next morning shortly after nine, I again asked for the phone. This time to my relief my grandmother answered. "Hi, Gram. Did you hear that I'm in the hospital?"

"Yes dear, I hope you're all right. It's nothing serious, is it?" The familiar voice was full of concern.

"No . . . it's nothing, but I need you to do me a favour. Would you phone Alberta Health Care and find out if I'm paid up and what my number is? They need it here at the hospital."

"I'll do that right away, you mustn't worry." There was a slight pause. "Is there anything else you need?"

"Yes . . . now that you mention it. Some cigarettes and stuff like toothpaste—so a little cash wouldn't hurt. Don't tell Mum I called. . . . Oh, and I wanted to let you know they're going to operate today. They found some cysts on my ovaries. But don't worry, they say it's no big deal."

"I'm sure everything will be fine. Remember, you're my special girl."

"Yah . . . thanks, and I'll call again when I know more . . . okay . . . bye." I replaced the receiver feeling reassured.

A small, youngish woman smiled at me from the next bed.

"Hello." I was unsure of how much the woman knew or had heard, or even how long she'd been in the next bed.

"Hi. I'm glad that you're having a better time of it than when they brought you in." The face flashed an even wider smile that conveyed much warmth.

"Thanks." I began fidgeting with my hands.

"I'm sorry, but I couldn't help but hear the conversation you had with your mother yesterday. A mother–daughter relationship should be one of God's gifts."

"Tell that to my mother! Just cut me out of her life, the bitch . . . just because I'm experiencing personal difficulties."

"There's nothing that can't be mended. I'm sure she'll come around. By the way, my name is Wendy."

"Nice to meet you." With that I turned away, wishing I'd thought to pull the curtain between the beds. My thoughts were on where I'd get the money for cigarettes or toothpaste or anything for that matter. Until my grandmother came through, I'd try to contact Sue at the rooming house. I began digging in my bag, and was rewarded with a scrap of lined paper. I left a message with one of the residents on our floor.

I dozed until the surgery team came for me. Afterwards it was a blur, except for the pain, as they wheeled me back to my room.

Later that evening, a well-dressed Sue made an appearance. Her London Fog raincoat was open, exposing her black pantyhose and one of her miniskirts. A flowered umbrella and purse was tucked under one arm and in the other she held a large green garbage bag.

"Jesus, Beth, I've been worried about you. Thought you might have run into a bad trick or something." She rushed over to the bed and placed a kiss on my cheek. "My God, you look like shit."

"Yah . . . whatever." I clutched the ten dollar bill Sue placed in my hand.

We smoked together in silence, until Sue started plumping my pillows and straightening my blankets. Through the half-opened slits of my eyes I stared blankly, watching this show of concern and thinking that I was owed at least this much. But after a few minutes Sue stopped. "Is there somewhere to put your stuff?"

With a jab of my index finger I indicated the metal closet in the wall and watched as Sue attempted to squeeze the bag into the tiny space. She left half the bag spilling to the floor and the door ajar. Then, as if she were embarrassed, Sue propped a card upright on the bedside tray. "Well . . . get better. I gotta go." She took a short step and then spun back around, a slight smile played at the corners of her little, pink mouth. "Did I tell you what I've been telling people?"

I shook my head, wondering why Sue seemed to be stalling.

"That I'm in the high-rise business." She made a pumping gesture with her hand and we both laughed. Then the long, tapered nails stroked her umbrella. "Have they found out what's wrong with ya?"

"Nah," I lied. "Still doing tests."

I listened as Sue's high heels marked her progress back down the hall.

Then I inspected the card. A picture of a smirking nurse with an oversized syringe stared at me. Inside was the inscription, "Damn those needles, Love Sue." I fingered the tight loops of the script, then opened the drawer of my bedside table and placed the card inside along with the ten spot. That was all there was until my grandmother came through by priority post the next morning.

> *Dear Beth,*
>
> *Sorry to hear that you have to go for an operation but it will be better to find out the source of all the trouble and have it cleared up. Your mother said you should not be calling collect in the daytime. Her telephone bill has been enormous, so many calls she said that you made to Peter? Write us, please. Also, she said that I could not send any money except for a dollar. I miss you very much and I am praying that you will take this opportunity to stay off drugs.*
>
> *I paid for your health number so all should be fine. I've called the hospital there and let them know. My prayers are with you. Also, a friend of mine from the church has friends in Vancouver who work with troubled teens. She is going to let them know*

about you, so expect a visit perhaps. Their name is Lawton.

All my love, Gram

P.S. I think of you so often as a little girl. You were so sweet and born into this world to spend your time on something special. Please be true to yourself.

I plucked the dollar bill from the scented envelope and grimaced, for there was also a letter there from my mother.

My Dear Beth,

I have taken a week's holiday and will be returning on Sunday. I thought with you in the hospital there would be no crisis to deal with and I had better have a break as my general health and well being has deteriorated under the constant worry about you and the need to deal with your delinquent behaviour. Your father told me that you have been operated on. I do hope the operation was a success and that you are recovering nicely. I would guess, although I did not ask, that you have been in contact with your grandmother. Your sister said she had been unwell since yesterday and she certainly looked terrible last night. I have asked you many times to leave her alone as she is too old to cope with the stranger inhabiting your body. You are shortening her life. You have the right to kill yourself, as you have been doing, but you have no right to kill my mother. It is sad to see someone destroy herself because she cannot accept the benefits of the experience and wisdom of those who have her best interest at heart.

We all send you our luck and best wishes for you to rebuild yourself.

Mother

I scrunched the letter and held onto it tightly, growling, "Bitch . . . bitch."

"What's the matter?" Wendy looked up from the book she was reading.

"Nothing." I rolled on my side and began rocking back and forth until sleep returned.

I awoke with a television set hanging above my bed and a carton of cigarettes on the dressing table. "Where did these come from?"

"I hope you don't mind," said Wendy, "but I thought I could make your stay a little easier. I hope I didn't overstep myself? Really, it's something I want to do. Please accept it and in the future, if you can help someone, then pass it on."

"Thank you. It's been months since the last time I watched television." I grinned at this new friend, noting that she was older than I had first thought, probably in her early thirties.

"Just enjoy." Wendy returned to her reading, as if to reassure me there were no strings attached.

With remote in hand I began to scan the channels excitedly. As I watched the Friendly Giant singing with Rusty the Rooster, and with my belly full of breakfast, a feeling of optimism surfaced. When Dr. Murphy entered, his face hidden behind a chart, I smiled. He cleared his throat and bent closer. "I'm afraid I have some bad news." He paused briefly, waiting for me to show some interest; seeing none, he adjusted his glasses. "We found your fallopian tubes have suffered scarring. I regret to inform you that you will probably never have children."

"Oh . . . is that all? I didn't want them anyway. So it will be cheap birth control."

He straightened and tucked the chart under his arm. "This is not the usual response. Are you sure you're fine with this?"

"Just dandy." I stared him down.

As soon as he left, I began sobbing quietly into the pillow. Wendy moved from her bed, her tan housecoat opening like the wings of a brown moth. She sat on the bed and wrapped her arms around me. She whispered, "I know . . . I know. Let it out. Let it out."

I resisted an impulse to push her away. "No . . . no . . . no," I whimpered. Again the quiet, "I know . . . I know."

"Oh . . . God . . . God . . . no babies . . . no babies," I sobbed against the woman's breast, who cradled me as if I was her own child. While I might be cut from my own family, I'd still had hope of children of my own. My despair was complete. "No babies!" I wailed once more and was silent.

◄o►

The pain in my stomach was barely noticeable and the Methadone silenced the withdrawal. I missed the vivid dreams that heroin offered, and the nod hiding me in its oyster shell. That sinkhole was gone, making my thoughts clearer but not yet focused. I examined my life without the usual sense of detachment, which was both puzzling and frightening. The hospital would, at best, keep me for another few days—and then what? There was nowhere for me to go except back to the street. I was well enough to make myself sick again. I crossed my arms tightly around my frame.

Junkies ordinarily didn't make get-well calls, but my only other visitor besides Sue had been Sandi. She and Blade rented their room by the month when in Van, which was risky. "If the narcs want you, it don't matter how often ya move—" this was how the pair defended their practice. The added luxury of a phone shared by all the residents on the fourth floor of their building made it easy to contact them.

One afternoon, Sandi had popped in while doing her wash a few blocks away from the hospital. She stayed only about fifteen minutes, a wash cycle's worth of visiting. Through her, I learned of Sue's return to Calgary and that Lanny was looking for me. Something about me owing him money was the best Sandi could recall. The idea was ridiculous, of course, but instead of laughing it off I felt a sense of foreboding. To avoid dwelling on the matter and getting more depressed, I turned my thoughts to Sandi. I was envious that Blade supported their habits. Sandi had never been turned out and was untouched by the nightly grinding of countless sexual encounters. While I was turning to compost, Sandi remained a flower child playing with cherry red cupids and dotting squares of construction paper. Some day Blade would get his from an angry customer, and then Sandi might fall into the same pit that I found myself in. But what difference did it make? We'd all be dead soon enough. The danger of an overdose was an occupational hazard, although I felt I'd more likely be strangled or stabbed at the hands of a bad trick.

"Halloo . . . Beth . . . Beth?"

A young man in his early twenties was bending towards me like a priest. His hair was the colour of straw, probably the same texture too, I reflected sourly, noting that it was both curly and cropped. The alertness in his eyes was so disturbing I looked away. He made me feel as if I was an exhibit in a sideshow, the bed my stage.

"What do you want?" I snapped.

"My name is John Lawton," he said. He was well spoken and his healthy face marked him as straight. I groaned inwardly.

"You don't know me, but my grandmother is acquainted with yours in Calgary. She is very concerned about you and was trying to find someone with relatives or friends in Vancouver who might visit you. So to make a long story short . . . here I am."

He'd been studying my face as he spoke and I returned the appraisal. He was of average height with a sturdy build. He wore blue jeans, and an old lift ticket dangled from the zipper of his ski jacket. As he turned to pull up a chair, I spotted the heavy, scuffed work boots on his feet. I pegged him for a Community Health Worker or something like that.

I searched my mind for some forgotten middle class manners. "It was very nice of you to come . . . and I'm sure you can pass along the word to my grandmother that I'm fine." The words sounded hollow, so I managed a smile. "She has been like a second mother to me."

He leaned closer and rubbed his face, which bore the telltale signs of a five-o'clock shadow. I noticed that his compact hands were still red from the cold outside. "Well, you have given your Gram and the whole family in Calgary quite a time of it from what I hear."

My smile disappeared. "No . . . I'd say they've given me quite a time."

As if expecting such a childish reply, he grinned, showing the crinkles that outlined his electric eyes. "I must say that you're down, but not out." He held his palm out, as if to ward off any brusque comment I again might make. "Now, before you go and get all riled up, I want you to understand I'm only here as a favour to my grandmother and it does look like you could use some company." He glanced around the room as if to point out its bareness—no cards, no flowers.

I rolled my eyes and extinguished the smoldering cigarette butt with such force that it sent ashes flying onto the wood grain of the tray. I emptied the ashtray into the wastebasket while John scooped the remaining ashes away into his hand and then dusted them off on his blue jeans.

"When I came in, I was surprised to see that butt held so close to the blanket. I thought for sure you would burn yourself up. Do you always doze off while smoking?"

I shrugged. "It's been known to happen. Look, I really don't know what concern that is of yours." John did not come across with the pseudo-caring of Shit Wormers, as I preferred to call them. Nor did he have the brusque, "get to the facts" of the health workers, or the brutal efficiency of the "I've got ya now police." I lit another cigarette and eyed him.

He pulled out a pack of gum and offered me a stick. "I really would like to get to know you better and perhaps you'd like to get to know me."

His sincerity alarmed me further. I tried to think of some excuse to rid myself of this uninvited visitor without appearing too nasty. "Are you a religious freak or something?" There could be no other reason for his proposal—unless he was a recruiter for a cult or a badly dressed pimp.

He chuckled softly. "Come on now, that's not what you think, really?"

"I can't think of any reason why we would get acquainted."

"Well then, you need a friend more than I thought you did." He stood up and thrust his thumbs into the front pockets of his jeans. "I'll come again tomorrow."

"If you're lucky and I'm still here."

"I just dropped in on my afternoon coffee break. I'm only a few blocks away—currently employed by Granville Square."

"Doing what?"

"Carpenter, labourer, pipe fitter, carpet layer, tree planter, jack of all trades . . . master of none, at your service." He saluted and was gone.

I was tempted to phone my grandmother and give her a piece of my mind. "All I need is another john in my life," I thought angrily.

I watched Wendy's husband, smart as always in his three-piece suit, stride across the room and pull the curtains between the beds. I strained to hear the whispers of the conversation and managed to pick out a couple of words: cancer and chemo. This interchangeable pairing and the resulting images of death and disease claiming Wendy made me angry. It was well after visiting hours before her husband left and I could confront Wendy. "I never asked, but why are you here?"

The directness of the question did not seem to distress the other woman, although her usually warm smile was stiff as she sat up.

"Ovarian cancer. It's spread and that's why I can't have children." She sighed heavily and the sound of it lingered in the squared corners of the room. "I'm going home tomorrow and will continue my treatments as an outpatient."

I was touched but unsure how to respond. "It pisses me off that you have this to deal with." This was not what I'd meant to say and I faltered, searching for the right words, the words that were out of my reach. "What I mean is, ah . . . sorry. Sorry . . . is such a pat thing to say, but I really am."

Wendy smiled, as if amused by my attempt at comfort. "It's okay. You don't have to be pissed off. I'm learning to deal with it."

"But I can't think of anything bad happening to you. I'd gladly change places with ya. I don't have much to live for and you do."

Wendy grasped my hand firmly. "Remember, there are plenty of good people; you just haven't met any for some time. And there are reasons for you to keep on living." The overhead boxed lights seemed to illuminate the woman's nightgown, casting a glow around her.

"I suppose." Unconvinced, I considered it as I extracted my hand and moved away. Then, rubbing the tip of my nose, I ventured, "Are you religious Wendy? I mean, what do you hang on to? I have Peter, my old man, but he's not here and doesn't seem very interested anyway, and there is my grandmother, but she's under the thumb of my mother and that's it."

Wendy's gold head bobbed, as if considering her answer. "I guess . . . my husband, my family, and my friends—it's their strength I hold on to. I've been lucky. Everyone must find their own pillars and maybe you do have a start with Peter and your grandmother."

"But I feel they've thrown me away too, like all the rest. I wish . . . I wish I could go home with you." I felt my cheeks burn with shame. I was a woman of the street. I had learned to sever myself from my emotions. I was tough and must not act like a lost child.

"I'll give you my phone number, and if you ever need me or a place to stay, just call." She scribbled on a piece of paper and handed it to me. There, in a neatly printed script, was an address and a phone number.

I felt a twinge of hope as I folded the scrap of paper and put it in my wallet.

◄◦►

After breakfast the next morning, the nurse said I would be going for more tests. When I returned to my room, Wendy's bed was empty and all her cards and flowers were gone. It was as if she'd never been there. I noticed the lined sheet of paper lying across my tray. "You can make it. I know you can. Love Wendy." This I propped up on my night stand, and then inspected the two letters neatly stacked there. Picking the first one I began to read.

Dear Beth,

I read an article in the weekend paper about a girl who was possessed by another person, who was trying to kill her because she was too nice. It made me think of you. I am sorry you are so lonesome, but you might as well face it, that it is part and parcel of the way of life you have chosen to lead. You can change, but only you can do it and my thought of no money was right. You will never do anything for yourself until you realize you are completely on your own.

What I want to ask you is to please not come back to Calgary as long as there are drugs in your life, and that includes Methadone. I cannot bear to look at my frail, emaciated daughter. The strain of having someone under my roof I do not understand is intolerable. The humiliation of facing people who are trying to help her has turned me into a grey middle-aged, old woman.

If you needed eyes, I would give you mine. If you needed a kidney, I would give you mine. If I could exchange my life for yours to get you out, I would do it. But I can do nothing to help you. I love you more than anything in the world, but since I'm helpless, I am telling you that your only hope is a firm commitment to change. A halfway house will help you make the transition.

Please don't come back until you have driven the devil out, are in control of yourself, and are your old sweet self. I suppose this sounds cruel, but all I can do is say I'm sorry if you find it so, I cannot cope with the whole situation any longer. There is nothing that means more to me and nothing I have less control over.

I have a letter from Peter at the house. I will send it on.

I love you and pray for you constantly.

Love, Mother

I lit a cigarette and tore open Peter's letter.

Dear Beth,

What's all this about not wanting to lay your shit on me? Of course I like hearing from you, shit and all. Do you think I've changed or something? Perhaps I've become a little more hard, but actually I'm still me and you know me pretty good. What I can't figure is you. It's like you're not telling me things. Listen, I promise that the first time I'm in Calgary I'll get in touch, so keep me posted so I know where you are!

Yeah, three years is a long time. I lost a bunch of good time for shooting pills and swearing at bulls, so the time just keeps being tacked on. But with any luck I'll be out by next Christmas. Why don't you write me a letter and tell me exactly what's on your mind? I'm not going to put you down for it or anything. You know I hate game playing. You know, too, that I used to really dig you and probably still do. I don't care what you've done or been as long as you're not a stool pigeon.

Do me a favour and write and tell me what's happening. Okay?

Love You as Always, Peter

With a wide grin I could not contain, I placed his letter under my pillow. Only then did I notice the note tacked to the side of the headboard.

Sorry I missed you. Catch you next time. Lanny

I ripped the memo into little bits and then tried to escape in sleep.

As a metal chair scraped across the floor I awoke. John smiled and made a valiant attempt to draw me into a conversation. He talked at great length of the pottery he made, the chickens he raised, and of the camping trips he planned to make in the spring. I feigned interest and was relieved when he finally left an hour later. If he felt I was a charity case then I would make him work hard to feel good about it.

Chapter Nineteen

I KNEW JOHN WAS MOVED by my plight, but he'd waited until the last moment to invite me to live at his house in Richmond, outside Vancouver. After hearing all his house rules, I'd accepted. I saw his offer as an a opportunity to buy time, and time was what I needed. But I couldn't believe I'd agreed to get up at 7 AM each day. And his reminders over breakfast about the virtues of a routine were as hard to hack as his home-made porridge.

"Early to bed, early to rise. That's part of what it takes to hold a job . . . adherence to a schedule. Reliability is the name of the game. The early bird catches the worm."

I'd begun to suspect he found pleasure in forcing me from my bed. Even on weekends he insisted I be up and dressed by eight. It was getting tougher to co-operate. I felt resentment with each, "Rise up . . . rise up and shine. Get out of the old fart sack."

I was to go into the city for my Methadone treatment and leave directly afterwards. "No fraternizing," was the way he worded it. After two weeks with just "Moralizing John" for company, I was beginning to feel restless, isolated, and edgy.

John quizzed me daily on how my job search was progressing. I could not expect a stranger to cover my expenses and knew I must pay for my room and board. But who would hire me and what could I do? How would I explain the long gaps in my employment history? Legally, I would have to say that I was on probation—and then what? More rejection?

From the security of my hospital bed, I'd welcomed this escape route. But as my health improved, I was increasingly oppressed by the rural atmosphere of Richmond and John's rigid expectations. I watched my language, tried not to smoke in front of him, and kept the place clean. When he was around, I made a dutiful attempt to smile and be attentive to what he said. Lighthearted was what I was striving for, but acting the part was hard work.

Along with my manners, my appearance was improving. My hair was clean and shiny from the daily showers I was encouraged to take. My face was plump, giving me a less angular look. Perhaps John's porridge was doing some good after all, I mused, staring at my reflection in the hall mirror. My skin had lost its sickly colouring and a hint of natural pink now showed on my cheeks. Knowing how much better I was looking, I kept waiting for John to make a move. I was prepared to pay for my keep with sex, and would have welcomed it. Instead, he grew more insistent each day that I search for work.

Pushing these thoughts aside, I made my way to the back porch where I picked up a small pail. One of my household jobs was to feed John's free-range chickens. They swarmed over my feet and caused the usual feelings of panic as I scattered the grain in handfuls away from me. Oddly enough, I did not mind the chores John asked of me, for I found them basic and satisfying. I laughed out loud at the absurdity: one minute I was a whore, and the next a chicken feeder. In the kitchen, I sat at the table by the window to better watch the antics of the excited birds.

What a strange hobby, raising chickens. I glanced over to the oak cabinets he'd made, which gave the kitchen its rustic feel. There seemed to be little that he could not do. Three years ago he'd bought this old fixer-upper, two-story house with two acres of land. The inside had been dry walled and freshly painted. This year he'd finished bringing back the beauty of the hardwood floors. Next year, he bragged, there would be a new roof.

John tried to interest me by showing the samples of shingles. I'd poked at them but offered no opinion. Although John's departure in the mornings for work was a relief, I did look forward to his return. He reminded me of a tightly coiled ball of controlled energy. His every gesture and movement was timed and plotted as he prepared our supper. He knew a great deal about odd spices, which he sprinkled over everything, all the while telling what he was doing and why, as if giving an informal cooking class.

I could hardly remember any culinary skills and was not interested in re-acquainting myself with them, but I did enjoy watching. What he served, however, I moved around the plate—my appetite had yet to return.

I butted my smoke in the sink and threw the butt down the drain, suppressing a sudden desire for a chocolate bar. A brown envelope on the counter with my name scrawled across it drew my attention.

Inside was a job application for E & S Fish Packers with a little note from John taped to the front.

Please fill this out and I will drop it off for you.
John

I ground my teeth and began climbing the flight of stairs just off the kitchen to my room, the first door on the left at the top. Here I found the window half way up. A breeze pushing against the curtains had knocked the lamp off the orange crate. Shaking my head, I shut the window and locked it. Then, kneeling, I pulled a pad of coloured paper off the floor and adjusted the sleeping bag that doubled as a quilt.

John's obsession for fresh air and his dislike of cigarette smoke had him opening the windows at every opportunity, so I generally waited until after he left for work to close them. I liked stale air and the familiar smell of old cigarette smoke. Besides, I hated the humid drafts of the great outdoors. I dug my nails into my palms remembering the one time John insisted I go camping with him. I could think of nothing I would like less, but I'd smiled, reminding him that I could not be far from my Methadone. Just this once I was glad of this daily inconvenience. I continued to grin as he expounded on how it would do me a world of good to sleep under the stars and develop an appreciation for nature. He vowed that as soon as I was weaned from the Methadone, he would take me for an outdoor experience I would never forget. I'd almost choked.

I squatted down, tapped a Bic pen across my teeth, and then began writing unsteadily on the flimsy crate.

Dear Peter,

It's been a long time since my last letter. I wish I could say I've been busy doing something worthwhile but I was in the hospital for twelve days. No big deal or nothing, but I did get put on Methadone. So I have the opportunity to change my life and get on with things, but I'm not sure that I really care anymore if I do or not.

I've been taken in by a complete stranger, John. This, in itself, is worth a good laugh. He's straight, of course, and believes he knows what is best for me. His first priority—a job. Can you believe that he wants me to apply at a fish plant? Even on a slow night, I can earn make twenty times the cash I can earn being covered in fish goo for eight hours.

I guess what I'm trying to say is I'm bored as hell stuck here in the middle of nowhere with only chickens for company. Going into the city for my Methadone is the highlight of my day. In the evenings, John drags me off for walks and drives in the country. As if I don't see enough of the damned country outside the window. I'm afraid that the next thing he'll want is for me to accompany him to church on Sundays.

I don't know if I'll be able to hack this, but I do need time to get myself healthy again.

Oh, yes, if you write me don't send it here as John inspects the mail and wouldn't dig the return address. As before, please send it to General Delivery, Vancouver.

I got that letter you sent to the folks' house. Thanks
Love Yu 2, Beth

◄O►

I took a place in the line in front of the wire cage, and waited to receive my Dixie cup of Methadone. After savouring the citrus aftertaste, I moved aside. Other bodies sprawled along the hallway. They were the same ones who seemed to be there each day, as if they reserved a seat.

Outside the building, another cluster of addicts buzzed around with seductive chants of "Wanna score?" Since I knew Methadone canceled a heroin high, I elbowed my way through them, shaking my head in a silent no.

I glanced at the posted bus routes, noted that they were running late, and twisted my purse strap around my wrist. A greying man in an expensive suit eased himself on to the bench and eyed me. I ignored him and studied the outlines of my partial reflection in the glass of the bus shelter. After a moment of silence the man touched me on the knee. "You ever go out?"

Did I have *whore* branded on my forehead? I did not see how I differed from anyone else. I wore no makeup except for some lipstick. My blue flared jeans were the style. My jacket was zipped over a sweat-shirt. It could only be the boots with their high wedge heels that gave me away. "Why ya ask?"

"I figure you must be clean, as you look healthier than what is usually down here, and I'd be willing to pay double the going rate for you."

What the hell, it wasn't like I'd never done it before, I thought, as I stroked my cheek considering his offer. "Sixty . . . and you provide the place."

"Done." The man reached for my hand.

I arrived later than usual, but ahead of John. It was all so simple I wondered why I hadn't thought of it before. For the first time since my hospitalization, I felt more secure. Now I had money and a plan. Instead of moping around the house, I'd go into the city earlier. By working the noon-hour crowd I could get a stake together. I could put John off, using my health as an excuse a little longer. There would be no fish guts in my future.

When John left in the mornings, I did the few things expected of me and hopped the bus into the city. Over the next few weeks this worked well, and I managed to hide close to a thousand dollars under my mattress.

On one of the daily walks John insisted I take with him after supper, he dropped in on a neighbour, so I could see their puppies. In a cardboard box retrieved from the basement were the most playful orbs of fluff I'd ever seen.

"What are they?" I asked, trying to contain my excitement.

"Maltese," replied the neighbour Ralph. Picking up one of the cotton balls, he offered it to me.

I hugged the little thing to my breast. "How much?"

"Seventy-five."

"I want one!" I touched my nose to the tiny furry face.

"You can't even look after yourself," John snapped, snatching the puppy away and returning it to its litter mates. I felt my face burn and I retreated through the screen door. In a few minutes John followed, his voice rising to catch me.

"When you can look after yourself and get your own place, you can have a dog. How are you going to feed it?"

"I'm such a loser, how would I know!" I tossed over my shoulder and cut across the hay field that divided the two homes.

Jogging to catch up, John shouted, "You haven't done much with your life . . . have you? Except to mess it up."

"What's that supposed to mean?" I stopped to stare him down, overcoming an urge to cuff him across the side of his head.

"Just what I said. You haven't got on with things. You're lost and there isn't anyone to point the way back. Not even your own family." He grabbed me around the waist and I wrenched free.

"I don't see you as a beacon of light . . . if that's what you mean." My lip was beginning to tremble. John, thinking I was about to cry, softened his tone.

"What do you want a puppy for?"

I studied him as if inspecting a fly I might tear the legs off. His jacket was open, exposing a white T-shirt, with a hole in the middle, his ever-present work boots were caked with mud, and his short wheat-coloured hair was standing on end. He was not particularly good looking. The look of confusion wrinkling his forehead made him appear stern and accentuated his broad nose so that it was out of proportion to his smaller cheeks and jawbones.

"Dense!" I muttered, scattering the chickens as I flounced through the yard and into the house.

As I flew up the stairs, John barked, "You never answered my question. Why do you want a dog?"

"Something to love," I yelled down, and then slammed the bedroom door.

The next morning I said my stomach hurt and waited until I heard the tires of his truck grind the stones of the driveway. Then I marched across the field. I found Ralph at home, and tried to hand him seventy-five dollars. I pleaded for one of the puppies. I swore I was getting my own place and no one would love a puppy more than I would. Ralph listened to my pleas and turned his hat around several times before agreeing. He ushered me into the basement to point out the little male that would be mine. He informed me he would not refund the money if I didn't get my shit together, and the puppies would be ready in a week.

For the next seven days I resumed the motions of my routine. I lied to John about promising interviews, listing all the places I'd applied for employment, courtesy of the Yellow Pages. I completed the application for A &E Fish Packers, which he dropped off for me. I agreed to go camping in a couple of weeks. With my change in attitude, John assumed our argument was forgotten. When the last morning came, I packed my belongings into a pillowcase, called a cab, and deposited a note on the table.

Thank you for having me but I don't think it's working.
Beth
P.S. the hundred dollars is for any inconvenience.

I directed the cab next door and collected my puppy. I wrapped him inside my coat, and after thinking he looked like a teddy bear peeking through the top, named him Teddy. That afternoon, in the same building Sandi and Blade resided in when in town—and where I was paid up for two months—I settled into a one-room apartment. I curled on the bed cradling the puppy: this time I would not be lonely.

Chapter Twenty

As I ambled up and down Granville Street, the May sun parted the morning clouds and gathered the city in light. At the unexpected warmth I shook off my plastic raincoat and tossed it over my arm. For the first time I'd been on the street I had a routine that was not based on a need to score. By working the lunch-time crowd, I could spend the rest of the day with Teddy. At four and half months, the ball of puppy fluff had grown into an even bigger one. I was grateful I'd stuck with the Methadone program, for it allowed a measure of freedom I hadn't known since falling into the cycle of addiction. Better yet, I was saving money. Today the sunlight seemed to have dulled sexual appetites, for no john had taken any interest in my overtures.

◄o►

Inside Granville Towers I scanned the index for MacKrow and Associates, Attorneys at Law. I found office 1402 and entered into a waiting room with comfortable padded chairs.

A receptionist with round glasses perched on her thin nose glanced up, "Can I help you?"

"I'd like an appointment with Mr. MacKrow." The woman behind the desk hesitated. "He was recommended by a friend of mine," I added.

"Very well, I'll check if he can see you now for a few minutes."

Before I'd finished sorting through the assortment of magazines in the wall rack, the woman returned. "You can go in."

"Wow . . . that's service."

"Not really, most of his clients don't keep regular hours, you know what I mean?" She went back to her paper work with a look that implied she didn't care if I knew what she meant or not.

A medium sized, slightly balding man opened the door and welcomed me into his office with a handshake. There were lines around his eyes and grey glinted in what was left of his dark brown hair. Observing the pictures of adult children in graduation gowns displayed on his filing cabinet, I guessed he must be around fifty.

"What can I do for you?" Mr. MacKrow inquired, as I lowered my rear end into the chair in front of the desk.

"I get into trouble from time to time, and Sandi Whalen told me how good you are. I was hoping that you might take me on too. I'm on probation for possession of heroin, although that will be up in a month, but I'll probably get busted again for soliciting." His eyes widened slightly. I shrugged, "A girl's got to survive. I'm on Methadone, so I'm not using. But that could always change." As I talked he began taking notes with a pen, which glided across the page.

"Sandi is an old client of mine. One of my regulars," he said, then looked over. "Now your name and tell me a little of your background."

"Elizabeth Hudson. Disowned by both parents. No help there."

"Be more specific."

"Father a doctor. Mother an accountant. Daughter a junkie."

"Unusual, but it ups the odds that you will find yourself out of this lifestyle eventually. What is your educational level?"

"Ah . . . one semester at U of C. I was going to be a teacher but I got sidetracked." I grinned, but Mr. MacKrow did not acknowledge the pun.

"Well, that's good, most judges tend to look leniently on young adults with some post-secondary education. Also, if I do see you in court, the first thing I will say is that your father is a doctor. This bit of information will almost always ensure that you get off lightly." He stood up indicating the interview was over, then added, "If you get charged with anything, I'll make it my job to keep you out of jail until you straighten up, which I'm sure you will."

"So what happens if I need you?"

"My secretary will give you my card. If you're picked up, call the number on it. Legal aid will cover my expenses on your behalf."

"That's it?"

"Yes," he acknowledged, and returned to his notes.

I left the office congratulating myself on visiting the famed Mr. MacKrow about whom Sandi raved so much. With any luck I wouldn't need him often.

My head bent in thought, I collided with a man who was speeding along. His umbrella clattered to the pavement. His reddish hair was pulled into a ponytail, revealing his fair face. He flashed a smile of recognition.

"Beth, isn't it?"

"Well, Chuck, I haven't seen you since The Broadway with Vie. "Why in such a hurry? You almost ran me over!"

"Me? You should look where you're going. I know now why your types only come out after the sunsets: you're blinded by the light."

"On Methadone. It seems to have dulled the dark side." I grimaced. "In a panic to score or what?" I bent to pick up his umbrella and hooked it back on his arm.

He finished adjusting his knapsack before answering. "Been evicted from my place on Hastings. I've an appointment at the Men's Hostel to grab a free lunch."

"Hungry, no place to stay"—I flicked at the sweat forming on his round face—"sick too."

"You don't know the half of it. The short-change business here is a bust."

"Short-change?"

"You know the old, 'But lady, I gave you a twenty and you've only given me change for a ten.'"

"Shit, I wouldn't think there would be much cash in that."

"And you would be correct, but a little late in pointing that out."

Out of the corner of my eye, crossing the street, I saw the black man who'd been pestering me the last couple of days. I grabbed Chuck by the arm. "Come. I'll buy you lunch and you can stay with me and Teddy."

"Teddy?" his forehead furrowed.

"My dog."

"But I gotta score later." Alarmed, he brushed off my grip.

"Listen, I'm sure I could arrange a loan. Now c'mon, I'll get you settled in. Just one thing—no sex, but right now you've got to pretend you're my boyfriend."

"A boyfriend that gets none?"

"You've got it—or in your case, you don't." We laughed together and hustled off down the street with the black man shadowing us.

◄o►

With my head propped against a couple of pillows I sprawled across the bed. My fingers butted against each other, as I tried to focus on the rented black and white television. The music trilled, as Captain Kirk managed to scuttle away from the lizard man who pursued him, while his crew watched helplessly from the Enterprise.

I'd not seen this episode but was distracted by Chuck who was slumped over the kitchen chair by the window. The blind was lowered, blocking the afternoon light and leaving only shadows to flash across the walls. I was trying to ignore the needle protruding from his arm, as a potent mixture of anger was stewing. "For Christ's sake, take the fit out."

Chuck's eyes cracked open, but he made no move to remove the spike from his arm. As his eyelids shut again, I leaped up and yanked it free. "This is bullshit! Haven't you ever done a full cap before? Fucking chippie." At the same time, I was having a hard time overcoming a powerful urge to slip the point into my own flesh. I traced my fingers over the zippered track on my right arm. Once abscessed, it had healed into a thick line resembling snakeskin that ran along the inside of my elbow and puckered when I moved it.

"Relax." Chuck's word slurred through his uneven smile. He attempted to stand but pitched towards the bed, missing the sleeping Teddy as he crashed down.

"Asshole." I gathered the startled puppy into my arms and banged the door with such force that a piece of the frame splintered. I flew down a flight of stairs, then ducked into a smoky hallway. Someone was cooking and it mingled with other stale smells, causing the bile in my stomach to shift. I stopped and knocked on a door. "It's Beth."

The door swung open and I did a double take. Perched on Sandi's head was a shoulder-length wig, cut into a long shag. The hairpiece seemed to bleach the pallor of her skin, making it appear translucent. As if to complete the effect, Sandi's blue eyes were surrounded by thick eyeliner that curled up at the ends. I gasped, "A little early for Halloween, ain't it?"

Sandi gestured to enter. Blade was sitting on the bed wearing a curly blond hairpiece that was feminine and accentuated his masculine features. I choked on my laughter, as Blade moved closer.

"Would you recognize me?" he demanded, turning his face sideways so I could better study his profile.

"I don't think so. I thought I had the wrong room." I tittered and dropped Teddy into Sandi's outstretched arms.

"Good." He turned and picked up a square brown package that resembled dried mud, wrapped in plastic. "I'll be going. Lock the door and don't be long." He shook a finger at Sandi and left.

I fastened the heavy chain on the door and spun around, "What's going on?'

Sandi was busy nuzzling the puppy, unaware of the traces of the black eyeliner she smudged along the white coat. I snapped my fingers. Sandi's voice, always raspy, rattled with ominous overtones. "Word is there's an undercover sting in the works." She placed the puppy on the floor, and he responded by lifting his leg and pissing. Sandi laughed and began blotting up the puddle with some Kleenex she pulled from the pocket of her jacket.

"What do you mean an undercover sting?" I asked, sucking on a cigarette.

Sandi lowered herself to the floor and rubbed the puppy's belly, "You know Gary Albert?"

I thought for a moment and remembered the good-looking kid who was a year or two younger than I was. He was known as the best booster in Calgary. I'd once bought a beautiful burgundy leather jacket lined with coyote fur for twenty-five dollars from him. "Yah," I answered, wondering where the coat was now.

"Well, he's got a brother on the police force and he warned him of something going down: undercover buys. Since Blade is a good friend of his, Gary passed the word along. We've decided to change our appearance so if something goes down, we'll be harder to spot. So what do you think?" She fluttered her heavily made up eyes.

"That you've been taking makeup lessons from Big Marie."

We both snickered. "You think there's undercover buys happening now?"

Sandi stifled a yawn, "Pretty sure . . . the source is good. But what brings you here? Don't need a complete make-over do ya?"

"No . . . I pretty much like the way I am. I got this letter from Peter the other day that has completely bummed me out; and second, I'm all messed up about bringing Chuck home."

Sandi interrupted, "What ya bring him home for anyway?"

I ran my fingers through my hair, burning the ends in the process. "Chuck might be all I need to deter the black son of a bitch who keeps dogging me."

"Well, first tell me about the letter and then we'll deal with the other, but quickly, as I don't got much time." Sandi took a cracker from a box on the counter and broke it into little pieces for Teddy, who wagged his tail in anticipation.

I took a crinkled piece of lined paper from my back pocket and began to read.

Greetings,

Right now I'm in solitary confinement and have been for quite some time. Nine days of it to be exact. Anyway I'm waiting to be transferred to PA, which hopefully will happen some time this week. The reason I'm getting transferred is 'cause I got pinched while I was loaded on bombers. You know what I'm like on bombers, and anyway they couldn't dig the action so they're sending me, North. It don't really make a fuck to me, the only hassle is they took another 30 days of my good time so now I get out on November 20, 1974.

Incidentally that's my birthday.

Anyway, my main reason for writing is to tell you a sad story. You see times change and people change and during the last few months I've been thinking a lot about you and me. I guess I've come to the conclusion that by the time I get out I'll have changed so much and you'll have changed so much that it's highly unlikely that we will still be compatible. Is that the right word? Anyway, I no longer think we have too much in common.

Ivan's been down here for a while and we've had a few talks and I kinda get the impression that anything we had was just a game with you anyways . There's no use grasping at something that no longer exists and that's probably where we're at.

As Always, Peter

Sandi gave a coarse howl of laughter as I tucked the letter back into my pocket. "That ain't nothing to worry about. He's bummed about the transfer. The guy's been in solitary for nine days, so of course his thoughts are screwed. I'm sure that talking to Ivan didn't help much either, but you'll see—once he's in PA and settled he'll be his old self again."

"I don't think so." I rubbed a thumb across my cheekbone. "What if it's over and I'll never know what I felt was real, or it just boils down to the old question of who was using who?"

"If he writes you the same letter when he's out of solitary, then you can take it seriously—until then forget about it."

"Umph, but it'll be over a year now before he gets out and we can sort things out."

"You'll sort things out before then. You know I'm right, and besides that's why you come to talk to me, ain't it? 'Cause I'm always right." Again the rumble of her laugh filled the room.

I smiled, and then was chuckling as Sandi rushed on, "Now on the Chuck thing. He's okay. You can't be by yourself forever, and with this bust in the works I might not be around long to give ya such good advice. So do yourself a favour and lighten up." She stood and grabbed her purse from the table. "I gotta go and be the backup man for Blade."

As we parted, Sandi cautioned, "Don't mention Chuck in any of your letters to Peter. The guy doesn't have to know everything, including who you drag home."

I stared after the retreating figure as she darted down the stairs and disappeared from view. Then, scratching Teddy's ears, I sank into the recesses of the hall to think. The stench of the place finally drove me to return to my own room. To my amazement, Chuck was sitting on the edge of the bed. He'd combed his hair with a wet comb. I could still see the drying traces in the dampened red ends. "Let's go for a beer."

I couldn't help but sneer. "I don't drink beer. Junkies don't drink beer."

"It's a figure of speech. I mean let's you and me go to the pub." He smiled and I noticed his white teeth, a rarity in a world where various shades of yellow and black were the norm, especially in the older hypes. Chuck had to be over twenty-five, I figured.

"I usually don't go out at night. I might run into certain people."

"I thought that's why you had me hanging around today. It can't hurt to have a little fun?" His face was glistening with nervous sweat that polished the freckles that arched across his nose. There was a nick below his left side burn indicating an attempt to shave. His cotton shirt was tucked into his pants and a silver belt buckle, depicting a sailing ship, seemed to anchor everything in place. Leather hiking boots that had seen better days gave him an assured stance. I stifled an overwhelming urge to ridicule him, for he looked more the part of a rumpled back packer than a junkie who only an hour before was in the midst of a deep nod.

Instead I kept my voice even. "I thought you'd had your fun for the night."

"Not the kind I'd intended."

Oh, what the hell, I thought, it had been a long time since I'd been invited out. I began to brush my hair and fix my uneven part, as I debated the pros and cons of making an evening appearance in a bar. I covered my lips in a white frost lipstick and slipped on a pair of leather thongs. Fear made me hesitate, then I followed him out.

As we sat sipping our Cokes, adding to the smoky ambiance of the Gastown Inn, he asked, "What's the story on the black dude? He's sure got your cage rattled."

"My guess, a pimp. Big Marie told me there was a bunch of them up from the States recruiting the white independents. Know what they call us? 'Snow Bodies.' Weird, heh? I got no desire to work for anyone but myself if I can help it. And by the way, I didn't dig how you almost OD'd on me."

"There's some powerful shit on the street right now."

"Yah . . . how'd you come out of it so soon. I thought you'd spend the rest of the night taking up all the space on my bed. Shit, when I get like that the last thing I want to do is straighten up."

"I was getting off on the wrong foot with you, so lots of cold water and walking brought me around."

"Well, don't let it happen again. Did you use my razor?" I sounded more irritated than I felt. Glancing up, I spotted Lanny cruising around the tables towards us. My face turned the colour of my lipstick, as I rose from my chair. Fear plugged my throat as Lanny lunged across the table and walloped me. My head snapped back, a scarlet dribble seeped from the corner of my mouth. Chuck pushed himself in front of me and landed an answering blow to Lanny's nose.

"You'll pay for that. She owes me money, you fuck!" Lanny cursed. He backed up, his hand covering his muzzle as the spouting blood spilled onto his tank top.

Chuck moved forward, his fists raised, and a waltz began with Chuck advancing and Lanny retreating. It ended in the foyer, where Lanny sprang forward and Chuck clocked him again with a double combination—a left, then a right. Two bouncers worked themselves into the fray and the fracas moved outside.

I moved back into my seat, just as Chuck returned, followed by the bouncers. He inspected my face and shook his head. "What a prick!" He took a Coke-soaked napkin from the table and wiped the blood from my face.

"He's why I don't go out at night. I've been so scared I'd run into him . . . the first time I take a chance . . ." I couldn't finish, and Chuck offered his arm. We escaped the stares of the other bar patrons through the side exit.

"Where'd you learn to box like that?" I leaned into his solid frame.

"The navy. Joined when I was sixteen."

"No shit. You must have been pretty square." Amused, I tugged at his long hair.

"I suppose I was," he agreed.

"I have to sit down." I dropped to the pavement and stretched out my legs. To my surprise, Chuck lowered himself down too, and we sat together—ignoring the passing pedestrians who sidestepped us.

"How you know Lanny?" Chuck asked, lighting a cigarette.

"Too long a story. All I can say is, of all the nightmares since Peter went down, he's the worst."

"Peter? I thought Ivan was your old man? That's what Vie told me that day in the Broadway . . . remember?"

"Ugh . . . another long story. No, Peter is who I'm with."

"Don't look to me like you're with anybody."

"He got pinched."

"Last name wouldn't be Stanhope?" I smiled feebly. Chuck cleared his throat. "I heard he and his old lady got screwed up on bombers and then just fucked up."

"That would be us, just two fuck-ups, but then you don't know the whole story."

He went to put his arm around me and I shrugged it off. "Let me tell you about the night Lanny and I decided to knock over a gas station." Not bothering to see if I was interested or not, he continued. "We had us a sawed-off shotgun and my job was to get the young guy on duty to open the safe while Lanny was to hold the gun on him. Well, he flipped after the safe was opened—began shaking and threatening to blow the kid on the floor away and I was sweating bullets trying to calm him down. I swear I thought he was gonna waste that poor bastard. I'll never forget the kid whispering the Lord's prayer. I felt we both walked through the valley of the shadow of death that night with Lanny's finger trembling, on the trigger. Funny thing, though, the kid never picked me out of a police line up, but he'd no trouble making Lanny. I think Lanny tried to make a deal by naming me, because he only got two less a day, but then the kid let me off. I never wanted nothing more to do with him after that. He's a head case and a rat."

I nodded and allowed him to pull me to my feet. Back in my room, we lay under the glare of the black and white images flickering from the television until Chuck nudged me under my ribs. "Do you ever think of getting out of this life?"

"I think you sink so far there ain't enough oxygen left to carry ya back up," I said, and reached for his hand.

We settled into a arrangement that seemed to suit us both. I continued to work the lunch-time crowd, but more confidently under Chuck's watchful eyes. Afterwards he slept while I visited the Methadone clinic. In the evenings, Chuck hustled for himself—how I did not bother to ask. But each night before he made his rounds I doled out twenty-five dollars, my part of our agreement.

Weeks into our lucrative relationship, Chuck returned home early. Not interested in why, and absorbed in *The New Avengers*, I didn't acknowledge his presence.

He crouched down beside me. "Things are shaking and I need another fifty dollars."

I glanced over, "The deal is twenty-five a day."

"If you haven't noticed, I ain't asked you for much and besides, it's a loan." He crawled closer and dropped his head on his elbow to stare wide-eyed.

"No," I said, swatting him away.

"You don't get it . . . I need it for a good score and I'll pay you back!" His usual mild face rippled with irritation and his lips whitened.

"In case you forgot, I'm the one who puts food on the table and keeps the roof over your head. I'll be God damned if I'll be responsible for anything else." As I climbed off the bed I couldn't help smirking, "You're well paid for what you do."

"Take your boots off," he ordered, bouncing up after me.

"Screw you!" I plucked Teddy from his basket on the floor and charged towards the door, but Chuck snared my legs in a flying tackle and brought me crashing to the floor. The dog yelped in fright and scrabbled away as I narrowly missed crushing him. His claws clicked across the floor as he clambered to safety.

"You fuck," I cried, spitting at him. The gob dribbled off his chin, but he ignored it as he twisted around and squatted on my legs. He pried my ankle boots from my feet. From the wad of bills that tumbled out he peeled off two twenties and a ten and threw the rest in my face.

"I don't need it all . . . just the 50," he said, and walked away.

Cursing, I scrambled to my feet and searched the room. I tossed his umbrella, his knapsack, and assorted toiletries into the hall. When nothing of his remained, I locked and bolted the door.

I balanced on one of the kitchen chairs and removed a loose ceiling tile. I reached in and withdrew a roll of bills bound by an elastic band. The money I'd picked from the floor was added and the stash returned to its resting place. I had two thousand dollars and I could afford to lose fifty, but not my pride.

This was my show, my room, my money, and no one was going to take that way from me—especially not some land-locked sailor.

I was still smarting when Chuck returned hours later and knocked on the door. "How about forgive and forget? I got your money."

I thumped across the room and, making sure that the safety chain was still secured, I opened it a crack. "I'll take the money, but you can go fuck yourself."

"You won't let me in?"

"God damn right I won't," I said, ripping the money from his fingers and slamming the door in his face.

"That's flimsy plywood between us. You're lucky I don't want to come in too bad," he warned. Aware of the implied threat, I chose silence.

I couldn't help thinking how odd it was that he hadn't taken everything when he had it in his hand. There was at least two hundred dollars in my boot, and I couldn't remember anyone ever paying me back. It was all very perplexing, but I was unable to dwell on it for long as the tenants in the next apartment began a drunken brawl. Someone was being slammed again and again against the wall, which vibrated as if it were going to collapse in on me. The profanity from many different voices drowned out the television while a woman's shrieks pierced the air. I covered my ears, longing to add my own screams to the chorus.

The quiet of the morning was welcome and I lingered by the window watching the cars clog the street. I dressed, listening to the growling of my stomach. Eager for breakfast, I did not see Chuck's sleeping form lying tight against the door. One arm was cradling his head and the other holding his umbrella as my foot caught under his ribs and I stumbled over him.

"Didn't you have no place to stay?" I tried to mask my irritation as I rose from my knees. Platform sandals weren't the best shoes to have a mishap in, and my jeans were so tight I was amazed the ass hadn't ripped from one end to the other on the way down.

"It ain't that . . . I wanted to be sure I saw you first thing. I did that all wrong. Look, I didn't mean to man-handle you. You can really piss me off sometimes, being such a know-it-all and miser, but things, they just got carried away."

"Carried away, that's what you call it?" I balanced on the balls of my feet but, perceiving his sincerity, I softened. "Listen, I've been ripped off more times than I can count and I don't trust nobody. But I gotta say, you're the first to repay so much as a cent. That's worth something, and if

I'm not mistaken, I think you're trying to apologize. Although I ain't sure I like being called a miser. Get in here and freshen up, but don't get no ideas about staying."

"You don't got much give left . . . do ya?"

As I accepted the cigarette he offered, my lips flexed into a smile of acknowledgment.

◄o►

I arched out a hip and rested my left hand in the hollowed crook. With the other I took a sip of Coke and wrinkled my nose as the foam bubbled up my nostrils. I'd slept in and missed the noon-time crowd. I would have to give up my habit of watching late night movies, however comforting I found the drone of the television.

Chuck and I had resumed our business arrangement. It was easy money for him and worth the added security for me. But seeing no sign of him today, I sighed. I'd missed him too.

Chuck was such a puzzle. Even his body shape differed from other male hypes, with his flesh still cleaving solidly to his bones. His face remained full in contrast to the hollow pits that marked the degrees of emaciation in his fellows. His looks and his ways were different. But I did not want to end up with another Lanny, so I was treading carefully. Chuck had displayed no other signs of aggression, but I still felt ambivalence about our relationship. Chuck had accepted his banishment from my apartment and was content to let me set the conditions of our partnership. "Not hollow yet," I muttered.

A few nights ago he'd arrived asking for a date, of all things. His copper hair was tied back with an elastic band and his clothes were laundered. I could still smell the faint odor of Fleecy on his checked shirt. He wanted us to see the movie *Deliverance* starring Burt Reynolds. He'd read the book and felt certain I'd enjoy the film. It had been over a year since I'd gone with Peter to see *Slaughter House Five*; since we'd smoked joints on the balcony, I could remember little of the film. But this time I'd enjoyed the outing and the popcorn, Cokes, and friendly banter. It was doing something, instead of the swimming gauged by the heroin's highs or the frantic flight of action brought by its lows that left nothing in-between.

To distract myself, I lit a cigarette, when a uniformed cop shoved from behind propelling me into a lamppost. He whipped me around and the contents of my purse splattered to the sidewalk. Watching his hands sorting through the Tampax, condoms, loose change, hairpins, and makeup was funny. I adjusted my black sequined top. "I'm not using."

"We'll see," the cop replied, as he spun me around once again and began patting me down with more vigour than was necessary.

"Name," he demanded, pulling a walkie-talkie from his belt.

"Elizabeth Hudson." The colour drained from my face as I realized my probation might have been pulled. Was it up or not? I couldn't remember when that noose was to be removed from around my neck. I still couldn't believe that my probation officer hadn't yanked it.

"Yah . . . I've got a Elizabeth Hudson detained. Any outstanding warrants?"

A lifeless voice from the dark box intoned, "Beth Hudson, alias Debbie Smith, alias Bobby-Jo Morrow, currently wanted for non-payment of fine. Known associate of Sue Harding, currently wanted for theft. Known associate of Sandi Whalen, wanted for assault. Known associate of Blade Rowans, wanted for assault with a deadly weapon. Known associate of Lionel Richards, wanted for questioning. Known associate of Charles Dion, wanted for fraud. Known associate of Peter Stanhope currently in custody."

"Nice crowd you run with," the cop remarked, slapping on the cuffs.

"What is this, Big Brother policing?" I was hustled to the waiting squad car and, as the door opened, I balked.

"You don't understand. My dog. I gotta feed my dog." But a push sent me sprawling into the seat and the door slammed shut.

◄O►

In the bleak holding cell of the city bucket, I paced. Diffuse light filtered through a dirty, slatted window near the ceiling. Steel frame bunk beds lined the walls. A fellow inmate coming off a speed run with wild hazel eyes, yelled, "Stop it! You're making me nervous." Several of the other women stirred from their bunks and nodded in agreement, a couple of them sitting up as if to reinforce the speed freak's plea.

"You want to make something of it? Then bring it to me." I raised my fists and watched the figure slump against the wall, while her dancing hands gestured me away.

I stepped to the open bars and screeched, my voice squawling along the narrow brick corridor. "I want my phone call. You hear me? I want my phone call. I've been in here for fucking hours and no phone call." My demands were met with silence, other than a few snickers from behind.

My sandals clacked against the cement floor as I resumed my pacing unchallenged, while my mind flooded with questions. Who was I going to call anyway? Who could I trust? No one, so what to do? My deliberations ended as I decided on Chuck. I could reach him through the men's hostel, but if I couldn't, then all that was left was to do the thirty days. Who would have thought I'd be picked up on that stupid soliciting beef again? The fine had slipped my mind. I tried to recall how long ago it was, but couldn't. I got picked up every three or four months by the stupid under-cover vice cops. All this hassle for a lousy one hundred and fifty dollars. Finally the matron escorted me out for my phone call.

Noting the slots above the black wall phone I reminded her, "I ain't got no money. You took all my change, remember?"

"Here," the woman said, her greying hair escaping in curls from the confines of a headband. She tossed a dime and resumed sorting through a stack of files on top of a cabinet pressed against the opposite wall. She was far enough away to give the impression of privacy but close enough to overhear anything other than whispers.

Now I faced another dilemma. Which hostel? That was something I'd never bothered to ask. Was it the YMCA or the Salvation Army, or even some city-run thing? I wasn't even sure if these were the only three possibilities. Chuck was heading east on Granville Street the first day I'd bumped into him. I turned again to the matron. "Is there a men's hostel somewhere east of Granville?"

The woman scratched her ear, causing another clump of hair to make its escape. "The Salvation Army's in that end of town."

I flipped through the tattered phone book and then listened to the sharp rings that went unanswered. At last I was explaining to a stranger that this was an emergency and I must speak to a Chuck Dion. As the minutes ticked by I was beginning to think that I'd called too early, too late, or Chuck just wasn't there. Then a younger, smoother voice came on the line—"This better be good. I'm missing out on roast beef."

"Food. It's always food with you. Isn't it? And why the hell don't they allow women to eat there? We get hungry too."

"Beth?"

"I'm in a jam. Can't think of anyone else. You know what I mean? Who is there in this world to trust?"

"Jesus, get to the point."

"You have to bail me out of the city bucket."

I heard an amused chuckle. "You know I don't got no money. That's why I'm eating here at one of our finer city establishments."

"I know you don't got cash. That's not a problem 'cause I do. I need you to fetch it and get down here. I'll take you to eat wherever you want. Understand?"

"I suppose. I don't relish coming to the cop shop. What if I'm picked up? I got outstanding warrants, ya know."

"I heard. Tell them you're my brother and just pay the damn fine for me. I don't want to do no thirty days, and I'll make it worth your while."

"Sounds like a bribe."

"It is a big one. At my place, above the table, is a ceiling tile. It's got a water mark stain. Inside is a roll of bills and if you wouldn't mind feeding Teddy. And Chuck . . . I need to know I can trust ya. Don't leave me hanging here—or Teddy alone?"

"Just how am I supposed to get into your place?"

"Christ sakes, you're a criminal—think of something!"

"See ya later."

I replaced the receiver, feeling more uncertain than before I'd made the call.

The next couple of hours I spent sitting on the floor where there was less chance of bed bugs, lice, or crabs. My tongue grew furry from chain smoking, and I hacked incessantly. When the matron finally gestured for me and unlocked the bars, I felt I'd never heard such a sweet sound. But my anxiety again increased when the male clerk pushed the release papers towards me to sign. "Where's my brother?"

"He left after paying the fine."

I flew out the main doors. I'd catch that son-of-a-bitch and beat the living shit out of him. I'd hire a hit. I raced by a sitting figure on the steps, did a double-take, and realized it was Chuck. Several cigarette butts littered the cement steps by his sandals. Sweat was trickling down his forehead between his freckles.

I reached for his hand and pressed it to my face, then, feeling awkward, I looked away.

"What are you carrying on for? You haven't got your money back yet," he said, pressing the crinkled wad into my palm. I peeled off a fifty and tucked it into his jeans.

"Ain't you gonna count it?"

"Nope." I shook my head. "What I am going to do after you're fixed is to take us to some swanky place, and we'll have a celebration of sorts—even Teddy will come. It's been a long time since anyone came through for me."

"Tell me something," he drawled, rising from the steps. "Would your old man, Peter, have done this for ya?"

"Sure, he'd have sprung me. But I wouldn't see my money again. He'd have some big plans for it or something." A smile played at the corners of my lips. "C'mon," I gestured. I felt a growing sense of hope, as I linked my arm through his.

"I almost didn't come," Chuck confessed, "I could have had one hell of a party."

"Ya, but you did come." I shrugged his confession away. "Did you know Lanny's real name is Lionel?"

"No shit!" Our howls of laughter reverberated along Hastings Street.

As if I'd never kicked Chuck out, our relationship resumed and now, at the end of September, the humid heat in the room was stifling. I was wearing nothing but my panties as the sweat from my body mingled with Chuck's—who was in a similar state of undress. I rolled away to escape the stickiness. The television was off and the only light seeped in under the cracks in the door. Breaking the sweaty silence, Chuck's scratchy voice indicated he was still high. "I'd like to take some bundles to Calgary and double our money. We could live pretty good. You get your Methadone for free and I could more than cover our costs and my habit to boot." He wiped a red strand of wet hair from his face and rolled me back towards him.

I tapped my fingers across his bicep, outlining his anchor tattoo. "Sandi and Blade said there was a sting operation going on. I don't think it's a good idea." I swallowed, as if something was caught in my throat. "Besides I don't want to lose ya, because, honestly, I think that *loss* is my middle name."

"You know we do have that in common. I lost my business, my wife, and my two kids—not to mention my self-respect along the way."

I yawned. "I lost my self-respect with my first trick."

"You're not wired. Why don't you get a real job?"

"Ha, and be paid a dollar fify an hour. I think not. One trick gets me more than I could make flipping burgers at McDonald's all day. Besides, as Sue once said, it ain't that bad once you get used to it."

I moved to the edge of the bed, unable to escape the heat that pulsed from the mattress. "What business were you in anyway?"

"Plumber. It was pretty good money until my habit got in the way." He rubbed his nose, making me wonder if he was still in the nod.

"I guess you could support us then, if I didn't work." I laughed at the thought.

"Yes, but not a habit." He stroked my arm. "But I could be more of a help if you'd front me for bundles."

"You want to take that risk? Remember the years that mark the difference between boosting or short changing and trafficking."

"I'll only sell to those I know. And you won't be sorry."

I got up, ran cold water from the kitchen tap, and splashed my face. "I'm sure I will, but that will be then and not now." He must have drifted off again and not heard. That was the trouble with junkies: you never knew if they were conscious or not.

My presence seemed to lift the fogginess of his nod, but this time he prodded in a different direction. "Don't you think we could have sex once in a while? Not that I want to pressure ya or nothing, but it seems strange to be this close to someone and never do it."

Male junkies, when they could get it up, never came—so it was a stupid request. I got fucked enough as it was. "That's what you got a hand for," I snapped, and turned away.

◄o►

I saw him off at the Greyhound station. He was wearing a raincoat that hung past his knees. It was tied at the waist, which should have made him look business-like—except that his sandals ruined the overall look. His umbrella was hooked over his right arm and he carried it with an air of importance. He had three bundles, and although I did not inquire where they were hidden, I could imagine from the rigid way he held himself. He stepped onto the running board of the bus, promised to be home in a few days, and kissed the top of my head.

That evening I decided to write my reply to Peter. I'd put if off for over a month and the pent up words flowed from my pen to the paper.

> *Dear Peter,*
>
> *One could argue that it was the drugs that made us feel the way we did, but even when I haven't been high and I think about you I feel the same as before you got pinched. What is love? I sure the hell don't know. What I can say is that I've never felt this way about anyone but you.*
>
> *I think that solitary and the change of scenery has been fucking with your head. But in the event that you see things differently now and your feelings have changed, then, as I have told you, I can accept that. I've been on the street for almost a year now, so I think I've proved I can stand on my own. Shit happens and I seem to get more than my share, especially from you. So for the time being I shall think of us in the past tense.*
>
> *Beth*

I placed the written page in the envelope without re-reading it, then dug around the bottom on my bag for a stamp, and stuck the dirty square on the corner of the envelope.

Chapter Twenty-one

I'D MISSED THE ACTION OF the nights, with the lights and the river of cars that slowed, looking and seeking. There was a feeling of belonging in playing a role in the nightly sidewalk stage, partaking in the cynical observations with the other working girls about the tricks, their performances, or lack of. Besides, the money was better. I could front Chuck four bundles on his next run and still add to my savings.

Pleased with my new-found sense of enterprise and the night's take, I returned home late to find the door wide open. The lock dangled from the door jam. My clothes were strewn across the floor, my shoes had been thrown at the walls, leaving heel marks and gouged-out pieces of plaster. The instant coffee jar was smashed under the table. The television was gone. I ran to Teddy's basket, and then checked the closet. I could find no trace of him. On the bed a butcher knife through the pillow held a scrap of paper.

> *Consider your debt paid. I've taken the dog and anything else I could find. Watch your back.*
> *Lanny*

"That mother fucking son-of-a-bitch!" I turned and wandered back into the night.

—<o>—

Later, I welcomed the return of the rush as I floated high above the weight of any feelings.

—<o>—

Two days after, Chuck returned and forced his way in by knocking over the kitchen chair secured under the door knob. The lock, hanging from one screw, popped off and clattered to the linoleum. His fingers combed his red hair into fiery spikes, then he gestured at the mess. Shards of glass from the busted coffee jar were scattered amongst the litter of the floor, the coffee grains were still sprinkled over the destruction like fine powder. "What the hell's going on?"

"Lanny took Teddy and busted up the place. Everything is gone. The TV too. I've lost my deposit and the guy I rented it from is gonna be pissed." I rubbed my nose, trying to wake from my stupor.

"You using again?" The question hung in the air as he lowered himself down to the corner of the bed. His hands unfurled until his palms were turned up with the unspoken *why?*

"Bought myself a bundle and been having a party. Not that I got very high the first night, but it's been getting better and better." I threw the balloon between my breasts at him. "Help yourself," I invited, and closed my eyes again.

"Pack up. We're moving."

"I ain't. This is my home."

He moved and whipped the sheet off. "Don't matter. Get your ass out of bed. It's too hot here . . ." he ordered, helping me into a sitting position while I continued to protest. With his arm around my waist he braced me and I began stumbling around, kicking at the strewn clothes and debris.

"Christ's sake get dressed. Put something on your feet, before you cut yourself," he said, losing his patience and plunking me back down on the bed. I began the process of deciding what to wear while he searched for his knapsack.

He found it under a pile of my clothes. Dog shit was smeared across it. He wiped it clean as best he could and heaved a sigh of relief that it was otherwise undamaged. He began to salvage what he could of his belongings, and began shaking out and neatly folding his shirts and pants. He accepted the handful of my stuff I pushed at him, leaving them for last. As he secured the bulging pack, he remarked, "You could have cleaned up the place."

"What for?" I leaned into him as he squired me away. On the street we hailed a cab. I didn't catch the name or address of the motel Chuck recited to the driver. I was not even aware of what direction we'd gone. Only later when the nod lifted did I inspect the clean surroundings. The rounded bed, the colour television, and the shining bathroom. "Why are we here? It's a long way from work and looks expensive," I said, returning to the bedroom with a basket of Holiday Inn toiletries.

"We can afford it. And besides, it's safer. What if Lanny came back?" he asked, burning a cap in a blackened aspirin tin.

"I was hoping he would and I could kill that son of a bitch." To reinforce my point I withdrew a two-inch switch-blade from my boot, flicked it open, and waved the it under his nose.

"Ain't your boots getting a little crowded? Money, knives . . . put that thing away. Any guy could take that off you." With that he hit my wrist and the knife plunged into the plush pile carpet. "You don't need another fix."

"That's for me to say, and it's my dope."

"You miss the dog that much?"

"Yah." I retrieved the knife and placed it on the dresser and accepted the needle that he pushed into my vein. The rush branched across my body and concealed me in the warm sleep it brought.

"You not interested in how much I made on the run?" he asked—but words were too far away for me to answer.

Chuck woke me with the news: he was going to buy a car. That way we could easily get back and forth from the downtown. I acknowledged him with a grunt and fell back asleep until late in the afternoon when he barged in and startled me awake. His tone was excited, "Come and see the 1967 Rambler station wagon I got for three hundred and fifty dollars."

I dressed and enjoyed a cigarette before walking around the exterior of the dark blue vehicle. Then, trying to raise my voice above my mood, I observed, "Nice colour."

"Bullshit . . . you could care less." His face grew slack, his lips scrunched at the corners.

"Well, I ain't had a test ride yet." I attempted a smile, which, despite my best efforts, erupted into a yawn. But he returned the smile and slapped my rear end. I tried to catch his enthusiasm as I jumped into the passenger side and settled into the cushioned seats. Rolling down the window, I relished the feel of the wind caressing my hair as we cruised along the wide highway to Chilliwack. After about an hour Chuck pulled over to the shoulder and put his arm around me. He pointed to the last of the sun's rays dripping into the horizon. His chest inflated. "Things gonna be a lot easier with wheels."

"I want to eat before I have to go to work, and it's getting late." I squirmed away from him. "Nice sunset though," I added, as I felt more was expected.

"Profits, all profits," he replied, turning the key in the ignition and swinging across several lanes of traffic in an arching U turn.

"Don't draw no heat," I said, digging my fingers into the seat and wondering why I seemed so out of sync with him since he came back.

"I'm leaving the dealer plates on. No tracing it, especially since I used fake ID to buy it."

I straightened my salmon-coloured top, thinking only of the fries, Coke, and the fix that awaited. At around one I finished work, and we wheeled away in the Rambler to the far-flung suburbs in search of a motel. I noticed the layers of tension peel away as we escaped from the noise and dangers of Vancouver's core. For the first time I felt grateful for the luxury of the car.

That night as I curled next to him, I pressed my ear close to his chest and fell asleep to the steady drum of his heart.

◄o►

I drifted into my relationship with Chuck as easily as a dandelion seed carried by a gust of wind. Although the highs and lows of my relationship with Peter were missing, I'd developed, over time, an appreciation for the more practical Chuck. His moves and scores were orchestrated like a business, minus the legality. His runs to Calgary were spaced three weeks apart, and he continued to dabble in the short change business with varying degrees of success. Between the two of us, our habits were well fed. But I could not forget that relationships on the street could blow apart leaving nothing. My life had emptied and filled with people in such rapid succession that my growing attachment to Chuck caused me to feel uneasy. I felt the steel thrust of a guillotine waited somewhere unseen.

◄o►

On the morning I dropped him off at the Greyhound bus station for another run, we'd been together for five months. He'd told me that there was no need to wait there with him, so I'd parked the car and gone shopping. I stopped on the fourth floor of the Bay for a cup of coffee, and chuckled at the clerk's shocked expression as I'd produced the wad of bills and skimmed off a twenty.

As I walked back to the car, a few wisps of cloud remained to empha-size the hue of the October sky. A slight breeze lifted the smell of salt off the water and I sucked it in, feeling the last of the summer's heat fleeing from the sun-soaked pavement. As I unlocked the car's door, I spotted the parking ticket tucked under the windshield. I moved to the Ford behind, lifted the wiper and replaced it there. I then spread the city map over the dashboard searching for the best route home to the Ramada Inn in Surrey and started the engine. With our policy of never staying more than a night or two, the rotations of accommodations was a maze of names and addresses that congealed in my mind. But I managed to maneuver the route safely, paid the bill for the day, climbed into the bed and fell asleep. Sometime around 4 PM the phone rang.

"Yah?"

"Beth, it's Chuck."

"Ain't you somewhere over the Rockies?"

"Got popped at the station after you dropped me off. It was like they were waiting for me."

"Oh . . . oh." I opened and closed my mouth as my breath came in and out in uneven wheezes.

"Don't suppose you could come and see me in the city bucket before they haul me off to Oakalla?"

◄○►

There was a sense of déjà vu, as I marched into the visitors' room with more confidence than I felt. The scene felt all too familiar with the barred windows distilling the light and the line of empty stools behind the glass. Always, always the glass, I thought as I waited.

Chuck was led in by two guards. His hands were handcuffed behind him, pulling his short-sleeved shirt apart and exposing glimpses of his smooth, white chest between the buttons. His hiking boots shuffled softly across the cement floor. His belt was missing and his blue jeans were dip-ping down to his hips. He stopped and struggled with his cuffs, trying to pull them up. One of the guards turned a key in the cuffs and freed his hands while I gestured to the phone.

"What happened?" I darted nervous glances at the uniformed guards who had withdrawn to the opposite wall.

Chuck's hair fell in damp red strands over his face. "Nothing and everything . . . I'm sorry," he said.

"They must have been watching us, but where? How else would they know? Do you remember if we told anyone? Who ratted? Why?"

Under the rapid fire of my questions Chuck spread his fingers in a stop motion.

"Questions without answers. It's too late to trouble with them."

I brought my thumb to my cheekbone and rubbed. "I brought your knapsack with all your stuff, and I gave the custodian a hundred dollars on your account, so you could get smokes and stuff."

He did not reply. "Is that enough? Tell me 'cause it's part yours too."

"I don't need more where I'm going. But I want to clear the air about some things before I go up. You never let me believe there was more than a partnership between us, but, unlike you, I really cared, and I don't mean to sound like some big wimp or nothing . . . I just wanted you to know."

I tried to smile but only managed to halt the downward curve of my mouth. "I think I figured that. Most of the time I don't feel nothing and don't want to neither. But you were the best thing that's happened to me since I hit the street. I'll miss ya. Honest, I will." I felt an odd sense of remorse. I knew this was the last time I would probably see him, and yet I could not express the emotions he evoked.

"Before I go I want to remind you that not every man is like Peter, running hot and cold." Before I could react, he concluded, "Don't look so surprised. I always knew he stood between you and me. If you're ever free from the fixation you hold for the guy . . . well, you know where to find me."

Dwarfed in the queen-sized bed, I stared into the darkness. I could not forget the picture of him walking away. The discipline of his Navy days was spelled in the dignity of his rigid back, the straight line of his shoulders, and the way his hair moved in time to the precision of his step. Only then did I cry—for myself, for him, for everything.

There were more of us than usual working tonight, and I was jousting for a place front and centre along the rim of Granville Street, when a young woman dressed in a business pant-suit elbowed her way through the crowd of women. Clean, she smelled so clean. I thought I could detect a faint trace of Zest soap still clinging to her. A tape recorder was strapped to her side. "May I ask you a few questions?" She handed me a business card and an obligatory smile.

"I'm working," I said, holding the card between my fingers. I gave it a cursory glance and then rocked back on my heels. She of the reddish streaked hair and perky little mouth was a student.

The way I saw it, I could reach into my heavy sack of shame and guilt and hand my stories over as if they were ripe tomatoes for her to savour. Perhaps my predicament and loss might be more real if compiled as a number, a statistic, in a paper to be catalogued, indexed, and filed. Instead, I did what came more naturally to me: I stepped back and spit in her eye.

◄○►

On the steps of the Broadway Hotel I sat ringed by cigarette butts and gobs of spit. A used condom was lodged against the curb, and I rocked back and forth as a cold gust of wind ruffled my hair. In an effort to avoid my huddled shape, an old drunk missed the bottom step and cursed. "Fucking bitch, move off !"

I was weeping as others moved past. The pimps, the prostitutes, and the drifters stepped over or around me as they went about their business. If I existed at all to them, it was only as a minor inconvenience. I remained oblivious to their movements as I wallowed in my misery. I sniveled repeatedly and my dripping nose mingled with my tears. I clutched at my throbbing head, knowing I must score, but I couldn't think how. In my present condition I couldn't work.

In desperation I'd called my parents. My father answered, and the operator duly asked if he would accept the charges from a Beth Hudson. "Daddy," I'd whispered.

"No, I will not."

"Please . . . Daddy, it's me, Beth, your daughter."

"I had a daughter once, but she's in a grave of her own making."

The line went dead. The operator droned, "The party does not wish to take your call." Leaving the phone dangling from the cord, I'd fled and somehow, in that mad dash, had found my way here.

I reached up and scrubbed at these fresh tears with my wrist. It would have been better if my father had aborted me in the womb, rather than wait till now. An unexpected spot of sunlight pierced the dense covering of fall cloud and bounced off my face. Red veins and puffy lids rimmed my eyes. I wore no makeup to hide the lines that filleted my once-full face into sunken flesh. My fingers trembled as I rubbed them together.

It was all too much—my father's declaration of my death, and then Vie and Terry ripping me off in the night. How they'd pleaded with me to take them in, as they had nowhere to go and no money. Like a fool I'd welcomed them. Grateful for the company, I'd even fixed them. But in the morning they were gone—along with my drugs, my money, and my leather jacket.

I was hours overdue for a shot and the real withdrawal agony was about to begin. What was I going to do? It was all so hopeless. I couldn't work when I wasn't fixed. A hand touched me on the nape of the neck, and I found myself staring into the eyes of Big Marie. "What the hell are you bawling about?" she demanded.

Normally I'd have moved a respectful distance away from the imposing figure, who used her physical advantage over most women and took pleasure in tormenting them. Instead, I croaked between sobs—"Got ripped off last night. I'm sick and can't work."

The jet-black hair piled in beehive fashion on the woman's head added to her height; because I was sitting down, Big Marie appeared even more colossal. Her eyes were circled with thick black eyeliner and her lips were covered in blood-red lipstick. The makeup enhanced the cunning and strength in her face. When she smiled, which wasn't often, she exposed a crooked set of teeth. On two inch spiked heels, the giant stood with her feet planted apart as if undecided about something. A pair of charcoal fishnet stockings covered her shapely legs, and above a miniskirt was topped with a ruffed floral blouse and sweater tied around her waist. Sue and I had often shared a good laugh about the Big M's fifties fashion sense, although at the moment nothing about the woman seemed funny.

Marie's biggest beef seemed to be with the hippie chicks. She was a

Rounder, prided herself on it and lived up to it. She loathed the idea that my ilk displayed our wares in bell-bottomed pants, T-shirts, leather thongs, feather earrings, love beads. Whether she saw us as a threat or just a nuisance, no one knew and no one dared to ask.

The woman was studying her large brown hands as if they held some answer. "Love" was tattooed on one, "Hate" on the other. I braced for the worst. But instead of kicking my butt, as I expected, she drawled, "Well, you done me a sort of favour once, so I'll do the same for you."

I stared wide-eyed and again tried to swipe my nose with the back of my sleeve.

"First thing, stop blubbering and shut up," the woman ordered, hoisting me up and marching me down the street. The big woman waved her muscular arms at a passing cab. The driver stopped.

"Gotta trip?" she asked. "No . . . good," and Big Marie roughly pushed me in.

"Where to?"

"Mayfair Road . . . hurry." As the cab sped off, she leaned over and confided, "Going to my mark's house."

I clenched and unclenched my fists in anticipation; it seemed we'd never get to wherever it was we were going. I was also feeling resentful. Big Marie should have fixed me in the hotel washroom rather than extending this agony.

As if reading my thoughts she muttered, "Not far."

The trip seemed an eternity, although it probably took no more than ten minutes before we arrived in front of a squat bungalow. Big Marie paid the driver and helped pull me out.

There was a picket fence surrounding the place, protecting the flowers and grass. Other than a giant red rose bush that impeded the opening of the gate, I noticed little. I was propelled along the walk to the front door, which Big Marie opened with a key she plucked from under a planter of carnations. I was ushered through the hall to the living room and then was eased on to an overstuffed sofa. "Please hurry," I whispered.

"I'm going as fast as I can." Though I'd seen the ritual thousands of times, it was taking too long this time as those huge hands painstakingly squirted water into the powder and then rummaged in her bag for a match. At last, the liquid boiled and blended, giving off its unique smell.

I wished now I'd stuck to the less-fuss Methadone program; as I clasped my right arm and, with my left, pumped. My exposed track, about six inches long, expanded and I looked away.

Big Marie plunged the needle into the vein. The rush! My brain stopped its silent screams. My tears dried up. My nose ceased dripping and the chills were gone. My stomach untied itself and I was at peace.

As my pupils retreated to pinholes I looked to my benefactor. "Thanks."

Yanking the needle from her own arm, Big Marie returned the smile. "Know why I helped ya?"

I didn't care but grunted in answer anyway.

"You done helped me once in Calgary, when a trick beat on me."

I frowned, remembering. It was the only time I'd seen Big Marie shaken and shedding tears. Moved by the sight, I'd gone and put my arms around her. I was surprised—the comfort I offered was accepted as the woman slumped over me, crying. A john had robbed her, savagely beating her with his fists until she'd turned over her night's take. Both sides of her face were bruised and puffy. Blood seeped from a corner of her mouth where one of her teeth dangled by a crimson thread.

"Don't worry, I'll fix you," I'd reassured the woman, knowing that if a man did this to Big Marie he might have done much worse to me. We'd walked to the Calgarian Hotel and there I'd held cold paper towels over the battered face, and then given her a few dollars for a cab home. Big Marie had not acknowledged the favour until now.

"I didn't forget. You must have noticed I never laid a licking on ya or ran you off like I do the other girls?"

"But you threatened to often enough," I replied, wondering why the woman was telling me this.

"Ya, but I didn't . . . and I've an image to keep." A rumble that passed for laughter filled the air. "Besides, Vie liked ya and then you helped me, but I really don't have much use for the likes of ya."

"I noticed . . . why?" I asked, thumbing my nose.

"Don't know. . . . Guess I grew up on the wrong side of the tracks . . . Rounders was all I ever knew and then all I wanted to know. Who ripped you off . . . a john?"

"Vie."

"Oh . . . that's a good one," another rumble forced its way from the woman's chest. "She probably figures you still owe her for that vacation she took ya on."

"She could have asked . . . she didn't need to rip me off."

"Ah . . . you'd be an easy mark for her . . . too trusting, I can see it in your eyes." Then she dismissed the subject with an shrug of her shoulders. Her scarlet lips puckered as she slid further down the sofa and began to stroke my hand. "Poor baby . . . you can stay here tonight, if ya want."

Unnerved more by the woman's manner than the invitation, I tried to think. I couldn't afford to offend her and I didn't dare stay. There were too many stories circulating on the street about Big Marie's sexual preferences. "No . . . I got to work . . . I've a big habit to feed," I said, removing my hand and adding, "That's nice of ya but, some other time perhaps?"

"Good, didn't really want ya anyway." Our earlier rapport vanished. "Okay, you're fixed, so we're outta here." She loomed for a moment, then whirled around and tramped off to the kitchen. Returning she announced, "Cab will be here in a couple of minutes." As we waited there was an uncomfortable twist to the new line of conversation Big Marie was taking.

"How come you wear such funny shoes?"

I looked at my feet. The brown boots with the platform heels seemed very fashionable. "I don't know," I muttered.

"You ain't got no style, girl. Men love a woman in spikes." She beamed, displaying her own black, pointed pair. "Why don't you get yourself a pair, and get rid of those things you call shoes? You can't make much money without showing a little leg, ya know . . . so how come you wear pants all the time?"

The woman was obsessed with what I was wearing. "They're comfortable."

"Boy, are you dumb," announced Big Marie, who appeared to be looking for another target when she ordered, "Well, don't just sit there like a lazy ass . . . get ready. The cab will be here in a minute."

"Mind if I use the can?"

"Make it snappy."

I moved past the kitchen, turned left, and found the washroom. From my bag, I removed a brush and tried to force it through my matted hair. After a few minutes with limited success, I turned on the taps, and using my hands, tried to wash my face.

A horn sounded. "Hurry up, the cab's here," the gruff voice boomed.

I heeded her abrasive call and hurried away. Once again, I found myself being propelled along, except this time it was out the door.

"Quit stalling," the woman said, storming past, and as I seated myself in the cab it was with a sense of relief. "Granville and Davie Street and make it snappy," Big Marie instructed, jabbing her silver-ringed index finger in the air.

With the woman's long, sharpened nail tip dancing through the air so close to his neck, the driver coughed in answer. During the silent drive I sensed that the woman really didn't want to let me go. So when Big Marie ordered the cabby to stop, I offered, "We'll have a coffee sometime . . . eh?"

"What, and be seen with the likes of you? We're even now . . . don't expect nothing again," Big Marie said and shoved me out.

Chapter Twenty-two

I PUSHED AT THE ROTTED window frame, leaned over, and hawked some phlegm to the littered courtyard below. Poised like a spider on a web, I could feel the sickness coming. These were dry times. The dope had vanished, leaving only withdrawal as a reminder of its power. Rip-offs and violence were escalating, adding to the frenzied sense of this panic.

I wished now that I'd stayed in Vancouver and not let loneliness and isolation chase me back to Calgary. I picked at a pile of mismatched clothes. I could care less what I looked like, but dressed in a pair of flared striped pants and a low-cut T-shirt. A burgundy pigskin jacket, recently purchased from Gary "The Boost" Albert for thirty dollars, and a pair of gold hooped earrings, courtesy of the Bay, finished off the outfit. Tonight I wore no makeup, knowing it would only run off with my sweat. Out on the street I shuffled next door to the Regis. As I entered, Sue appeared, barring the way. "I've been looking for ya. Thought for sure you'd by here by now. I got great news."

If it were about a score, Sue would have spit it out already. "What?"

"I just seen Sandi at the Summit and guess who's there?" With a slightly superior cocking of her head, Sue smiled.

"I don't really give a fuck," I said, blowing my nose on a used Kleenex.

"Oh . . . I think you do."

My lips compressed in irritation. "Well . . . who?"

"Peter."

I considered the possibility, then cackled with disbelief. "Bullshit!"

"See for yourself, then," Sue replied and looked at her watch. "I'm going back over now. Rumour is Rick will hit there tonight."

Unable to hide my interest, I picked up the pace as we began the five-block walk to the Summit Hotel. I peered over the endless line of tables that spread along the extended length of the bar. I followed as Sue threaded our way to a table at the rear, repelled by the clash of loud voices filling the smoky place and competing with the live band. The smell of the beer we ordered made me queasy and I pushed it away.

The last I heard, Peter had been transferred to PA But then I hadn't written in months, so perhaps he was playing the game for a change. With a quiet resolve, Sue and I continued to scan the crowd. Sue gave a nudge, pointing to a group of boisterous young males emerging from the men's washroom on our left. My jaw dropped. There he was, slapping his friend Larry on the back. His dark hair was tied into a long braid that accentuated his high cheekbones and made him appear almost native. He looked healthy, and from the width of the smile on his face, he was enjoying himself.

Uncertain, I muttered, "I think I'm going to go."

"But why? There he is. Ya fucking well talk to me enough about him . . . now go talk to him." Sue said with a scowl.

"I can't . . . I just can't . . . I'm outta here." I stood to leave, but Sue clutched at my arm.

While trying to extract myself from Sue's claw-like grip, Peter sighted me. He broke away from his group, moving and pushing himself through the crowd. Apprehension and doubt jostled each other, for I knew I looked like shit—and what was there to say anyway? With a frantic jerk, I escaped Sue's hold and began to jog towards the exit, but he overtook me with long, loping strides.

"That's some greeting—ya spot me and try to take off !" he said, swinging me around to face him. I was forced up against the wall where he leaned across my upper chest and with one hand, supporting himself, pinned me there. "Well, I can see you didn't tie no yellow ribbon around no oak tree for me." He laughed, but his brown eyes remained inscrutable.

At the mention of that song I remembered the bleak ride back from Drumheller and lashed out, "Fuck you."

"No, my dear, I fully intend to fuck you. After all, what kind of pass is it if my own girlfriend wants me to fuck myself ? I can do that quite well enough in the joint." He nuzzled my hair and the warmth of his breath on my neck made me feel more edgy and confused.

"You could have at least sent me word you'd get a pass," I said, refusing to look him in the eye and smothering an urge to shove him away.

"And tell me where I'm to get a hold of ya? I never know if you're in Van, the hospital, or here. Besides, I sent Sandi to get word to ya."

Before I could answer, Larry came up and tapped him on the shoulder. "We gotta go."

"I'll be there in a minute," he replied, wrinkled his forehead, and then ordered, "Go ahead."

"See, ya don't plan on spending no time with me." I shrugged.

"Ah, ya got it all wrong, baby. We're just going to score. I'll be back. So wait . . . okay?" He released my arm and I ducked under it.

"You ain't gonna score. There's no stuff. Ya think I'd look like this if there was any to be had?" I could not hide the contempt in my voice.

"Contacts, baby . . . contacts." He winked, ignoring my tone.

"Hah . . . you ain't got none no more."

"We'll see, won't we? By the way, what number are you in the Beverage Block?"

"Room 46. Ya should have known that if ya talked to Sandi."

"Just checking—I did get that was where ya was at, but I can't visit. If I get caught there I could be bounced back with no chance for another of these little holidays—that's why I sent word for you to come." He turned to go. "Promise you'll wait."

He looked so sincere that I considered. "Ya sure this ain't a con job?"

"Yah . . . I'll be back."

"I'll wait then."

He moved and disappeared out the exit. Irked at his usual glibness and the vanishing act, I returned to my table.

"Well, what did he have to say for himself ?" Sue asked, raising her well-shaped eyebrows as she tried to hike down the miniskirt that was forever inching up her thigh.

"He said wait. He'll come for me," I said, trying to sound more certain than I felt. "I just hope I'm not being played for a mark."

"Ya always said you two had something. He'll come, but . . . you'll wait alone. The dope ain't coming here, else Rick would have been here already. I'm going to try at the Imperial. Crash at your place?"

I nodded and settled into the chair. The band was blasting over the speakers an old rock and roll number, "Move over Beethoven." The drunken voices curdling around gave me a splitting headache. I tried over the next few hours to sip the beer, but it made the bile in my stomach rise. My chain smoking aggravated the hacking cough I'd developed in the last couple of weeks. Occasionally I'd spot another hype and wave them over to get the latest on any dope leads, but otherwise I remained alone, feeling more terminal as the night dragged on.

The bar was emptying as the band played its last set. The sweat was flowing in rivulets down my face while my chilled flesh contracted into upright tiny spikes. The waitress approached for last call, and my anticipation was replaced by a burning hatred as the staff began to clear the tables. I left, promising that he'd never fuck me around again.

Along the emptiness of Ninth Avenue, my boots slapped hard against the squares of cement that I wished were his face. At the Beverage Block I stepped over a sleeping drunk in the foyer and resisted a violent urge to kick him. I did stop to fumble through his pockets and was rewarded with a ten spot. I made the long climb to the fourth floor where the darkened stairway swallowed my footsteps.

I turned the key and Sue rose up on an elbow from the bed. Her sweat-stained face was an easy read. There was no dope again this night.

"Fuck," I snapped, and then, wanting to avoid her questioning look, added, "No, he didn't." I flopped down next to Sue, who brushed my hand in sympathy. Her touch seemed to bring on another bout of coughing. It took a few minutes to catch my breath before asking, "Did you get that Mandrax from Jacob?"

From under the pillow Sue produced a full bottle of the blue and white pills. "Well, I guess I can OD on these," I said, fingering the plastic vial. I peeled off my sweat-stained clothes, punted them against the wall, swallowed four of the downers, and then slid between the dirty sheets. I was comforted after a while by the sounds of Sue's shallow breathing. I stared into the dark, waiting for the pills to moderate my own suffering. The tight muscles relaxed but my racing thoughts would not be stilled. With only the ponderous action of the pills to slow them, they went round and round and would not allow any rest. I inched closer to Sue and, reassured that she still slept, wrapped an arm around her wafer-thin frame and pressed myself tight against her.

At about ten the next morning a pounding on the door startled me from an uneasy sleep. "Beth, wake up. Beth," ordered a male voice.

I made for the door, and tilted my head to the keyhole to listen. "What ya want?"

"If it was narcs the door would be down already."

"Okay . . . okay." I unbolted it and Peter elbowed his way past. He took in the dirty room in a quick glance: the nicotine-stained wallpaper curling as if it bled from the insides, the rusty sink in the corner that doubled as a toilet, and the smell of the urine seeping up from the drain and fouling the room. Adding to the stink was the accumulation of take-out dinners left on the counter to rot. Clothes encircled the walls, mingling with the candy wrappers and pop bottles that littered the floor.

He frowned at the girl in the cot beginning to stir. "Not exactly the Ritz," he noted, then angled himself against the door and popped a cigarette in his mouth. He recognized the bag of pills on the metal-framed night stand and said, "Well, at least ya got some good downers."

"Get out," I screeched, trying to push him through the door, but he remained fixed. He was not moving. "Tell him to fuck off," Sue said, clutching the thin covering of the sheet.

"I don't think we've had the pleasure." Peter advanced towards Sue and held out his hand. "This of course, as you know, is my old lady, who ya sleep with." He gestured towards me, then added, "Nude, yet." He appraised the naked form beneath the discoloured sheets that reeked of sex. Sue returned the appraisal.

I moved and jerked him away. "How dare you? It's not what you think." Sandwiched between the two of us, I taunted him—"Not that it's your business, anyways!"

"Well, my business or not . . . I want to talk to ya and I can see that we ain't going to get no privacy here, so get dressed. You're leaving." He picked my purse off the floor and threw a pair of pants at me. But I sat down on the bed. "You couldn't pay me enough. You lying fuck."

He bent over, warning, "Watch the language. You haven't seen me in over a year and I was hoping for something more romantic from you than 'lying fuck'." He took the brush from my purse and I held up a hand to ward off the downward strokes on the tangled mess. I opened my mouth for a remark, but he held his forefinger to my lips. "Well, naturally the romantic stuff can come later. Now you're going to get ready. I'm giving ya exactly three minutes to get dressed, else I'm hauling ya out of here . . . whether ya like it or not." He laughed in an easy manner that only seemed to enhance the threat.

"Just try it!" I snorted, turning my head and looking to Sue to intervene.

Following my lead, Peter glanced to Sue and warned, "Don't even think of it." In one fluid movement he yanked me to my feet, flung me over his shoulder, and made it to the door. "Now I will take ya out like this . . . or I can give ya one more chance to get dressed."

"You prick!" I screamed, pounding on his back.

As he turned the knob, I conceded, "All right, you win." He dropped me on the floor and I shimmied into the pants. Over my grubby bra I put on the first T-shirt that came into my hand, a tie-dyed thing. I guided my bare feet into my platform boots, splashed some water over my face, retrieved my jacket, and stood tapping a foot.

Peter shook his head as he withdrew a bottle of brown-coloured liquid from his jean jacket and unscrewed the top. "Take it," he said, holding out the foul smelling stuff.

I waved it under my nose. "What the hell is it?"

"Poppy juice . . . it'll take some of the sickness away."

I held the bottle to my lips and retched in the effort to drink it. Peter then offered the bottle to Sue. "Okay . . . let's go already. I can't afford to be here any longer." With that he grabbed my arm and nudged me to the door, where he paused to smirk at Sue. "Been a pleasure . . . I'm sure," then slammed the door.

In the dust of the hallway, he opened his hand and gestured for me to take the three yellow Valium held there. I downed them with the poppy juice.

A Mustang was parked behind the York Hotel, and Larry waved as I approached. I did my best to imitate a smile and bared my teeth. "Larry, here, is going to drive us around and see if we can score," Peter said.

I spent the rest of the day squished in the front seat with the two men while they visited all their contacts and find nothing. Peter doled out the opium juice at regular intervals. If only the juice wasn't so hard to get down, it would have been the perfect tonic, for it did help lift the sickness.

The conflicting feelings inside me circled each other like bloodied boxers in a small ring. I made little effort at conversation and spoke only when spoken to. As I listened to the banter and shared companionship between the two men, my jealousy spiked. I declined an offer of lunch and watched disinterested as the men downed their A&W burgers and shakes. I also refused to enter any of the houses or apartments where we stopped, preferring to wait alone.

I did not fit among the chippies, these occasional suburban users. I knew from past experience that my presence would only arouse anxiety about the heat they thought I brought with me. With my dress, speech, and being, the street had claimed me. Although Peter pretended otherwise, "junkie whore" might as well be burned into my forehead. The exception to my refusals was a short stop at Sandi and Blade's apartment on Thirty-third Avenue. At last, around the supper hour, with my head on his shoulder, Peter instructed Larry to drop us off at the Westgate Hotel.

He registered us as Mr. and Mrs. Brown. The clerk looked dubious at the long-haired man, who looked more like a member of some hippie rock band than a sedate Mr. Brown, while I, as Mrs. Brown, was covered with a layer of perspiration and felt as if I was suffering from some wasting disease. My clothes, although expensive, were sweat-stained and wrinkled, and my hair hung down in a long, stringy mat. He did not challenge us, however, except to demand payment in advance.

The room was neat and clean, smelling like sheets on a summer line. There was a queen-sized bed and a full bathroom, luxuries I was not accustomed to—unless I had had a good night and treated myself. But with my habit consuming most of my earnings, it was a rarity. I made my way to a small winged chair by the writing desk. Here, Peter pressed some Valium into my hand, and, as I accepted them, he said, "You know we got a lot of catching up to do, but first I want ya to have a bath."

"Fuck that!" I turned my back to him, appalled by the suggestion.

"Believe me, Beth, I'm not judging ya or nothing—and shit, I saw where you are living, but ya need a bath."

I threw myself onto the bed and buried my head under the pillow, feeling—for the first time in a long time—shame. Undisturbed by my hiding, he pushed on. "You need a bath and you're having one." With that, I was hoisted off the bed and carried into the bathroom. There, as if scaling a fish, he striped off my clothes and then lowered me into the tub and ran the water.

I suppressed an urge to struggle. I'd nowhere to go but the Beverage Block and I'd return there soon enough. He was also supplying a good assortment of drugs. If a bath was the price, it was a fair enough exchange.

His hands moved the face cloth hard, as if he wished to remove every trace, every smell of the street. He alternated this by sponging slowly, his hands lingering over my breasts and between my legs. The poppy juice and the Valium swam together in my mind and, closing my eyes, I relaxed.

Peter turned his attention to my hair, which he scrubbed with equal vigour, using a sample of Halo shampoo provided by the hotel. He worked up a sudsy lather and then I was told to stand, as he opened the shower-head to rinse the shampoo away. I saw him grit his teeth as the water cascaded over the ribs poking beneath my chest and between my jutting hipbones. He wiped his eyes from the water that splashed him and helped me from the tub.

Towel drying my hair, I noted that at least it had not lost its fullness or sheen, when clean. I moved away and began preening in the mirror above the dressing table, scrunching my hair to make the waves more pronounced. Working at being attractive was something that I had almost forgotten how to do. Men, I learned, cared only about the hole between my legs. I stared at my reflection, searching for the signs of beauty that had once graced my face.

I focused on my flinty eyes gleaming like blue stones and contemplated my options. I'd a clean bed to sleep in and he was here. Perhaps we could sort through our differences and find a connecting bridge, but I wasn't sure if I wanted to. It all seemed somehow irrelevant—sort of like losing something for a long time and then finding it, but retaining no memory of its usefulness. I tried not to think of him as a john, but then I'd never been with one who'd given me a bath before.

He appraised me coldly as he inclined against the wall. "Remember, cleanliness is next to Godliness. Ya do look better." Then he produced a plastic bag from his pocket and the smell of hash filled the room. As the smoke was exhaled, he offered it.

"I'm sick, not dirty," I said, refusing the pipe and moving to the bed.

He followed and sanded his hand across my hollowed stomach. "Beth, you'll probably take this the wrong way, as we seem to keep getting our wires crossed, but ya have to take better care of yourself. I mean, you look like a refugee from some Biafran camp or something." This time I took a turn with the pipe but made no answer, as the hash further distorted my troubled thoughts. "I think you've made the point that you're royally pissed, but this silent treatment is ticking me off. I got better things to do these last two days than to spend them with a mute. As it is, Larry can't understand what the hell I see in you and you didn't help much today. Did ya say three words to the guy?"

"What the hell do I care what he thinks? He's your friend. Where were you last night? You promised me ya'd come back."

He took another hit from the smoldering pipe. "I did come back . . . just a little late."

"Don't give me that shit. Where were you?" My mouth puckered, as I maneuvered to pin him down.

He ambled off and looked out the window. "I was screwing a sixteen-year-old, if ya must know."

"That's your excuse. I sit in a bar all fucking night waiting, sick yet . . . and you're off screwing a bopper. It's not enough that ya don't hardly write. That ya treat me like shit, and now you're screwing jail bait. That's it . . . the final fucking straw!" I jumped up.

"I don't think you'll get far," he said, again concentrating on the street scene below.

I ran to the bathroom and saw that he had hand-washed my clothes. They hung folded over the shower rod. "Shit . . . shit," I screamed.

He called out after me. "I know that you're freaking, but I came for ya . . . didn't I? I'm here and I'm all yours. Don't ruin this pass for me. It happened . . . okay . . . that's all. I would have come for ya . . . if I could have. Larry didn't want to leave the party, where we went to score. As it turns out they didn't have no dope, just cute chicks." He sauntered into the bathroom, glanced at the wet clothes and offered, "I'll buy you new ones if I've ruined these."

I hauled off and slapped his face. "You washed my clothes. Were they too dirty for you too? You arrogant fuck."

Anger curled at the corners of his mouth as he grabbed and shouldered me against the wall. "I thought I was your old man. I thought I gave a damn about you."

I threw myself against him with my fists slamming into his chest. "You ain't my old man, you made that clear . . . remember?" But he linked my wrists together and bent me to the floor where he held me as I twisted underneath the weight of his body. Furious, I opened my mouth and bit his lip. As

I tasted his blood in the mix of saliva, my teeth released their hold but he made no move to acknowledge the pain or release me. With only the sounds of heavy breathing to mark our rage, I unwrapped my legs from around his waist.

He rolled off and stretched beside me on the tiled floor. "Jesus . . . what ya have to do that for?" He wiped his sleeve against his punctured lip. "I care . . . although you got a painful way of showing your feelings. I'm still looking out for you . . . ain't I? What is it ya want? A contract or something?" I wheezed trying to catch my breath and he laughed. "I'll never promise that." I stiffened and he stroked my cheek. "I don't know what it is about you that pulls me to ya, but I've always come back. Remember how we first met at Tina's? I came in to talk to ya and you were so cute in that striped uniform, red and white. You whipped the hat off pretty quick though."

He'd teased so many times about this incident that I snapped, "Shut up," and closed my eyes.

"No . . . I don't think you want me to shut up. Ya need to smooth some of those sharp edges, but ya need me. I'm the only one left who gives a Goddamn. Don't ya see that?"

"Yah . . . I've seen this last year about your Goddamn!"

"Open your eyes for Christ's sake! I wouldn't spend these few days with ya if I didn't care? C'mon talk to me. Let's make up and don't let no stupid chippie that didn't mean nothing come between us." He helped me to my feet and we moved back to the bed.

Snug in the pit of his arm, I ventured, "I don't do much talking these days. If ya don't tell people what's on your mind . . . ya ain't likely to get shafted."

"Talk to me. Tell me what's going on in there." He tapped my head lightly.

"Talk about it . . . talk about it . . . isn't that what the shrinks say?"

"It's just too damn shitty to talk about. I'm not sure I'll ever be able to, and there's nothing you or anyone can do that will make it easier." This was as close to a confession as I could come. They were my ghosts, my nightly horrors, the violence, the bad tricks, the smell of 'cum' that clung to me.

"What of the joint?" I countered.

"Nah . . . I can't say."

"Me neither."

"I suppose some things are better left unsaid."

Covered by the weight of his body, I let him have me. He moved his hands expertly under me while his tongue circled my nipple. I struggled to enjoy him but could not. He asked, when done, "Don't ya dig sex no more?"

"Why?" I said, trying to hold the pretense, but thinking instead of the poppy juice that beckoned from the bedside table.

"Ya don't respond the way you used to. It's like you're not really giving yourself to me."

"I get fucked all the time. It's work."

"Aahhhh," he answered, and fell silent. He lowered his head to my stomach and I cradled his head between my rib cage. I probed his face and traced its outlines with my fingers, trying to read all the new lines that tracked across his profile. I traced my own facial outlines in comparison until he moved and enfolded me in his arms. With a lost sense of safety, I slept.

We awoke around lunch time and he resumed an exploration of my body. I obliged, forcing myself again to respond. When he finished we shared some cigarettes.

"Why don't we run to Toronto?" I ventured. "I could work there and support our habits. You might not like the line of work, but the jail time is considerably less than anything you might think up."

"Don't tempt me. Don't." He buried his head in my hair. "I'm shaking such bad time." It was as close to a confession as he would come. "I want ya to stay here. I'll leave the juice and some pills, and you just watch the telly. I got to check back in at my folks and do some other errands."

"Like fuck some sixteen-year-old. I'll not stay and wait for you again."

"Ah . . . yes you will, as I'm taking your clothes to make sure you stay put." With that he dressed himself, and, taking my clothes, wadded them up in his jacket. "Trust me . . . I won't be long."

I took some sleeping pills, had a good swig of the juice, and slept until six o'clock. When I awoke I wondered if it was all a dream, him being there. I shook my head to clear it, grabbed the phone beside the bed, and called the Regis Hotel asking to have Sue paged. To my relief, she picked up a few minutes later.

"What's up?" she asked. "Or is *he*?" The sound of her high-pitched giggle followed.

I saw nothing funny in my situation and complained, "He's up and been gone for hours, and took all my clothes, too. I think you're gonna have to bring me some. I gotta work. I can't stay here."

"Don't worry about work. There's no dope yet. The rumour is it'll hit in a few hours. If I score, I'll call and we'll work something out about the clothes. By the way, what a hunk."

"Now that's just what I need to hear."

"What's wrong with that? Fuck, it ain't every day that a guy pulls you from the Beverage Block and then leaves ya buck naked in a hotel room." She giggled again. "Give me the room number and I'll check with ya later." Sue hesitated and then asked, "You got any more of that juice? Good stuff that."

"Yah . . . it ain't bad. At least I'm not too sick."

"Later then." Sue hung up.

"Shit," I grumbled, feeling my options ranged from bad to worse. I drained the last of the juice, turned on the telly, and began watching *Quincy Jones*. As Quincy was wrapping up his case, my agitation mounted. I thought of calling a cab and leaving with a towel draped around me. But before I could carry out such a plan, I heard the key turn in the lock. Peter made his entrance holding several bulging paper bags.

"Looks like quite the shopping expedition," I called from the bed.

"Here . . . I stole some of my sister's stuff," he said, dropping a bag at the foot of the bed.

"Where's my stuff ?" I said, grinding my teeth together.

"I threw those old rags out. Anyway, these are pretty cool and they'll just have to do. Now you be nice and I'll show ya what else I got."

"What?" I stood to sort through the bag. There were several cotton panties, a couple of long sleeved T-shirts, a pair of bell-bottomed jeans and a belt. At the bottom was a half-empty bottle of L'air de temps. I began quickly changing, observing that they were at least a size too big and commented, "Well, at least you approved of my boots."

"Where do ya think you're going?" he asked, sitting on the chair and watching my march towards the door.

"Leaving."

"Really?" He smiled, holding out his palm. There lay two white caps.

I stepped back to him. "Shit . . . ya just get out of the joint and ya got more contacts than me." I went to take one, but he jerked his hand away.

"Are you staying?"

"Of course," I said, locking my arms around his neck.

After we fixed, he went to another of the bags and pulled out several big pops and wrapped burgers. "You gotta eat." He pushed one of them at me. The drug had settled my stomach and I obliged. As I chewed, I asked, "Why were you so mean to me . . . when I visited you in the joint?"

"I ain't going to let them use you against me again. Let'em think I don't care. If you believe I don't dig ya, then there's nothing that can change your mind. Remember the setting, and who ya came with. Let's face it, they couldn't have pinched me if I wasn't such a pussy for ya."

I smiled and finished the burger. Kneeling on the floor I huddled against his legs, letting the drug carry me away.

"What about you, Beth? Do you ever think about what's going to happen to ya?"

"No . . . I'm just walking the pavement."

"But . . . the pavement ends somewhere."

I traced round patterns on his jeans before admitting, "I used to wish for the white picket fence and kids and all that straight stuff. But it ain't going to happen." I rushed on, the drug loosening my tongue, "I mean, there just ain't no lonely hearts club for hookers. Fuck . . . they even told me I couldn't have no kids." I wiped at my eye. "I thought I was pretty bright and now my vocabulary consists of three phrases, "Fuck that, fuck it, and fuck. You tell me what I'm going to do?" I motioned to the wrappers on the dresser, "Get a job flipping burgers. There's nothing for me."

"There's me."

"Yah . . . I suppose, when you're not screwing sixteen-year-olds, but I don't believe in happy everafters anymore."

"Me . . . neither," he said, and pulled me to him. Like dried petals on the bed we curled together, leaving only the mindless black of the drug to hold us together.

Chapter Twenty-three

MY FINGERS RIFLED OVER THE magazines and plucked a *Chatelaine* off the rack, then I edged towards the window in the corner. Here I could spot the heat from any direction, and, with a feeling of safety, I spit out the balloon into the now-opened pages. Spittle dotted across the pages as I worked my cold fingers to untie the knotted rubber. I cursed as the rubber refused to release the capsules. The others would be here for the meet any minute.

I questioned my stupidity in agreeing to hand out these drugs for Jacob. There were undercover narcs on the street and a free cap at the moment did not seem like such a big deal if I accidentally handed over one of these babies in exchange for eight years. My desperation for more, always more, was driving me crazy. The last of the chalky capsules passed through the compressed opening and lay exposed in the seam of the magazine.

Gloria's nails, shaped into artfully long points, wagged a fifty dollar bill under my nose. I glanced behind and was relieved to see the clerk was bent over, cleaning the Slurpee machine. I delivered two of the caps for the bill that Gloria dropped onto the book, and then watched as Gloria sprinted towards an idling Camaro parked outside. The car squealed away and a few seconds later Jeff or Gerald, I was never sure which one of the twins it was, shoved three twenties at me. I dropped a couple of caps and a ten spot into an outstretched hand.

Behind the twins stood Vie and Terry poking my shoulder, and I saw that Sue was just coming in the door, followed by the chippies Jane and John. They crowded around and it was as if I was in the middle of a feeding frenzy—as the money came at me from all directions. I handed two caps to Jane and John and was busy counting the wad of the bills when a hand rested on my back. I shrieked in fright, jumped around, and stood face to face with my mother.

My mother's ringed fingers stroked my wrist, and her words were spoken as if she sensed that I was posed to run. "I've been worried about you."

"Christ . . . you nearly scared me to death." I shook off her touch and zipped up my jacket. I tossed the magazine back into the rack. "Didn't anyone ever tell you it isn't nice to sneak up on a person?"

"I didn't mean to scare you. I just couldn't believe that it really was you."

"Yah . . . it's me, alive and kicking. Surprised?" I moved to walk around her, but my mother threw out an arm to stop me.

She was searching through her shoulder bag and then extended a business card which she tried to tuck into my pocket. "The dentist . . . please see him. You've got such beautiful teeth. If you'll go, Dad's arranged for him to bill us."

"You can't be bothered to pay my health premiums and you want me to go see a dentist. You've got to be kidding." I threw the stalling arm back and proceeded to the door.

"Beth, wait . . . listen. I'm trying to do what I think is best. I know it doesn't seem that way to you. But I am." Tears were swimming in her eyes and leaking over her rouged face, which seemed older than I remembered.

"Throwing me out. That's what you call best! Go fuck yourself," I shouted, and stormed out the door with red-headed Debbie following, demanding her cap.

◄○►

I propped a callused heel on the edge of the night stand and unscrewed the bottle of pink nail polish. I held it up to the bulb that was dangling from the ceiling; in the syrup of the polish, flecks of fluorescence sparkled. I began stroking each toenail, noting that my hand held steady. The last fix had done little but straighten me and I longed for more. I wriggled my toes to help them dry and became lost in my thoughts.

I seemed to recall unimportant details like smells and colours. I licked my chapped lips, remembering the cups of coffee Chuck used to buy. I pictured the two of us perched on the stools at the all-night cafe on Hastings, our elbows digging through the grime on the counter, and drinking from thick china mugs. In my mind, too, were the Players cigarettes and the Turkish Delight chocolate bars, my favourite, that he always kept in his pockets.

I moved towards the bureau standing against the faded wallpaper and sprayed myself with Cinnabar cologne. As the mist lingered, I closed my eyes. I saw Chuck's hand position the fragrant package on my pillow as I lay in a drug stupor. It was wrapped with white tissue paper and held together with a wide red ribbon. I'd been so lost in the nod I'd thought it was a dream. I reprimanded myself: "Poor Chuck. The only gift he gives and I'm too damned stoned to know it's real."

I undid the two braids that ran down my back and tossed the elastics into the ashtray. The tricks wanted girls younger and younger, as if seeking their daughters. From the image in the mirror, I knew I looked older than my twenty years, even with the bluff of pigtails.

There was a slight knock on the door. I moved backwards. "Who is it?" I whispered, searching through my purse and moving the aluminum covered caps in my cigarette package to my mouth.

"It's Sue."

I unlatched the door and ushered her in. "Where you been? Look at ya, ya get skinnier every time I see ya. Just think, some beads and a twenties style hat and ya would make one hell of a flapper." I laughed and lit a cigarette.

"Just rubbing it in again that you got a set and I don't," Sue replied, bending and placing two cups of hot chocolate on the floor. Then she removed her sheepskin coat and tossed it on the unmade bed. "I'm blowing this scene. I've come to say good-bye."

I twisted the plastic lid off one of the cups and asked, "Why? Where ya going?"

I watched Sue stretch leopard-like on the stuffed high-back chair by the window and become more serious. "Peter and Chuck are gone. Sandi and Blade are in hiding from that drug round up. Shit, they even got Big Marie on that one. You, girl, are just about all I got left."

"Don't matter. Think on it—we're old timers now, you and me . . . hardly in our twenties . . . and old timers. I want to go some place new. Somewhere where there aren't any panics and no one knows ya. I'm going to Los Angeles."

"No way! Not Lost Angeles."

"Keep your voice down. No need to announce it to the world," Sue cautioned. "I got my ticket and I'm leaving in the morning."

"Ain't ya afraid? I mean, you're a small town girl. What are you going to do in such a big city?"

"Couldn't be any worse than Van," Sue countered, smoothing her cropped hair back into place.

"Well, I guess I can't change your mind," I scuffed my foot over the carpet, waiting for Sue to disagree. When this didn't happen, I reconciled mysefl to the idea and offered, "I don't got no goodbye gift to give since ya didn't tell me till tonight, but I'll share my caps."

"You know Jacob sold out tonight. It'll be dry tomorrow," she warned.

"Don't matter. It always comes in sooner or later."

"It's the later part you should be worried about," Sue said, shrugging as I popped and unwrapped the silver treasures from my mouth.

Soon we were fixed and lying side by side together on the bed. The drug was having a greater effect this time and I confessed, "I wish ya would have tole me more about yourself. I don't hardly know nothing about ya."

Sue patted my thigh and whispered, "It's better that way. No need to relive all that crap."

"That's what I'm talking about. I go on telling you everything there is to know about me and you won't tell nothing." I felt somehow used.

"Drop it, okay?" Sue warned, as she wrapped her arms around her chest.

Turning away, I bitched, "Who cares anyway?"

Sue grunted and asked, "You ever think you was just born unlucky?"

I rubbed my nose, "Nope, I just fucked up." I paused to take a drag on my cigarette. "Sometimes I can't believe I've been so stupid. I mean really . . . really stupid."

"Don't you get it? It's unlucky, I tell ya. Being in the wrong place at the wrong time. Being born into the wrong family. Being the kind of person who has the wrong friends. Being raped and beaten. Being used again and again." The words were forced through her mouth with such bitterness that Sue panted with the effort.

I fingered my hair, looked at Sue and reiterated, "Ain't that what I said . . . fucked up and stupid." We tittered together. Then I sighed and began to ask about something that was very much on my mind since the night with Peter. "Do you ever think . . . er . . . ?" I wavered before managing. "Do you ever think this life kinda turns you off men."

"If it didn't before, it sure will after. God, I can't believe you're still such a baby. Didn't you listen to the rumours? Some of us never did like men."

"Well, I did. And I don't think I will again . . . the dirty fuckers."

Sue murmured something under her breath, crossed herself, and then slipped her hand into mine. Our fingers locked together as our heads slopped towards each other and rested there while we retreated into the solitude of the nod.

◂◦▸

In the morning, there was no trace of Sue except for the empty styrofoam cups in the wastebasket. I couldn't believe she'd packed and gone without waking me to say goodbye. I had to overcome an urge to cry—whether from feeling alone or because I felt the sickness coming I didn't know. I refused to dwell on it as I dressed for the opening of the York Bar.

I ordered a lone beer from a waitress wearing scuffed shoes, and watched the butts pile up pyramid-style in the ashtray. Around lunch-time, I was joined by Jeff and Gerald, the identical twins. Their large noses bulged from their small egg-shaped faces as if to give them definition. High cheekbones and brows overshadowed their green eyes. Rarely were they seen together on the strip and so I amused myself by studying them and trying to sort one from the other. It was, I concluded, no wonder that they were successful in ripping people off and then blaming each other. I could find no difference between them and, becoming bored with it, gave up.

As the afternoon dragged on, a few more acquaintances drifted in and joined us. None of them had any leads and everyone, it seemed, was looking. Terry and Vie were the last to arrive. Even in his misery, Terry was still smiling as if his lips had nowhere to go but up. Vie was wearing a jump suit several sizes too large that accentuated her chalky colour. Terry put his arm around her and Vie rested her head on her hands.

I rose up on my elbows and leaned towards the pair, charging, "You ripped me off!"

"Shit happens," Vie muttered, as Terry stood and raised his fist. "Want to make something of it?"

"Ya, I do," I said, then reconsidered. "Another time maybe?" I eased myself back into the seat.

No one had news of any dope. There was not even a rumour of some. The word was that coke and speed were also in short supply. There would be no alternative to mask the sickness. The mood at the table became grim. By five, the sweat was running down my forehead in mini-rivers, joining the snot that streamed from my nose. I began to think of returning to my room to face these miseries in private. Just as I was gripped with another round of chills, Rick's pock-marked chin rested on the back of my neck.

"Come." He crooked his finger under my nose and I rose. This action caused a stir of consternation among the others and a ripple of anticipation worked its way around the table.

Rick's black leather jacket was zipped against the November cold and a wool scarf was corded around his scrawny neck. He stopped in the foyer of the bar. I stumbled into him as he leaned over and said, "You wanna fix?"

"That's a stupid question," I snorted and stepped back.

A smile played along his skinny lips. "All you got to do is come to a little party I'm planning with a few of the boys. I'm only inviting the better looking whores."

His back was hunched, making him appear vulture-like. "You expect me to fuck you and a few of the boys for a fix?"

"It's what you do ain't it?" he replied, then barked—"There ain't no stuff to be had except for me, and ya either do it or go sick." A grin crinkled his eyes into slits.

"But I got money!" I protested, my hand wiping some of the snot from my face.

"That's just it my dear, everyone in there has money and it ain't money I want. So think this offer over before I make it to someone else."

"Fine," I puffed, "But I get fixed first. I ain't fucking sick."

"Who'd want you sick?" Rick said, as he pinched my arm and led the way to an old Lincoln Continental parked in front of the hotel. The engine was running and a stream of fog was escaping from the exhaust. I got into the back seat beside Margie, a working girl new to the strip. Vanessa, a high-end hooker who usually worked the better class hotels, was in the front passenger side with a fur hat pulled over her head. Neither of the two acknowledged me. "Things must be rough all over," I spat.

We were driven to the Midnight Motel on Macleod Trail. Rick parked near the back of the building and hurried us into a room on the ground floor. Once the door was closed and bolted, he ordered, "Get undressed."

We obliged, stepping out of our clothes and discarding them in piles on the carpet. We stood clustered together, avoiding eye contact and staring at our feet. After what seemed an interminable length of time, Rick called Margie into the washroom and fixed her, then Vanessa. At last it was my turn. I refused to speak as he motioned for my arm and grunted as the liquid was pushed into my vein. I returned to the bedroom feeling much better and sat on the bed with the other two. The silence was uncomfortable even with the calming effects of the drug. I darted back into the bathroom, interrupting Rick's fix. "Do I at least get to buy a couple of caps after this is over?"

"It depends on how good you are," Rick replied, drawing blood up the dulled point of the needle.

I retreated. What did that mean, I wondered? How good did it have to be? I did not have long to wait for the answer, for there was a knock on the door. Rick welcomed in two men with handshakes and laughter. One was familiar, Neil, a chippie that I had seen at some of the bigger meets. The other was an unknown, who looked close to thirty. They'd been drinking, I could smell the alcohol on their clothes.

Rick thumbed to the three of us sitting on the bed. I noticed that all our thighs were pulled tight, as if to hide our thatch of pubic hair. I stifled an urge to fold my arms across my breasts, and instead gave the men a glare. The other two women lowered their eyes and dropped their heads, as if they had already submitted to whatever the men had in mind.

Rick ran a comb through his greasy hair and pointed me out to Neil. "Told ya, you'd have your hands full with that one. Independent and willful. Needs a strong hand—like a back hand." Rick raised his palm and waved it at me.

"Nothing I can't handle," Neil replied.

My mouth stretched into a rigid line while Neil hung his fur-lined coat in the closet. With exaggerated movements he unbuttoned a cotton shirt with a wide collar, exposing his fleshy body. His breasts were engorged with fat and hung down his hairless chest. His dress pants slid to the carpet and chimed as a silver belt buckle bounced. He strutted in front of the three of us on the bed, moving his hands to lift his flaccid penis. "Ladies, you will soon get a personal introduction to Big Willy."

Rick and the man they called Shawn laughed and followed Neil's example. Shawn's build was toned and smooth. Rick's was gaunt and stringy, straight down to his pointed, bony toes. The pock marks also covered his torso in puckered pits. An ulcer oozed pus on his left leg. I turned away. Amused, Rick chuckled and kneeled down beside me, moving his face along the inside of my leg. "Don't worry, you're not my type," he whispered and leapt across me to grab Margie. They tumbled off the bed and thudded to the floor. I watched as arms and legs twisted, moved and cemented into a rocking beat. Margie was all but lost beneath Rick's gyrating body.

Shawn pulled Vanessa down on top of him, rolling her next to Rick, who laughed and began licking Vanessa's breast as he continued to plough into Margie. There were now four people in an L shape grinding and butting into each other. I scouted for an escape. Neil, who had finished strutting, was pulling me off the bed by my ankles. I held a hand up in a stop motion and pushed against his chest. "Ya know," I drawled, as I landed on my back on the floor, "it's pretty bad when one's own kind takes advantage."

"It's the golden rule. Who's got the dope makes the rules, and these are my rules." He twisted my nipple and I winced.

"Tell ya what, go wash Big Willy and I'll play." I tried to smile through gritted teeth.

"Why don't you do it for me?" he said, nibbling the top of my ear.

"After what I got in mind, it's the least you can do." I ran my finger tips along his spine and gently caressed his buttocks.

"Shit, if that's all it's gonna take." He heaved himself up and waddled towards the bathroom. When I heard the water running, I scooped my clothes from the floor and bolted.

In the parking lot, I wriggled into my jeans as the frost in the ground found its way into my feet. I realized I had no shoes. Like a long-toothed rat, Rick's face peered around the door as I struggled to pull my sweatshirt over my head. His tone was ominous. "You're finished. No one will sell to you and if I get my hands on ya, I'll kill ya myself."

The door shut with a loud thud and I sprinted towards Macleod Trail, the sweatshirt still plugged around my neck. I struggled to hold my coat and purse, while flagging for a cab or a passing motorist. I ran and waved at the steady stream of rush hour traffic. The soles of my feel were burning with cold as I put as much distance between myself and that room. At last, a youngish woman pulled over and offered a lift.

Back in my room, I smoked half a pack of cigarettes to calm myself and then began packing. Rick was right, I was finished. I had no one to score for me; since Rick was the man, my only option was to return to Vancouver. My street life in Calgary was over.

I wondered as I buckled up my suitcase if running had been worth it; it was, after all, only a fuck.

Chapter Twenty-four

THE BEDSIDE LAMP CAST A feeble light, outlining Sandi and me huddled in the middle of the room, slowly circling each other, as if playing some girlish game. My hands were flying through the air, as I insisted, "You gotta go . . . something's going down. I can't explain it . . . I just feel it."

Sandi's husky voice growled back, "If you want to be rid of me . . . say so. Don't give me this crap."

I threw my arms up in exasperation. "What are you talking about? I like having the company. I know you need a place to hang, but ya got to trust me on this one."

"We've only been here three days. No way have they tracked me here. I ain't hardly even gone out." Sandi cracked her gum then tucked her tongue into the centre of the wad, blew a bubble, and popped it loudly.

"You think because you and Blade split up it'll be harder for the narcs to find ya and I keep telling ya they got ways to tell them who ya hang with. They could track me. I'm working every night." I retreated to lean against the window sill, and after taking a deep breath added, "It's a bad feeling I got."

Sandi advanced and, undeterred by the difference in our height, snapped: "It's one thirty in the morning. Where am I supposed to go?" Her jaws worked up and down. But receiving no response, she conceded, "All right . . . I'll go after we get some sleep."

I pulled myself to my full height and towered over the smaller girl. "No . . . it has to be now."

This action didn't seem to register on Sandi. "If you're wrong about this, I'm gonna be some pissed off. You'll get your next licking from me. Besides, if you're so fired up about this feeling, why don't you come with me?"

I licked my dry lips searching for the right words. "It ain't me with the warrants. If they come, it'll be better for them to draw a blank."

Sandi pushed her face into mine and rumbled, "And I never heard anything so stupid! You expect me to believe that they're on to me? Seems more likely you're a rat that got a conscience?"

"Why does everyone have to be so fucking paranoid? I do get these feelings once in a while and they're always right." I lit a cigarette and exhaled the smoke in the other girl's direction. "A rat, my ass!"

Her voice lowering, Sandi acknowledged. "It ain't a big deal, I guess, especially since, according to you, it's my ass on the line." She spit her wad of gum into her hand. "I'll fix first, though." Her compact body had grown fuller and her jeans puckered around her thighs, making it difficult for her to fish the small wad of tinfoil from inside her pocket.

We each injected a cap, which didn't affect either of us much. It acted as a barrier to hold the sickness at bay for another few hours. I began to wipe the spoon with the edge of my T-shirt but Sandi grabbed it, cranked open the window, and tossed the bloodied fit and the blackened spoon to the street below.

"What ya do that for? Where am I gonna get another fit? A kid could find that!" I cupped a hand over my mouth in disbelief and stuck my head through the opening only to jump back as Sandi slammed it shut again.

"If you think I'm going down, then I ain't going to have nothing on me and neither should you. When I'm facing eight years, I should give a damn about some kid or where you can score another fit?" Sandi pulled a pair of work socks over her bare feet. Over her long-sleeved shirt she slipped into a man's cardigan with deep pockets on the sides and, lastly, placed her long black wig on her head.

Within minutes she gathered her possessions into a battered canvas bag. "I don't know if I'll see you again if they're as hot on my tail as you think, but take care of yourself, Miss, I can see the future." Sandi made a movement as if she was peering into a crystal ball.

I smiled and ignored her attempt at humour. "If everything turns out fine, I'll meet ya at the Gastown Bar tomorrow around five o'clock." I grasped the shorter woman's forearm and we hugged.

This show of affection tilted Sandi's wig over one eye and I found it hard to hide my amusement as she adjusted it. Then, resting her hand on the doorknob, said, "Hopefully later, then."

More like a prayer I repeated, "Hopefully later."

➤◯➤

I reached and turned off the almost useless lamp, and in the enfolding dark a swell of doubt washed over me. It did seem stupid pushing Sandi out into the street at 2 AM on nothing more than a feeling. The walls of the small room seemed to tilt, as I tossed on the bed hoping to let sleep claim me.

Less than an hour later my mouth parted into a frightened *O* as I was hurled to the floor. There was a loud crack as my nose took the brunt of the fall. A man wedged his knee into my spine and my head was held down with the flat of his hand. My arms were wrenched behind my hips and steel cuffs were locked around my wrists. Unable to see what was happening, I heard my lungs whistle in and out. The search began in earnest and the sounds of destruction intensified.

"We're too late. The bitch we wanted is flown and this one's fixed," one of the men complained. Their determined hunt turned up nothing; the evidence they wanted littered the sidewalk below.

With a sense of satisfaction at Sandi's foresight, I parted my lips and sucked in dust as I attempted a smile. But it vanished as one of the men removed a loose wallboard in the closet and there was a snap of splinters as his fist pushed through. From inside he produced a rotted dun-coloured cloth and examined the glass fit scrolled inside.

The insistent pressure on my back was released and I was yanked to my feet. The four plain-clothes men clustered around and one of them recited my rights in a memorized monotone, his words detonating in my brain.

◄○►

Confined in the humid cells of the city bucket, I was racked by the sickness of withdrawal. The place was crowded with thirty occupied steel bunks and I was disoriented by frequent bunk changes as the number of inmates fluctuated in a continual ebb and flow. Some were released while others were shipped off to Oakalla Prison. All the confusion, combined with the smoke and the noise, augmented my misery by inducing splitting headaches.

One of the older women, once a country and western singer, crooned the lonesome twang of heartbreak from a nearby bunk. The songs were comforting and gave voice to some of my own hurting as I lay in pools of my vomit.

I'd phoned Mr. MacKrow, my lawyer, on the day of my arrival, but in court on my second day he'd been unable to convince a judge to release me on my own recognizance. My only option now was a stint in Oakalla until my trial date, set eight weeks away. On the third day I was transported there along with four other women.

It was an interminable ride as we sat bunched and shackled in the transport van. The sense of gratification I'd experienced in escaping the bucket mingled with anxiety at where I was going. My hair slithered down my back in a greasy mass. My clothes absorbed the stink of the sickness and mingled with other foul body odours, making my skin crawl.

Through the window of the van I saw that we'd stopped in front of a square building positioned on a sloping hillside. Manicured grass just turning brown under the waning sun of early winter stretched as far as the eye could see. Further below, dipping slightly with the gradual incline, was a larger building in a *T* shape. As I stared, the woman beside me wiped brown fingers across her lips and muttered, "The men's prison."

Two female guards ordered us out. We converged briefly before being shoved into single file and led along a fenced corridor. At the end, a thick steel door was buzzed open and we were inside the prison.

Fluorescent lights glared, hurting my eyes and making the headache worse. We arrived in an enclosed cement room. Shower heads lined the wall while, below, a great steel grill was fitted for drainage. Here we were directed to undress and shower. Each inmate was issued a bar of Ivory soap and handed a white terry towel. When finished, we were guided into the next room and ordered to bend over the wide white sinks that stretched along three of the walls. Latexed hands scoured my head and pubic hair with Klewalia Shampoo.

I could smell the crisp clean uniform of the nurse, who, afterward, examined each of us in a cursory manner. Next I was presented with a smock dress the colour of ashes and a pair of matching felt slippers. Then I was taken and locked into an over-sized dorm room. Of the six steel bunk beds only one remained vacant—a bottom berth next to the barred window, where the darkening light squeezed through the iron bars. I tried to ignore the silent appraisal of curiosity and the contempt of the other inmates as I crumpled on the bed. The sickness left me too weak to care or respond. Rustling above me, a bunkmate snuffled, "You too."

"Yah." I managed, trying to cut off the snot that leaked from my nose with my fingers. It was already staining the scrubbed white covering in a wide pool.

"Tomorrow the Doc comes and we'll get Methadone."

"Another day," I groaned. "I've been sick for days."

The withdrawal made sleep impossible and the long night dragged on. Suddenly the screams of a woman pierced the air: "I can't piss and it hurts. It hurts. I can't stand it."

In the ensuing fracas, between the howls of the woman, two female nurses managed to hook up a catheter. As the bag began to fill, the woman ceased her frantic cries and a semblance of peace was restored to the dorm.

◄○►

After my visit with the prison doctor the next morning, the Methadone ingested, I finally ate. My plastic tray held a small bowl of thick stew with a crusty roll. There was a glass of milk and two pads of butter. The lime Jell-O with whipped cream was a special treat: I licked the bottom of the bowl.

Later I was moved upstairs to a small rectangular cell where the cinder blocks were painted a light yellow. The floor was a neutral tile and a built-in desk bordered the length of the room. On the other side were the two bunks. The top one was obviously mine, as an oversized woman occupied the bottom bunk. I guessed that my roommate must be least two hundred and fifty pounds. The last bit of a perm fizzled on the ends of her silver-streaked hair. Her cheeks were as round as plump tomatoes and stained with tears.

"Hi, I'm Beth." I held out my thin hand, which was swallowed by a wet, wide palm.

"I'm Doris." More tears streaked across her face and splashed on the shapeless fabric of her uniform.

I smiled, uncertain how to respond, turned my back, and began rifling through the drawers in the desk. This was more out of curiosity than any-thing else, since I'd no belongings to fill them. Then I scrambled to the top bunk and squeezed the ends of the pillow together to prop up my head. Below, the woman began weeping. I covered my ears with my hands. This was going to be a lot tougher than I first thought. A face appeared in the reinforced glass of the cell door, a key turned in the lock, and I was now confined for the night with the sobbing woman. I reached for my tin of tobacco and began the laborious process of rolling cigarettes while beneath me the rasps and wheezes of my cell mate subsided.

"I suppose you think I'm nuts," Doris sniffled, while her voice edged higher. "I'm headed to Kingston Penitentiary . . . so far from my kids." With renewed vigour another rasp ignited the woman's weeping.

I lit the first of my cigarettes, and in an effort to slow the woman's wails, asked, "What ya do to get pen time?"

Doris stopped for a moment and blew her nose. "My brother is a big-time heroin importer and he asked me to cut and bag his stuff. The money was good and I've got six kids. The rest of the story you've probably guessed. They busted us and charged us with trafficking. Got eight years."

"That's a bitch," I replied, becoming more interested in the woman and remembering my father telling me once: everyone has a story. One only has to listen.

Another round of grief gripped the woman's frame making the bunks rattle. After a few minutes of silence Doris asked. "What's your beef ?"

"Busted for a glass fit. Some relic they found in the closet. Funny thing was I could feel those bastards coming. I warned my girlfriend Sandi to hightail it out of there. I guess I was more worried about her, 'cause she's wanted, when I should have been thinking of myself. I mean I was clean and they find this stupid antique from the fifties."

Receiving the woman's attention with her spaced, "Un-hah's," I continued. "Got busted almost two years ago with this dealer friend of mine. They caught me with eight caps and it was the same play—they were his. So I know kinda how you feel. It was my first beef and that, coupled with a good lawyer I paid for out of my education fund, helped. Only got a year's probation, but my friend got eight years."

Doris shifted and the steel frame groaned. "Got a husband? Any kids?"

"No. My old man got popped for an AR but he doesn't. . . ." I faltered for a moment. "I guess I'm on my own."

"You a hooker?"

"Don't see any other way to support a habit without having to do eight years. This other friend of mine got popped at the bus station a few months ago—same deal, eight years." I finished and butted out the cigarette. My tongue was burning with the unfamiliar shit end.

"Well, don't worry. I'll take you under my wing while I'm here," the woman said, blowing her nose again.

"Thanks. But I look out for myself."

"Suit yourself." The woman muttered. "Better get undressed, 'cause it'll be lights out in a half-hour."

The days smudged into each other in a predictable, monotonous pattern. Breakfast was at eight, and at eight thirty I was placed in a large hall with a pile of wool socks. These I darned for three hours. There was the occasional whisper or low giggle, but otherwise the place was still as each woman applied her darning needle—some more skilled than others, but each willing. If not, you could be transferred to scrubbing floors, washing windows, or polishing doorknobs. This work, though tedious, was easy enough. After lunch, I returned to darning for two more hours, and then it was free time. During these hours you could watch TV in the common room, or sleep, or, in my case, smoke endlessly and think.

The freefall of my life never quite seemed to be over, and how I wished it was. When I turned my mind to it, and I hadn't for a long time, I had nothing. No children, no husband, my friends were either in jail or skipping around so much that I could not find them. My mood was further burdened by Doris's nightly sob sessions. The woman was inconsolable. Even as she darned her socks across the table from me her tears would run, streaming down her cheeks. I could feel myself slipping down a rocky slope, finding it impossible to maintain my angry stance, my shield. Vulnerability was working its way to the surface, which would mark me for persecution by my peers. They left Doris alone; I assumed it was due to the woman's age or because of her brother's connections.

Yesterday morning Sheri, a 20-something with brown hair braided straight down her back, had refused to pass me the toast. This was the first test. We were forbidden to stand once seated, so I'd thrown myself across the table, snatched a piece, and given the woman a dirty look. The cocky girl responded by making a gesture of ringing a chicken's neck, and I'd drawn a line across my throat. But inside I'd quaked and tried to remember the words of others who'd been in the joint. "Be tough. Don't back down. Take a licking, but fight back." But it was the same code as the street and therefore not much help.

I'd called Mr. MacKrow's office the first chance I got, demanding to get out of this place. The receptionist told me firmly that Mr. MacKrow was in court. There was nothing that could be done until my trial. No, my court date would not be moved, and I must call back in a few days if I had any further concerns.

"Any further concerns," I fumed, returning to my room. I longed to sit beside Doris and cry along with her, but, instead, I paced. I would not allow myself to be weak.

The next morning Doris was transferred to Kingston. I'd tolerated the woman's grief for over ten days and I found it a relief not to listen any longer to the whimpers of her fear and loss. That afternoon with my thoughts more settled, I asked the matron for paper and a pencil and began a letter.

> *Dear Peter*
>
> *I got picked up for possession again. An old fit they found in my room. So, I'm cooling my heels in Oakalla. I don't think much of it, but I am getting a small idea of what it is you go through.*
>
> *I missed you when I got up in the morning at the Westgate Hotel on your last pass, but then you always said you hated good-byes. I would have liked the opportunity, as sometimes I fear that we may never see each other again. I mean bad shit seems to be going down all the time. If I'd known what would happen to me and to you, I would have cut the scene when I still could.*
>
> *Not hard to tell that I'm unhappy and I'll have my first fight on my hands soon. The set up is in place. Having all this time to fill certainly makes me ramble and I always did like to ruminate. I suppose you heard from those gossiping hens in Prince Albert that I hung out with Chuck for a while. He's a nice guy and I feel bad he got popped. He was the best friend I've had since you left.*
>
> *Anyhow, since I'm settled in here until I go up I thought I'd send this. I'll go now and see if they'll let me post it after the matron reads it. I'd like to say more but it seems inhibiting having someone else read my stuff first.*
>
> *So until later, Beth,*

I decided not to inform my family of my latest predicament, and slowly I picked another piece of paper and jotted a short note to Chuck.

> *Dear Chuck,*
>
> *Hope this finds you. I don't really know where you are so I'm addressing it to Oakalla—and by the way you'll be surprised that I'm in here too. I sure miss you and I wanted to thank you for everything you did for me.*
>
> *It's a mess the way things worked out. I haven't heard if you got sentenced yet. Let me know okay?*
>
> *Sandi and Blade are still on the lam. They were right about the undercover buys. I guess being disguised helps. Too bad we didn't think of it. The strip is pretty bare. Big Marie and Old Jimmy were in on that scoop as well. Young Jimmy got killed up north on some rig accident. Sue is gone to Los Angeles, so it's more lonely than ever.*
>
> *Love and Friends, Beth*

I flopped down on the bottom bunk, which I had claimed for myself since Doris's departure, and wondered how I'd endure the next six weeks before my trial. The monotony of the hours seemed to extend endlessly into the boring days, like a lead sinker weighing me down. Our schedule never varied. I'd no choice but to accept the dreary routine of my incarceration.

Daydreaming my way to lunch one afternoon I was caught off guard. Sheri cornered me and slammed me against the wall, hissing, "Your ass is mine. Understand?"

"It ain't going to no toast miser," I snapped, shoving her away, but the woman's strength was surprising. I managed to escape the other girl's wedge of weight and, when I was safely down the hall, gave her the finger.

Now my anxious thoughts ran in circles about when and where the next attack would take place. Danger lurked in the hallways, the dining room, the common room, and the work room. Sheri seemed to shadow me everywhere, always in the background. It was a relief when the matron's key turned the bolt and locked me in for the night. The woman's words, "Your ass is mine," was chilling. I couldn't understand why I'd been singled out.

I refused to be intimidated in front of the other girls, but alone at night I was more fearful than I ever had been on the street. Thick and heavy, my cigarette smoke was my only comfort.

—◄o►—

During free time the matron unexpectedly handed me a couple of letters. One was from my father and the other from Peter. Surprised, and thinking I'd get the bullshit out of the way first, I opened Dad's. On the plain paper I detected the faint smell of Old Spice.

> *Dear Beth,*
>
> *Even if that means having to do jail time, I am praying that you will find it worthwhile to get into the routine of a normal life. It will take time, dear, but you can make it "a day at a time" until you are really steeled in your determination to avoid (like the worst of demons or plague itself) anything or anyone who might be in or near the subculture group with whom you are associated. You must know there is no way you can see your friends and not get dragged back.*
>
> *Remember there is no such thing as just one more time or now and then. Just once is back all the way to the bottom in jig time— it's a toboggan slide with death at the end of the run and misery all the way down.*
>
> *I hope you can see now that individuals just have to conform to some of the rules if they want to be free to live a decent life. I'm not going to go on and on with moralizing or philosophizing— you might call it preaching—but to summarize: We love you. We pray for you and we are made happy when you face up to your just punishment. I know one is never cured of the curse of addiction in the sense that one must face years of being determined, and cut off every contact with the past in order to fashion a new life. I pray for you. I pray for others, too, who are trying to break away and to become valuable to someone.*
>
> *I know you can never be what you were as a little girl. You are a woman now. Please do your best for you and for us and for society and what it can mean to you in the long run.*

I love you little girl.
Sincerely, Dad

As if, I thought, wondering how Dad knew about my stint in Oakalla. But smelling the paper one more time, I placed it gently under my pillow. Next I opened Peter's letter.

Dear Beth,

As usual I have no idea how to get a hold of you so I've sent this on to your folks. You see, a funny thing has happened and I am not the person I was and, for sure, neither are you. What I mean is that you have to have respect in order to have love and I just can't respect what you're doing to yourself. I don't think you even respect yourself. The time we spent together was just one big farce on my part and I always wanted to be up front with ya and that's the way I see it.

So I guess that's it then.

Peter

P.S. Thanks for the gift that keeps on giving.

I threw the paper down in a rage and stormed off to see the matron. Minutes later I was carving my words into the paper.

Dear Peter,

How dare you think it was me when it could have been that sixteen-year-old chippie you two timed me with! I go to the health clinic once a month to be checked and I can assure you that although I might have needed a bath, I was clean.

Of course we're not the same people. What do you expect? I will never again be that girl and you will never again be that boy. Those two stupid fucked up kids are gone and in their places are two stupider fucked up adults.

As for everything being a farce—if that's what you call the time we spent together, then that is what it was, a farce. Thanks for enlightening me. It won't happen again.

Beth

I went to my bunk and cried as hard as Doris ever had.

—◦—

One grey morning my routine was disrupted by the matron who pulled me from the darning room and told me to pack. My trial date had been moved up. Within the hour I was escorted back to the city bucket for my trial.

A day later I was free. Mr. MacKrow came through: another probation, six months. It was a miracle, a gift.

Chapter Twenty-five

THE RIDGES OF THE BRICK, steel, and glass office towers funneled the rain in cold torrents along the flooded streets. The sky, darkened by the ominous cover of clouds, grumbled. With a faint hum, the street lights sputtered and came to life. The splash from the rush hour traffic doused my boots and I could feel the moisture flatten my hair against my head. Oblivious to the downpour I angled along, carrying a umbrella hooked on my arm and ignoring the curious stares from those smart enough to huddle in doorways and overhangs.

A leftover Santa peered from behind the tawdry window of a pawnshop. Its round face, adorned with leftover tinsel and framed with twinkling lights, was a reminder of yet another Christmas spent alone. I turned away. Out of the joint for over a month and I'd yet to run into anyone I knew; even the dealers' faces changed nightly, I thought, stomping through a puddle. I preferred not to venture too far from the safety of my austere room or the familiar sidewalks of Granville Street, but my body's continual need forced me into the night. The neon signs and shuttered shops were left behind as I snaked my way through the back alleys heading towards the smoky bars of the city's decaying core. Once there, I was surrounded by the other creatures of the night—the hustlers, pimps, and drunks.

I slipped into a bar and stood for a few minutes by the exit, stifling an urge to shake myself like a wet dog. I scanned for a familiar face or an indication from some stranger that they knew why I was there. Tonight everyone seemed to have features that reminded me of someone else. The man leaning against the wall next to me had Peter's eyes; the woman hurrying from the washroom, Sandi's hair; the petite waitress rushing by, Sue's figure.

"Christ," I muttered. I was acting more like I was on an acid trip than a junkie coming down. I tried to shag off my edgy feelings but there was something going on. I'd begun to have panic attacks, feeling as if the tricks were suffocating me, and I was finding it increasingly difficult to work. More disturbing was that the soothing effects of the heroin did not purge these irrational fears. A few times I'd flipped out and pounded on a slicked chest greased with fervid sweat screaming, "Get off. Get off!" It definitely was not good for business. I'd tried to reassure myself that the sensation of drowning under the johns would pass, but it hadn't.

Rick's voice, dripping with sarcasm, played over in my mind: "It's what you do, ain't it?" I lit a cigarette and sucked on it hard, trying to distract myself from these troubling anxieties. As a red-frocked waitress approached with a smile, I skirted around her and began circulating between the crowded tables asking, "Have you got?" One of the groupings I approached, seasoned toughs sporting biker colours, parted to make way and enclosed me in their midst. Our transaction was quickly made.

I waited to fix in my room and then changed into a comfortable short sleeved T-shirt that hung down to my knees, the word "Pussycat" printed in red was now barely visible under the grimy grey of the garment. The nod escaped, and I stared blankly at the fracturing walls. Once painted green, they'd blanched to a lifeless pasty colour. A wool blanket covered my cold feet against the damp of the place. I lay on the bare mattress trying to imagine the warmth of another body lying next to me. My hand rolled into a fist as if holding on to the emptiness. My nails dug into my palm as a loud rap on the door pounded its way into my consciousness. I grabbed at my dope, and with the wad of tinfoil safely in my mouth, I yelled, "Yah . . . whaya want?"

"It's Lanny."

"Get lost," I growled, while a cramp of alarm doubled me over.

"Let me in. I got something to tell ya."

"Nothing I want to hear." Why hadn't I the foresight to have a room with a phone? I twisted on the bed seeking a way out, but there was only the small window and a drop of four floors to the street below.

"Honest, I won't hurt ya. Just listen to what I've come to say." His voice took on a quality reminiscent of a used car salesman's pitch. "You and I got off on the wrong foot is all. One chance to talk to ya is all I want. C'mon, what's there to lose?"

"The wrong foot, my ass, and my dog . . . I lost my dog because of you!"

"That dog got a great home with some good folks in Chilliwack. Middle-class straight johns. Think on it for a minute. He got a better life than with you, going from one hotel to another, and, to boot, it squared up what you owe me. Besides, don't think I don't know who stole my car and rammed it into a pole. You and that prick, Chuck. I'd say we're even. Now, are you going to open the door or not?"

I savoured again the sweetness of revenge, remembering Chuck hot-wiring the old Chevy we'd seen Lanny driving around in and imagining the crunching of it into a crumpled mess.

Lanny's pounding chased the memory away. "Are you still there? Jesus, I hate it when a woman don't answer back. You gonna let me in?"

"No, I'm not."

"Well then, I'm sitting right here and you'll have to come out sooner or later."

I heard a shuffling noise and a black form covered the crack between the door and the floor. I rubbed my nose. Then, overcome with anger, I swung the door open. With the bedside lamp gripped in my hands, I swung it at Lanny's head as he fell into the room.

He rolled out of the way and, regaining his footing, waved me off. "I tole ya . . . I ain't gonna hurt ya, but don't push it!" His hair was clean for a change, but full of static that electrified his split ends. His clothes looked as if he'd lived in them for months and I wrinkled my nose at the stink.

"Well! What the hell do you want?" I asked, and then began laughing as I realized what an ineffectual weapon the lamp was. It was nothing more than a four-inch stick with a bulb on the end of it.

He chuckled as he vaulted past and shut the door. "Sit and put that stupid thing down. I got a deal for you. There's a mark looking to score some high-grade stuff, a real bozo with more money than brains. You could play the part of the mule. I'll split the take—should be a couple of thousand each or more. Besides, I know you ain't been working much and could probably use the money."

I flung a arm across my chest. "How do you know what I'm working?"

He smiled, exposing his crooked bottom teeth. "I know a lot of things."

I eyed him, then, deciding it didn't matter what he knew, changed the subject. "You sure this guy ain't got no street connections?"

"None whatsoever." He thumped his thigh and pulled his drooping shoulders straight.

"I'll think on it," I responded, but knowing my other alternative was more men climbing on top of me, I patted the bed. "Tell me more."

He perched on the corner and coughed—a deep wracking hack that folded him over while it worked its way up from his lungs. After a few minutes he wheezed, "You hear that Rick and a few of the boys held a party months back and one of the girls OD'd?"

"No," I answered, trying to hide my intense interest by looking at my chipped red nails. "You should do something about that bark. It don't sound too good."

"It's nothing that won't cure itself," he said, lighting a cigarette. Then clearing the phlegm from his throat and inhaling deeply, he continued. "A new girl—Margie I think was her name. Died anyway. They threw her in a dumpster in some alley off Fifty-eighth in the industrial park area. I also heard you was there," he said glancing over.

"Yah, right, me and Rick." I puffed, hoping he wouldn't notice the slight tremble in my hand.

"Stranger things have happened. My God, who'd have thought that out of the old crowd it's down to practically just you and me. Old Vie's on her last legs and Goofus got popped for robbing a bank. I guess he didn't get his name for nothing." It was his turn to chortle, "You heard that Sandi and Blade got picked up?"

I shook my head, as he rattled on. "Yah, the cops staked them out on Macleod Trail. Held up traffic both ways. Ten cop cars to take them down, is what I heard. Wild, eh?"

I shrugged, trying to hide my apprehension and a biting sense of loss. "Just before I went to the joint Sandi said we probably wouldn't see each other again. But I can't figure why she went back to Calgary. She knew they'd be easier to catch if they was together," I said, and holding the end of my T-shirt, scrubbed at my misty eyes.

"Probably got lonely," he concluded and then asked, "you written to Chuck?"

My throat felt constricted. "Once in Oakalla."

"What about your old man, Peter? You hear from him?"

"What business is that of yours?" I snapped, sitting up rigidly.

"Just curious is all," he replied mildly and continued his chatter about the latest panic Calgary was now only coming out of.

I knew the only reason I let him talk was to be near another being. I'd been alone for so long and desperate for the sound of another human voice, I mused, even Lanny's raw-edged monotone seemed consoling. As he droned on, I relaxed into the thin pillows and drifted into the nod.

When I surfaced, I picked up something about a job he'd held at sixteen. "I don't want your life story."

"Well, if you want me to shut up just say so. I didn't mean to put ya to sleep." He sulked for a couple of minutes. "Did Sandi tell ya why they knew those guys were narcs? Asked for horse . . . everyone knows only narcs use that kind of language. They knew better," he said and then ventured. "You mind if I crash here? I'll sleep on the floor. Won't be no trouble."

"Lanny, you're always trouble." I threw him one of the pillows.

In the morning I insisted he take a bath. But when we looked into the bathroom at the end of the hall, we saw the toilet had overflowed, spreading fouled water across the floor. "Good thing junkies don't have to go often," he said, pleased to have an out.

"You reek something awful," I said as we walked away and he agreed to sneak a shower at the YMCA. When he returned a few hours later I found him less objectionable and so said nothing about him continuing his stay.

He began setting the scam in action. It was three and half weeks before the rip-off was set and in play. To keep his habit fed, Lanny did some free-lancing as a B&E artist in the evenings, as I refused to support him. I'd a hard enough time to turn enough tricks a night to keep myself fixed. On more than one occasion I'd bolted from the first john who'd approached and returned empty handed. When he asked about it I could only mumble, "I can't is all. I just can't."

He frowned, and I knew he didn't understand, but then neither did I. He'd jimmy me with the understanding that I'd return the favour when I pulled myself together.

◄○►

The end of January slowly slipped forgotten into February, and I became used to Lanny's presence, even allowing him after the first few nights to sleep on the bed. We lay side by side, never touching, locked in parallel worlds, but the sound of his breathing was reassuring. I was still leery of his fists but he hadn't tried to push me around. I assumed this was because he thought of me as his partner and not his whore.

The rip-off was to go down the day before Valentine's Day, and so the night before we stayed up stuffing empty gelatin capsules with icing sugar. When that was finished we painstakingly made twenty bundles, and a cloud of the white sugary dust coated our clothes and faces. My job was to remember the off-coloured purple balloon and to appear to naturally extend it for the tasting. The top caps inside held a salting of the real thing, so they would easily pass a taste test. If the mark wanted to fix I'd be in trouble, but that was unlikely, Lanny assured me, as the transaction would take place in his car.

The next morning we were off boosting for my clothes. I decided on a pair of dress pants, a white blouse, and a checked blazer, all easily lifted from Eatons. I wanted to wear my funky leather boots with the four-inch heels but he observed, "Remember you're supposed to be a professional person. Only working girls wear those kind of things." Instead, I purchased a pair of black leather pumps he'd spotted a few days back at a thrift store.

With everything prepared, I packed the bundles into a plastic Safeway bag, tied the ends, and tucked it into my purse. Lanny began cursing our stupidity and blundered out, leaving me. But he returned a half-hour later with a charcoal briefcase in his hand. Some initials were engraved in gold letters by the lock, which he easily opened. We threw away the important looking papers inside and he transferred the bundles into it.

In silence we sat, the air growing thick with our smoke until about twelve thirty. Then he gave the A-okay signal and I split. With my out-stretched thumb, it was only a matter of minutes before a van stopped, and I was clamouring over the camping equipment that was crammed into the back. The young couple in the front informed me that they were on their honeymoon. I extended my best wishes as they dropped me off at the west entrance of Stanley Park.

Here I watched for a cream-coloured Mercedes. To the man driving I would say, "Nice day," and he'd respond with, "What do you expect from the Caribbean of Canada?"

I walked in a tight circle, waiting. As the minutes dragged by, my stomach gurgled with tension. I stopped and rubbed the briefcase across my middle, willing it to settle. Then I noticed the crocuses were blooming. Today was a typical West Coast day; and with the winter clouds blocking the sun, I took the mauve blossoms as a good sign.

A horn sounded and I spotted a white Mercedes breaking to a full stop. I ran forward, heard the automatic locks click open, stuck my head in the passenger door and said, "Nice day."

A thirty-something man with black hair and wide sideburns responded, "What do you expect from the Caribbean of Canada?" and indicated for me to get in. He didn't exude any warmth, but at the same time he didn't seem threatening either.

I kept the edges of my lips turned up. I wanted to be pleasant and approachable, the way I thought a real estate agent might look. But my demeanor did not affect the man, for we drove along in silence across the bridge to Richmond. Once across he remarked, "You're not what I expected."

I wondered if I'd left the tag on my thrift store shoes and sneaked a peek at my feet to be sure there were no telltale signs. Reassured, I turned to him and asked, "And what exactly were you expecting?"

"Nothing . . . nothing at all," the man said, and steered the speeding car along a gravel road. Flying pieces of rock rat-a-tat-tatted against the undersides; I found the sound aggravating. As the car skidded to a halt, I could see bulldozers and graders clearing lots in the adjacent fields. The sky was brown with the blowing earth. The man scratched his thick jaw with his hands and said, "I need to taste it."

"Of course . . . of course," I replied, and hoisted the briefcase to my lap, offering a small smile of apology as I fumbled with the lock. It finally released and I lifted the purple balloon out and placed it into his outstretched palm, then watched as he squeezed two capsules from the rubber compartment and pried them apart. The muscles in my neck tightened and I gripped the sides of the case to steady myself. Next he licked the exposed tops, and I held my breath and stared at his brown loafers. A shiny penny glinted in the middle of each and I took it as another sign of good luck. Satisfied with the sour taste, the man puckered his lips and produced four thousand dollars from under the leather seat. The bills, mostly in twenties, were stacked together and bound with thin elastic bands.

Not sure if my hands would hold steady, I did not count the money, but rather quickly placed the wad in the case and snapped it shut. "And your name is . . . ?"

"It doesn't matter," he replied, then added, "just call me Murray." He did not ask for my name as he put on a pair of sunglasses he retrieved off the visor. I studied his profile and, with his eyes obscured, he seemed more foreboding.

The transaction completed, he revved the engine and, squealing the tires, accelerated away. I was relieved that I was not to be fertilizer in these bronzed fields of Richmond. I stroked the briefcase in my lap praying he wouldn't stop to fix as we sped back to the city.

I assumed Murray was going to fix after he returned me to the park, for he wheeled away without so much as a backward glance. I hailed a cab, and from Hastings Street walked briskly back to my room in Chinatown. It felt strange carrying a brief case and I thought a cop would spot my deception, frisk me, and confiscate the cash. No one took any notice, and my anxiety decreased once I was inside the gloomy rooming house. Before I'd even placed the key in the lock, Lanny yanked me in, wrenched the case from my hand, and clicked it open. As his warty hands fingered and caressed the money, I saw the look of greed wash over his face. "Don't think on it too closely," I warned, snatching what I considered to be my half. "Remember it was my ass on the line."

"You ain't such a dumb old whore as I thought." He waved some bills under my nose.

"If that's a compliment I'm not buying it." I grasped my money so tightly that my knuckles were turning white.

"You know what I meant," he said, gesturing for me to begin a count of what I had.

"What? . . . that I'm only good for the occasional fist in my face . . . and because I'm a whore . . . that I'm too stupid to have a thought in my head!" I stormed, calculating my portion and tossed him three twenties, as he edged towards the door.

"You don't have the stomach for screwing no more. Don't tell me you're not fucked up. I'm out of here, and if you had any sense you'd head back to Calgary, too. And Beth . . . you're lucky I didn't bash you over the head for your share, but you played this part well and now you can just go fuck yourself."

I scrambled after him as he loped down the hall. "I hate you. You fucker. I hate you." But my words only bounced off his back as he ducked into the stairwell and disappeared.

I paused only long enough to catch my breath. With Chuck's warning—"A junkie can't move often enough"—ringing in my head, I began packing and changed rooming houses.

I purchased a box of Clairol hair colour from Rexall Drugs and dyed my hair a rich, deep red. For added insurance, I also bought a pair of sunglasses. My plan was to lie low. With only myself and a needle for company, my life continued much as it had before Lanny's visit.

As February passed into March I was broke again and standing on Granville Street under the ever-present drizzle of the leaking sky. I struggled to overcome my fear of men and still bed them, while the tedious wet nights blurred together, distinguishable from each other only in the number of men I fucked. Their faces spread before me like grainy mug shots at the end of each night while I tried to blot them out with each jab of the needle into my arm.

I'd been milling around for over an hour on the same square of pavement, when an Aboriginal girl remarked as we jostled for position, "You hear, there's a reward for info on a broad who ripped off some crime syndicate's relation, a nephew or something. I guess the guy got took for twenty bundles or so. They say there's a hefty price on her head as well as on the guy who set the thing up."

A bad feeling worked its way into the pit of my stomach as I rocked back on my heels. "A sucker born every minute and one to take them." We snickered, but that night I moved rooms again.

As May approached I did feel a measure of safety. I'd not moved in three weeks and had stopped wearing my hair pulled back. Although I continued to keep the red colour that Clairol provided, I'd long since lost my dark glasses. I heard or saw nothing of Lanny since the rip-off, and no other news reached my ears.

The smell and feel of men grinding into me continued nightly, but instead of panic as I lay under them my thoughts were now filled with violence. I pictured my vagina as a giant pair of garden shears; imagined thrusting a knife through a ribcage or down a throat. This rage was an effective weapon against the fear that had almost paralyzed me.

Under the talisman of spring, my lungs cleared and I coughed less. The first morning light of June stirred something deep within, waking me early. I tried to catch the sunlight in my fingers, then stretched, and yawned, and moved to stand and wash at the little sink in the corner. I dressed and fixed the last of my dope. On a hunch I left and walked the eleven blocks to the downtown post office, promising myself that it didn't matter if there was nothing there.

A postal worker dropped a letter on the spotless counter. "One more day and it would have been sent back unclaimed." I ignored the clerk and studied the return address. It was from Prince Albert and I recognized the familiar handwriting.

This was completely unexpected. I'd hoped for a letter from my grandmother, perhaps even Chuck, but not this. A part of me wanted to tear it to shreds, but overcome with curiosity I slipped it into my pocket. Outside the building I paused to watch a dozen or so fat pigeons waddle in circles, pecking at the pavement. Through the middle of the flock I suddenly ran laughing, watching the birds flutter into the sky.

I decided I would score before reading the letter and I headed east towards the Broadway Hotel, my arms swinging loosely by my side. Whatever Peter had to say, the junk would help, I thought, side stepping around a pool of vomit. Today, even Hastings Street looked good, with its grim buildings losing their shadows under the dousing of sunshine.

As I pushed into the smoky bar, I spied ole Tommy. Vie's rheumy friend, who had once repelled me with his weakness, had been looking better over the last couple of weeks. He was fixed. I smiled and started towards him when a young man with a small gold loop in his left ear broke away from a taller man in a pinstriped suit and threw himself in front of me. "Looking for some good stuff?" he asked. I saw the dagger tattoo on his right forearm as he reached for me and it reminded me of Peter's, so, instead of breaking away from him as I'd intended, I smiled. But the man, intent on getting my business, pointed towards ole Tommy dozing in the corner and bragged, "My stuff is better than that old fart's."

I saw him flash a thumbs up signal to the man in the pinstriped suit as he herded me back towards the entrance. Here, one of the battered doors stood propped open with a broken stick. I tried to gauge him, thinking something was not quite right. The earring and tattoo did not go with the green golf shirt and tan shorts. They didn't harmonize, but before I could think any further about it, as if sensing my hesitation, he offered, "Look, my stuff is so good that I'll sell ya one cap for ten. But it'll be twenty next time you come crawling back."

"Great," I responded, taking this as a sign of better things to come, and moved through the doorway into the light. Again I saw dealer give the man in the suit the A-Okay signal as he moved to follow. Framed by the door, and in the open, I felt something was wrong. But on the steps where once I'd cried so hard that Big Marie had taken pity on me, the cash and dope were exchanged.

I hummed a tuneless song and, relishing the warm rays of the sun on my cheeks, I moved towards my tiny quarters in Gastown. It was now June and I'd been away from Calgary seven months. Perhaps, I brooded, Rick would forget about me and that ugly incident. It wasn't such a big deal. Not like I ripped him off or nothing. I'd check things out and fly in for a trial run in a week or so. Perhaps someone there had news of Sue and I could catch up on some gossip from Vie, if she was still around.

I pried open the window in my stuffy room to freshen it and a breeze moved the tobacco-stained curtains, bringing with it the faint smell of the salty Pacific. I paused to breathe in the welcome scent and watched a crow march across the sill. The bird cocked its head to peer at me. The gleaming eye refracting the light was unnerving and I clapped my hands to frighten it away. It spread its wings and let loose an ear-piercing cry before flapping away. Uneasy, I backed away to sit in the chair that doubled as a garment rack. Unable to wait any longer, I read the letter.

> To Elizabeth,
> On warm sunny mornings
> And cold dark nights
> I sometimes find myself
> Thinking of you
> And I remember the way

Everything seemed so right

When we were together

And you know . . . sometimes I still miss you.

    Well, who else but me. I hope you're well and keeping yourself healthy for a change. I haven't heard from you since I got stabbed. Didn't you hear?

    Anyway, I'm healing up just fine, although I have a scar on my cheek—but fear not, I'm as handsome as ever. I'll be out in another couple of months and you can see for yourself. How about we get some wine then, and catch up with one another. What ya say?

    I guess that's it, but do keep in touch so I'll know where you're at.

    Love U's

    Peter

    P.S. What I wrote before was bullshit and you know it.

This was unbelievable. After all the crap of the last couple of years, he was telling me, in a poem yet, that he missed me. Since his conviction, the miles of sidewalk I'd walked had carried me into all the broken places and there I'd stayed. I appraised myself in the small wall mirror, brushing my fingertips across a junk sore erupting on my forehead. I leaned closer; the angry pustule was unsightly but would clear, I reassured myself. The harder, older face stared back, and my grandmother's words came to mind, "a woman can never be too rich or too thin." Well, I at least had the thin part down. I pinched my cheeks to relieve the shallowness of my skin, but otherwise I concluded I didn't seem too badly worn. I'd been right about Peter and that was all that mattered. I could feel a change coming, as sure as the spring that called me out this day.

I sighed with a hearty feeling of satisfaction and puckered my lips as I fussed with the flared sleeves of my T-shirt. I kicked off my platform sandals, spread my freed, callused toes, and sat straighter in the Shaker-style chair. As if I was presenting a tray of fancy sweets, I held the letter with both hands and reread the poem aloud, emphasizing my name, "To Elizabeth."

It sounded good to my ears, an affirmation of being alive. I said it again. But the crow on the windowsill and the dealer's hand signals to the man in the pinstriped suit had combined to spook me. I would sample this new dealer's dope. I cooked a few grains of the white powder finding I couldn't shake my feelings of uneasiness. I readied my arm and pumped. The stuff hit my brain like a rocket rush hurling me into a black nothingness. Gasping for air I toppled from the chair, the fit, leech-like, still dangling from my arm. I quivered and became still. As a wasp butted against the window screen, I remembered to breathe.

◄o►

A day later I was standing in front of the Air Canada booth. I explained to the Vancouver agent I'd lost my ID. Receiving a student standby ticket, I tossed twenty-five dollars on the counter and was on the next flight to Calgary.

◄o►

I'd been working Calgary's Eighth Avenue since my return in June. Now at the end of October, Rick would still not allow me back on the main drag. I'd heard from Gloria my admission ticket back to Seventh Avenue was a beating with a wire coat hanger.

The sky was clear and there was a little warmth in the air that fall afternoon when, tired and discouraged, I stopped to sit on one of the many benches that lined the outdoor mall. I should have felt grateful that Rick didn't want to kill me, but to submit to a brutal beating had no appeal either. I couldn't return to Vancouver. I couldn't work the drag. My friends were all locked up or gone. I stretched out a leg, jiggled my foot, and wondered if I should just disappear like Sue to Los Angeles.

Suddenly a young man with long, blond hair and brown eyes plopped down beside me. "Beth where the hell have you been? You look as if you stayed there too long." He laughed and put his arm around me.

"Jack," I said, happily leaning into him. "Nowhere. I don't have no place to go."

"You're homeless?" He sounded like he couldn't believe it. "Come and stay with me." He jolted down an address on the back of his cigarette package and tore it off. "Here, take this," he said, pressing the jagged paper into my palm. He stood. "My roommate is home so you can come anytime. I'm late and gotta run. See ya later at the house?"

He'd been like that since I'd known him in high school. Running off someplace and always late. I watched the distinctive movement of his shoulders as he walked away, fingering the scrap of paper he'd given me. It had been about a year since my stay in Richmond with John. Now another invitation. It hardly seemed possible. Within the hour I was at Jack's door.

When I attempted my climb out of the street in 1974, I believed there would be no place for me in a society that had shunned and marginalized me. There was no one to show me the way, or join me on my journey up and out, nor were there any social agencies in existence that were equipped to guide me in my quest for a different and, I hoped, possibly better life. It seemed all but impossible—and looking back now, almost impossible.

I was twenty-one the day I bumped into my old hippie friend Jack. Jack, fortunately, did not think about the considerable amount of baggage I brought with me or how long I'd extend my stay. But, as there were no shelters in the Seventies for homeless women, my quick acceptance of Jack's offer granted me what society could not—a place to withdraw.

For four months I was either in a drugged stupor from prescription drugs and/or intoxicated, or both. I do not know how Jack tolerated me for as long as he did, for I was more feral than human. Yet breaking the vicious cycle of addiction fed by my prostitution is, and remains, the largest of the many toeholds I secured for myself on the long scramble out.

At the end of my time on Calgary and Vancouver streets I was a young woman full of rage. With no resources, I grappled with my negative emotions until grasping that the essence of my anger hid my fear. Then a miracle: Mrs. R., an old family friend, encouraged me to write, and over many a written page I have squeezed my anger.

It has been part of my life's work to find some inner peace and rebuild my relationships, especially with my mother. Only once I was a mother could I understand her tough love approach—a bitter experience for anyone who's had to enforce it or been subjected to it. But what was defined as love for me at the time was interpreted as rejection, and I remain committed to the belief that tough love is, and was, a one-way ticket to the graveyard. I did reconcile with my mother during my first pregnancy, and our relationship since has had its share of ups and downs. She is, however, still beautiful and stoically resigned to my articulation and exposure of "those terrible years."

I carried no identification with me during my time on the street. If I was picked up by the police I could and would, whenever possible, be someone else. My letters, especially the ones from Peter, acted as a bridge connecting me with who I once was. I had my last fix in 1974 with Peter, after he was released from Prince Albert Penitentiary. Rebuilding my life has come at a cost measured in regrets, and Peter is one of them.

At no time was my recovery easy, neat, or clean. It was ten years before I stopped thinking about fixing every day. There were overwhelming obstacles, and the worst were my psychological feelings of isolation, which I deal with to this day. Coming off the street and then trying to live the straight life was like jumping planets and keeping the leap a shameful secret. In spite of these deficits I have managed to have a full and rewarding life. I went back to school and graduated with honours from Mount Royal College's Social Service Careers diploma program. Obviously, the doctors at St. Paul's Hospital misdiagnosed the seriousness of my condition, for each day my two children fill me with a sense of thankfulness for the Universe's forgiveness. My husband, friends, and little dogs, and digging in my garden are great sources of contentment.

I do bless the few who have been my stepping stones, but sometimes I stop and ask—Why me? And the voices of my lost companions always whisper back—Why not you?

Author's note

As for the people mentioned in this telling, I have been unable to locate any information about Peter. Sandi died of a brain embolism. Gary the Boost was stabbed to death in prison. Rick died of unknown causes. Ivan succumbed to pneumonia before age thirty. Both Young and Old Jimmy died. Of the others—Sue, Big Marie, Vie and Terri—I can only guess. I believe only Blade and Chuck and myself have survived.

ELIZABETH HUDSON was born in Halifax, Nova Scotia, and grew up in England, Montreal, and Campbellton, New Brunswick. At age 13 she moved to Calgary, Alberta. This picture was taken when Hudson was a young woman living in Calgary and Vancouver in the 1970s.

Hudson attended Mount Royal College, where she was awarded the Lorraine Hill Award and the George Kirby Scholarship. Her poems have been published in *Tower Poetry, Other Voices, Pottersfield Portfolio, The Amethyst Review,* and *Herspectives,* and she has written articles published in *Wildflower, Homebase,* and *Maclean's.* Hudson's two sons have both graduated from university, and now she lives in the deep suburbs with her husband, three dogs and a cat.